Ayrshire &

AN ILLUST ARCHITEC GUIDE

FOR AN AYRSHIREMAN there is no greater pleasure than to be asked to pen a few words in tribute to the county of his birth and upbringing.

Ayrshire folk are a couthy lot with a distinctive personality. The architecture of the place is no less distinctive. From the douce Victorian dwellings of the settlements on its coast, to the elegant public buildings in its inland towns, to the sturdy architecture of its rural marches there is much in Ayrshire over which to enthuse.

This volume is an essential companion to any study of Ayrshire, its people and its places, and is a splendid adjunct to the other titles in this excellent series of RIAS guides.

G B HORSPOOL, BARCH, RIBA, FRICS, FFB

© Author: Rob Close
Series editor: Charles McKean
Series consultant: David Walker
Cover design: Dorothy Steedman
Editorial consultant: Duncan McAra

Royal Incorporation of Architects in Scotland
ISBN 1873190 06 9
First published 1992

Cover illustrations:
View from Culzean (photo McKean),
Crossraguel Abbey, Maybole (photo Paton),
Burns' Cottage, Alloway by Sam Bough, RSA
(courtesy of Glasgow Museums and Art Galleries)

Typesetting, page make-up and picture scans:

Print *h*

A

Z020366

Of the thirty-three historic counties of Scotland, Ayrshire ranks seventh in size, and fourth in population. No county outranks it in both size and population: it is the largest county south of the Highland Line. These dry statistics underline essential truths about Ayrshire: that it is a large, and, in general, densely settled county which, while being remote from the centres of political life and artistic development, still has a great wealth of architecture worth seeking out. This ranges from the many surviving farmsteadings (often of courtyard form) and weaving villages to mercantile centres and great mansions.

Ayrshire, as part of the Region of Strathclyde, straddles the boundary between the Central Lowlands and the Southern Uplands: Girvan marks one end of a line which stretches across Scotland to Dunbar: south of it lies southern Carrick, Ayrshire's empty quarter, a wilderness of remote glens, and secluded hills. Despite Bruce's connection with – and alleged birth at Turnberry, this area, the fiefdom of the Kennedys, was only nominally under the control of the Scottish kings. It is no surprise that the coast road between Ayr and Stranraer should have given rise to the legend of the cannibal Bean and his awful family. The dangers of travel must have been real enough.

The contrast between the true hill lands of the southern province of Carrick, and the rolling farmlands of the north, rising to moorlands to north and east (the provinces of Kyle, between Doon and Irvine, and Cunninghame, north of the Irvine), reinforces Ayrshire's complex personality. Indeed it seems sometimes to be a series of dichotomies. Ayrshire cows and the industrial Garnock Valley: Dunlop cheese and Ardrossan: Muirkirk and Culzean: James Boswell and Johnnie Walker: Straiton and Irvine New Town.

Both industry and agriculture have a long pedigree in Ayrshire and there is harmony in the relationship. It is prime dairying country (mild winters and plentiful grass growth assure that) and the russety Ayrshire cow is Scotland's premier dairy breed. It was also an early industrial area as the monks at Kilwinning exploited coal and salt on their estates. The county has had many generations in which to resolve any conflict between agricultural and industrial-extractive needs; although now that deep mining has ceased, the scale of open-cast extraction may upset the balance.

Opposite: *Streets A-K, Esplanade, Ayr Shore (photo Kyle and Carrick Libraries)*

The distinctive rich brown and white Ayrshire cow, one of the leading dairying breeds in Britain and elsewhere, has a misty pedigree. Likely progenitors appear to be the black, white-spotted, Cunninghame cattle, short legged and allegedly of Dutch or Danish origin. The Cunninghame was a mixed dairy/beef breed, though selective breeding had moved towards a single-purpose breed by the late 18th century. This trend had been accelerated by the introduction, earlier that century, of light brown Teeswater bulls by Bruce Campbell, factor for Lord Marchmont.

The shore at Troon, 1890

There is another dichotomy between the coast and the interior. Sandy links and raised beaches from Skelmorlie to Ballantrae made Ayrshire a prime resort for Victorian and later pleasure-seekers, creating a chain of towns – Skelmorlie, Largs, Troon, Prestwick and Ayr – with a substantial commuter trade with Glasgow. They provide the county with some of its most distinctive urban and, especially near Troon, suburban architecture. It also attracted tripper trade, not only at Ayr and Largs, but also at Girvan, Saltcoats, Irvine and, in the 1930s, Lendalfoot. Ayr itself is a mass of contradictions: county town, mill town, holiday resort, coal port. The shrieking of gulls on bright winter mornings is the only indication in the High Street that the sea is within 200 yards. The money trippers brought underpinned the town's prosperity and, with the decline of such holidaymakers, Ayr, and the other coastal towns, have turned to other specialities. Ayrshire is a county with a distinct personality, which takes a pride in itself and displays a sturdy, self-willed independence.

This guide is designed to help Ayrshire folk and visitors alike try to reach an understanding of the county's character and history through its built environment. Many people have helped in the preparation of this guide book. They are listed on p.211. Errors and inaccuracies are the sole responsibility of the author.

Sequence
This guide covers four post-1975 Districts: Cumnock and Doon Valley [CDV], Cunninghame [C], Kilmarnock and Loudoun [KL] and Kyle and Carrick [KC]. Starting with Ayr [KC], the guide follows the coast north through Troon [KC] and Irvine [C] to Largs [C], before turning inland to Kilmarnock [KL], then southward to Cumnock [CDV]. Thereafter we follow the valley of the Doon, from Alloway [KL] to Dalmellington [CDV], then deal with Maybole [KC], and the

valleys of the Water of Girvan [KC] and the Stinchar [KC]. Finally, we visit the islands in the Clyde: Ailsa Craig [KC: reached from Girvan], Arran [C: reached from Ardrossan] and the Cumbraes [C: reached from Largs].

Text Arrangement

Entries for principal buildings follow the sequence of name or number, address, date and architect (if known). Lesser buildings are contained within paragraphs. Demolished buildings are included if appropriate. Entries in the small columns highlight interesting biographical, historical and social aspects of the story of Ayrshire.

Map References

Maps of Ayrshire, Ayr, Irvine, Kilmarnock and Cumnock are included. The numbers relate to references in the text itself. Owing to the area covered, the maps give no more than a general indication of locations.

Access to Properties

Many of the buildings described in this guide are open to the public, or are visible from a public road or footpath. Some are private, and readers are requested to respect the occupiers' privacy.

Sponsors

This guide would not have been possible without the support of Enterprise Ayrshire, Kilmarnock and Loudoun District Council, Kyle and Carrick District Council, Cunninghame District Council and Irvine Development Corporation whose generous financial assistance has lowered greatly the cover price.

The Comrys (Cumbraes) with the islands of Bute & Arran

RCAHMS

The river (Ayr) name belongs to a group whose roots lie in early Bythronic tongues, sharing, with the Yorkshire Aire, a meaning close to *strong river*, and the many advantages of the little hills overlooking the river mouth were surely not lost on those who named the river.

Kyle and Carrick Libraries

AYR

Capital of the province of Kyle, and the social, cultural and economic centre of the county, Ayr's growth derived from its position at the mouth of the river. The River Ayr's debouche forms one of the few safe anchorages on the long eastern sweep of the Firth of Clyde, and allows reasonably straightforward landward communication. It lent its name to the settlement which grew up in the shadow of William the Lion's castle, St John's Town of Ayr. Historical evidence and folk memory unite to suggest a Roman route up Nithsdale towards the coast, with a fort of some kind on the intriguingly named Castlehill.

In 1205 William created a royal burgh adjacent to a castle founded c.1197, which, with Dumfries, marked the limits of the then regal influence, secure points from which efforts could be made to quell the hill men of Carrick and Galloway. The Castle was on a small sandhill, alongside a medieval church possibly on a Celtic site among the sand dunes. The burgh developed on an L-plan, with the heel nearest the castle, at the present junction of High Street and New Bridge Street. High Street was the upright, paralleling the river before bending sharply inland: Sandgate is the foot of the L: it has been suggested that this was the original burgh, but that the windblown sand quickly encouraged a major reorientation. Riggs ran backward from the streets, for the fortunate to the river and the wharves, elsewhere to back lanes whose modern

Close

successors are Mill Street, Carrick Street,
St John's Lane and Fort Street. Medieval
extension stretched the High Street southward
to the gushet where Alloway Street and Kyle
Street divide. Medieval Ayr remained
comfortably within these limits, though it
witnessed the growth of Newton across the
river; the only major change until the coming of
the New Bridge was the sweeping away of
William's castle and kirk during the
Commonwealth, to allow the erection of a
Citadel; while a new church was provided out
of government funds on the site of the
Franciscan Friary. (See p.C4)

Ayr from the north

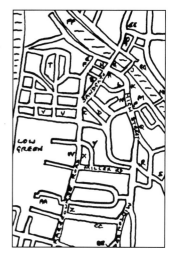

In about 1800 Ayr came into its own as a
town of fashionable resort, the centre of an
integrated and effective system of civil and
legal administration. Both the burgh and the
McNeights (owners of the Barns Estate which
abutted the burgh on its southern flank) began
to feu land, after which the neat terraces of
Wellington Square, Barns Street, Alloway
Place and Charlotte Street rose quickly. There
was also a major rebuilding of the main streets;
while the street pattern of *c.*1200 persists, the
houses are largely Georgian, mostly rebuilt in
the forty years between 1780 and 1820.

In the 1850s, feuing of the Citadel area
began, under the eccentric *Baron* Miller, an
Indian returnee. Nabobs found the social life of
Ayr considerably to their taste and comprised
many of the new feuars throughout the 19th
century, as further swathes of the burghfield
south of the town were opened up. They

The Air Bank, formally known as Douglas, Heron & Co, collapsed disastrously in 1772. It had been founded in 1763 by John McAdam & Co, passing to Douglas, Heron & Co in 1771. It had 136 partners, capital of £150,000, and liabilities estimated at £1,250,000, including £400,000 owed by various partners. Injudicious lending forced the firm into an ever-increasing spiral of issuing new notes against bad debt. The bubble burst spectacularly: it is estimated that the Air Bank Crash was directly responsible for forcing £750,000 of property on to the market.

Thomas Hamilton's decision to forfeit his fee for the Burns Monument at Alloway was a shrewd move, ensuring that he would be regarded with favour when further commissions arose in the county. Ayr Town Hall is the most spectacular of his subsequent Ayrshire work, its majestic tapering steeple – unrivalled in Scotland – a potent symbol of Ayr.

Hamilton's perspective of Town Hall spire

Kyle and Carrick Libraries

preferred detached villas in commodious grounds (a trend hastened by the cholera outbreaks of the 1830s) and thus grew Ayr's enjoyable Victorian southern extension; Racecourse Road, Midton Road and Victoria Park, from 1848, and Southpark Road, from 1852, each became the spine of a new feuing area. Oddly, this district has no generic name, always known, in the days of Ayr Town Council, as the First Ward.

The 20th century has witnessed rapid expansion of the town in all directions, leapfrogging the publicly owned policies of Belleisle and Rozelle to engulf Alloway beyond which suburbia sprawls onward. Central redevelopment has cost much and the rigg pattern has been largely obliterated. The High Street has been affected as much by visually intrusive façades as by total redevelopment. Modern Ayr bustles: a holiday resort whose main streets turn their backs on the sea, a place where red-faced trippers in search of presents look oddly out of place in the High Street; a town of great antiquity, and yet with no museum; the seat of a sheriff yet a coal port. Ayr is a real place to enjoy; and it is not too late to save it from further despoliation.

A **Town Buildings**, 1827-32, Thomas Hamilton
The ideal symbol for the town, at the heel of the L. Astounding neoclassical Grecian façade of great assurance, topped by a griffin-guarded steeple; composed of a massive basement surmounted by a cornice. The façade of the principal storey is formed of pilasters, with mouldings, circular-headed windows, the whole finished with a massive entablature, dentil cornice, and blocking course. Rusticated base to the spire, massive pilasters surmounted by a heavy entablature and cornice, and elegantly enriched on the external angles on which stand four eagles. The third storey is octagonal with Tuscan columns and entablature. The dials of the clock are surrounded by eight coupled Roman Doric columns, upon the entablature of which stands a lofty and elegant obelisk supported by consoles and crowned with a fine capital, the whole surmounted by a gigantic figure of a Triton. Extended along High Street, 1878-81, Campbell Douglas & Sellars, and reconstructed internally in 1901 by J K Hunter, in an imposing but coldly mannered classical idiom, after fire had devastated Hamilton's interiors.

Sandgate

Much of Sandgate consists of narrow classical frontages dating from the period 1780-1830. **No 3**, the former Ayr Arms, rebuilt in 1829 by Thomas King, is a three-bay, two-storey house, harled with stone dressings to the windows; **13**, 1929, Thomas O'Beirne, is respectful infill, repeating the details within a neo-Georgian stone façade; **27-29** is an oddity, an exuberantly ornamented red sandstone interloper, c.1880; **37**, c.1790, is altogether grander, with elaborate Venetian-windowed façades to both Sandgate and Newmarket Street. The Registrar's Office, **43** (the former post office), 1893, W W Robertson, is excellent Scottish baronial; **67-71**, 1911, J R Johnstone, the former Liberal Club, wonderfully florid with dynamic corner tower and startling baroque doorpiece, luxuriantly sculpted.

Above *Sandgate*. Left *Lady Cathcart's House*

B **Lady Cathcart's House**, 22 Sandgate, 17th century onwards

The lower crowstepped wing, with doors and small window openings irregularly placed in the thick walls, led to recent investigation uncovering a barrel-vaulted ground floor, and evidence of a house of c.1600, the upper floors jettied out over a postulated arcaded ground floor, in the manner of Elgin (see *Moray* in this series) or Gladstone's Land in the Lawnmarket (see *Edinburgh* in this series). Restoration, by Simpson & Brown, for the Scottish Historic Buildings Trust, began in 1991. In the 19th century, the building was the Ayr branch of the City of Glasgow Bank; its neighbour, the Bank of Scotland, 1877, Alexander Petrie, being the least confident of the banks clustered here, and

Lady Cathcart's House was acquired by the Scottish Historic Buildings Trust in 1989. There is a persistent, but unproven, belief that **John Loudon McAdam**, 1756-1836, pioneer road engineer, was born in this house. There are other claimants, such as the McAdam family seat at Craigengillan. What is certain is that much of his life was spent in the county. He was a partner with Lord Dundonald in the tar works at Muirkirk, and his first experiments in macadamised roads were on his estate at Sauchrie in the Carrick Hills. These were roads made of compacted layers of small and crushed stone – easily laid and easily repaired. It was only in the late 19th century that the idea of strengthening them with tar was developed.

Gale's plans were accepted after being submitted to the approval of Mr Thomas Hamilton, *the celebrated Edinburgh architect*, and on the assumption that it would cost no more than £1 4s per sitting. William Bryant, an American tourist in 1845, passing through Ayr on his way to Alloway, recorded that *we heard a great hammering and clicking of chisels, and looking to the right we saw workmen busy in building another of the Free Churches, with considerable elaborateness of architecture in the Early Norman style.*

Wellington Chambers is the major memorial to Henry Vincent Eaglesham, the Ayr engineer and architect, 1861-1901, who died suddenly in Florence: it has great presence and rare quality and, in its use of advanced constructional techniques, is an engineer's building. It leaves us to ponder what Eaglesham might have achieved had he lived longer, though he considered himself first and foremost an engineer. Engineering business took him abroad for much of his life: to Spain and to Tasmania. His elder brother John, *c.*1856-1922, trained with John Mercer and succeeded him as Burgh Surveyor, resigning in 1899 to join with Henry in J & H V Eaglesham.

Right *Wellington Chambers.*
Below *Holy Trinity*

no match for the former Commercial Bank at **34** Sandgate – a typically impressive Italian Renaissance palazzo by David Rhind in 1863. The **Royal Bank of Scotland**, **30**, 1973, Gratton McLean & Partners, picks up some of Rhind's details, especially the console, in a bold but self-conscious attempt to marry old forms to new materials and new methods. **Bridge's Bar, 8** Sandgate, reasserts the mode of *c.*1800, the thin prim harled tenement, expression confined to the window surrounds: a traditional bar beneath, increasingly rare in Ayr. **14** Sandgate, *c.*1820, fills its narrow first-floor frontage with a huge three-part window with console and pediment. **Sandgate Auctions**, 1845, by William Gale, occupies a former Free Church in ignorant but cheerful neo-Norman. The block finishes with single-storey shops, 1881, which the Police Commissioners greeted with disappointment that such paltry-looking buildings should be erected on such a site.

C **Wellington Chambers**, 1895, H V Eaglesham
A most splendid red stone tenement block, strongly horizontal in feel, which demands your attention. It is not only the flat roof that makes one think of New York, but would the effect, the deeply recessed joints, the obsessively unornamented openings, have been the same in grey Giffnock stone, as originally proposed?

D **Holy Trinity**, 1898, John L Pearson
A soaring, powerful essay in 13th-century Gothic, Scotland's major example of the work of this scholarly church architect, designer of Truro Cathedral. Completed by Pearson's son, its proposed 92 ft tower and 92 ft spire, replaced by a truncated tower in precast concrete by Roger Pinckney. Dark interior in the Anglican tradition, the numinous light through stained glass by, among others, Clayton & Bell.

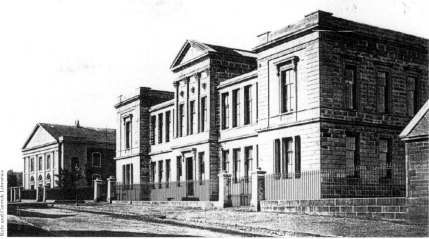

*Academy and Dansarena
photographed by G W Wilson*

E **Ayr Academy**, 1880, Clarke & Bell
A plain but massive Grecian two-storey
structure, with rustic basement, centre and
wings, the Corinthian portico of which is
adorned with medallions of Wilkie, Watt and
Burns. In 1907 James Morris added a large art
school overlooking the river, its debt to the work
of Mackintosh clear to see. Academy Street,
formerly School Vennel (and what a lot lies at
the root of that name change), is the most
evocative of the lanes linking Sandgate with the
back of the burgh; still setted, enjoyably
narrow, with one good run of stuccoed and
painted houses, **10-22**, of *c*.1780. Cathcart
Street is similar, but wider, allowing greater
contemplation of the late 18th-century houses,
5-9 and **10-20** the most rewarding, while **6**,
1890, John Mercer, is an attractive coachworks
of the *modern warehouse type*, of polished
Sevenacres stone. The street concludes with the
former **Cathcart Street Relief Church**, 1816,
plain thinly detailed classical.

F **Dansarena (former New Church)**,
Fort Street, 1807-10, David Hamilton
Built to accommodate the overspill from the
Auld Kirk. Behind a 20th-century gateway
Hamilton's church presents an assured, five-
bay pedimented front to Fort Street. There is a
notable, three-piece, pilastered entrance. The
church was well converted to a dance studio by
J & J A Carrick, 1984. Elsewhere Fort Street
mixes its metaphors: at the south end late
Victorian tenements in grey and red mingle
with decent early 19th-century semi-villas,

Aiton was clearly not a Relief
Church man: *Oratory in the
preacher, and a disposition in
the members to contribute to the
support of the Gospel, are the
leading qualifications required.
Seat rents cover a multitude of
sins, and are the sine qua non of
membership. One man expects
eldership there which he had
long sought in vain in the
parish Church, and another,
baptism for his child, which he
could get nowhere else. Some
have quarrelled with their
minister, some pretend to
superior sanctity, others wish to
bring more customers to their
shop. Some follow the
multitude, others their
sweethearts, and many cannot
tell how they are gathered
together.*

such as **47-49**, 1824, Thomas King, and **52-54**, also King, and the **Baptist Church**, 1817, a classically fronted former theatre. **2 Fort Street**, *c.*1810, was the town's Custom House. It is a two-storey ashlar box lent interest and character by the pair of shallow, full-height, bow windows.

Ayr drawn by Henry Duguid

National Galleries of Scotland

G **1-3 New Bridge Street**, 1787, Alexander Stevens

New Bridge Street forms the serif at the angle of the L: its alignment with Main Street, Newton, marking the original ford across the river which was made redundant by the Auld Brig: given renewed importance when the first New Bridge reasserted the direct connection between Sandgate and Newton in the 1780s. **1-3** is a most attractive, highly decorated composition with a double-bowed river frontage: Stevens was the architect of that first New Bridge: his house built in an elegant manner so as to ornament the bridge. The second **New Bridge**, 1877-9, Blyth & Cunningham, is engineer's architecture, plain and simple. Opposite, is **2** New Bridge Street, *c.*1834, John Kay, whose plain classicism is a suitable foil for Stevens' house.

Loudoun Hall

H **Loudoun Hall**, *c.*1513

A real gem: the earliest surviving example in Scotland of a town house designed as the comfortable dwelling of a rich merchant. A three-storey block to which the Campbells of Loudoun, hereditary sheriffs of Ayr, added the congruent north wing in 1534. Rubble built, slate roofed, hall over the normal vaulted basement. Rescued from slum clearance by the Marquess of Bute, and restored from 1948 by Robert Hurd.

South Harbour Street has two good groups: simple classic houses, of *c.*1800, **1-13**, and,

23-41, a mid-19th-century range of plain, generally stuccoed, bars and warehouses. **Ayr Baths**, 1970-2, Cowie Torry & Partners, dominates the harbour: delicate foundation stone (to the right of the entrance) by Frank Dunbar.

Dunfermline Building Society,
New Bridge Street, *c.*1830, Thomas Hamilton A powerful neo-Grecian, monumentally colonnaded partner for Hamilton's Town Buildings. Built for the Ayrshire Bank, it is another of the major commissions in Ayr that Hamilton won as a direct result of the favourable impression he made on the Burns Monument Committee.

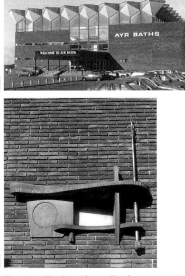

Top Ayr Baths. Above *Baths: foundation stone.* Left *24 New Bridge Street*

High Street
13-21, *c.*1825, set the pattern for much of High Street: façades based on the old rigg frontages, with three bays and two storeys of domestic accommodation over ground-floor commercial uses. **13** is broad, upper windows within prominent surrounds, middle-floor windows having deep aprons; **17** is slightly narrower, again with prominent window surrounds and aprons, though one first-floor window is, oddly, bipartite; **21** is noticeably narrower – but still three bays – no aprons, but an original shopfront and a consoled surround to the central window. A walk along the High Street produces variation most obviously in the treatment of the window surrounds. Here, the opposite side took the brunt of 1930s redevelopment: **12-18**, **Woolworths**, 1933-5, **34-40**, **Burton**, 1936-7, and **42-48**, James M Monro & Son, for Marks & Spencer. Finally, two assured red sandstone blocks of great quality: **50**, 1879, Allan Stevenson, with Queen Anne cornicing, and the free Italianate **54**, 1880, John Mercer, built of finely detailed Mauchline stone.

The Ayrshire Bank was founded by Quintin Kennedy, *c.*1830, on leaving Hunter's & Co (the Ayr bank set up by James Hunter, cashier to the ill-fated Air Bank). In 1845, the business was taken over by the Western Bank, and the subsequent failure of that bank in 1857 is generally regarded as having been caused by the Ayrshire accounts that the Ayrshire Bank had brought to the Western – good value but quite unrealisable – which had been the cause of the disagreement which had caused Kennedy to leave Hunter's & Co, taking these accounts with him.

Fish Cross in early 19th century

RIAS Collection

In **The Brigs of Ayr**, Burns
foretells the collapse of the first
New Bridge: *I'll be a brig when
ye're a shapeless cairn!* The
New Brig gives as good as it
gets, banishing the Auld Brig
and all that it stands for thus:

*Fine architecture, trowth, I
needs must say't o't!
The Lord be thankit that we've
tint the gate o't!
Gaunt, ghastly, ghaist-alluring
edifices,
Hanging with threat'ning jut,
like precipices;
O'er-arching, mouldy, gloom-
inspiring coves,
Supporting roofs, fantastic –
stony groves;
Windows and doors in nameless
sculptures drest,
With order, symmetry or taste
unblest...*

Auld Brig

Close

Fish Cross
Where the High Street widens at the first
bend, creating an irregular square, partially
cobbled enclosure, is the Fish Cross – all that
remains of the medieval market area –
enclosed by a variety of architecture including
further examples of the High Street standard,
and **35-39**, a commercial block of *c*.1870, of red
sandstone and plentiful glass, handling the
corner with ease.

J **Auld Brig**, *c*.1470
Massively constructed, and for many, the
symbol of Ayr, this narrow bridge was for many
centuries the only crossing of the River Ayr.
The hero of Burns' poem needed a trenchant
rearguard action orchestrated by James A
Morris, to prevent its demolition in the first
years of this century. This icon has four rubble-
stone arches, the most southerly seemingly
squeezed into place, and big triangular
cutwaters, but is built without corresponding
refuges or passing places.

K **Buttermarket**, 1984, Ian Burke & Partners,
indulges in the façade retention of **86**, 1883, by
John Baird II in severe neo-baronial, and **88**,
1883, by John Mercer, in hunched-up
Renaissance style, like his contemporary **92-98**.
Note the Jacobean details on **112-114**.

L **Tolbooth**
The tolbooth, which stood in the centre of the

market place (and from which William Wallace is said to have escaped by means of an upper-floor window), is long gone. Development of the market place from *c.*1780 has left High Street, Hope Street, Fish Cross and a faint echo in front of Winton Buildings to mark the site. The resultant buildings form an eclectic gathering. **57** High Street, *c.*1790, a large corner site tenement, offers severe elevations to High Street and Fish Cross; **61-63**, 1893, H V Eaglesham, a delightful Flemish Renaissance former bar; **67**, 1937, Eric A Sutherland, an excellent meticulously detailed Savings Bank of Glasgow mixing Northumberland, Aberdeen and Kirkcudbright stone in its miniature Tuscan façade. **75**, 1886, Allan Stevenson, a multi-turreted Scottish baronial confection, houses William Reid's 1810 statue of William Wallace. **Winton Buildings**, 1844, is mannered, round-shouldered in provincial classical, *a great embellishment to the town.*

Newmarket Street, 1767 onwards
Cut through the back riggs to allow more effective development, its current demeanour is mainly simple harled two-storey houses of *c.*1830, though **27-35** and **4-10**, *c.*1780, give some impression of the original houses: 4 was a Kennedy town house. Note John Knox as keystone, Wallace and Bruce as springers on **30-38**, **MacNeille Buildings**, 1869, James I McDerment, a late classical façade with curious mixed motifs.

Tourist Information Office, 1857,
Peddie & Kinnear
At the junction with Newmarket Street; a good Italian Renaissance banking palazzo of Dunaskin stone. The doorpieces have delightful shell tympana. Alongside is **Queen's Court**, the former County Club, 1873, John Murdoch, a Scots baronial snecked rubble block to Sandgate, plainer crowstepped flanking wings to the inner courtyard, the whole beautifully restored in 1975 by Patrick Lorimer to create a civilised shopping complex.

M **Old Parish Church**, 1652-4,
Theophilius Rankeine
The approach is through Kirkport, a narrow setted street with a good group of well-restored 19th-century houses on either side of the street, some rubbly (**9**, **14**), others harled

Top *Wallace Statue in original position.* Middle *75 Newmarket Street.* Above *MacNeille Buildings*

Ayr Auld Kirk

A plaque records the site of the garden of **John Welch**, the son-in-law of John Knox who continued his proselytising work. Born at Dunscore in 1568, he came to Ayr in 1600, and quickly gained a local reputation for pertinent intervention in master-and-servant disputes. His sermons, often directed at James VI, ensured that he was banished to France in 1606.

(**10-12**). The street terminates in the massive **gateway**, 1656, to the kirkyard. The church is a characterful T-plan kirk, paid for by the Commonwealth Government – which had requisitioned the medieval church – with chunky, powerful, Gothic windows. Alterations and additions, most obviously by a youthful David Bryce, 1836, have left the original pattern still clearly visible. Interior of high quality: three fine lofts on provincially detailed Corinthian colonnades, and splendid contemporary pulpit.

N **Bank of Scotland**, 119-123 High Street, 1902, Peddie & Washington Browne
An excessively elaborate neo-Georgian design, it reinforces the conservative nature of its seaward neighbours, **85-103**, the best sequence of early 19th-century town houses in Ayr, of the pattern familiar in the town of a relatively narrow frontage of two bays and three storeys, harled with painted margins, individuality provided by differing treatments to the window surrounds; 101-103 was rebuilt in 1834. **105**, 1964, Alex Cullen & Co, is an uncompromising but effective concrete insertion. To the landward side, the unabashedly contemporary **Littlewoods**, in two stages from 1968, the later partially clad with huge chunks of red sandstone, and **Mothercare**, **145**, 1973, by Boswell Mitchell & Johnston.

Halifax Building Society,
128-130 High Street, 1856, Robert Paton
A fine Grecian building, originally the Union Bank, in the palazzo style pioneered by Charles Barry. It dominates this section of the High

Street, and must have done so even more before its neighbours were rebuilt later in the 19th century. The Creetown granite façade was added in 1963. To its left, **116**, 1905, J K Hunter, with three-part windows recessed within its red stone ashlar, and **126**, two plain storeys in beige ashlar. To the right, the feus were all redeveloped from 1883, set back to widen the street line: the narrow **146**, *c.*1884, topped by a curved and broken pediment, interrupted by a pedimented aedicule; **148-156**, 1893, H V Eaglesham, excellent free form design with two curly Flemish gables. Both Allan Stevenson's 1883 **158-160**, and John Mercer's **168-170** of 1885 use conservative classical motifs which would not have been out of place 40 years previously. The latter was rebuilt behind the façade in 1971-2 – the first major development in this manner in Ayr. **172-176**, 1886, by John Mercer is Tudor in style.

P **Wallace Tower**, 1833, Thomas Hamilton
The street widening left this Tudor Gothic folly stuck in the street. It is an excellent composition, with a niche for James Thom's primitive statue of Wallace, and complementary to the great steeple both in style and outline. It was built on the site of an earlier tower, possibly that of a friary church, jutting out into the High Street like some medieval totem preserved amidst modern improvements. It was also a sign of Scotland's growing consciousness of her history – though obviously not as yet of the precise forms of her historic architecture. **Turner's Bridge**, an ornamental cast-iron footbridge on sandstone piers, dates from 1900 by John Eaglesham.

Top *Halifax Building Society.*
Above *Wallace Tower*

Kyle Centre, 1987, Shepherd Robson with Cowie Torry & Partners
New shopping complex breaking through into the High Street in a colourful modern gabled and banded idiom: concomitant rebuilding has left **209**, 1862, James I McDerment, undemanding but within the scale of the town, and **213**, 1909, Murdoch & Lockhart, pleasantly astylar, as façades only. **219-223**, 1894, William Kerr, well-detailed ashlar free style; Italianate **225-231**, 1884, by John Murdoch, **237**, 1904, J & H V Eaglesham, florid baroque, and **239-241**, 1904, William Cowie, more restrained, carefully controlled Renaissance.

The **Tam o' Shanter** cannot be conclusively identified as the setting of Burns's poem. There is nothing in the poem which allows even tentative identification with any of the many inns which existed in the late 18th century. It is probable that the name was bestowed on the bar by an enterprising publican, John Glass, who recognised the opportunity to benefit from the increasing interest in Burns.

The current fare at the **Gaiety Theatre** – the hugely successful annual pantomime, the summer *Whirls*, touring shows and local operatic performances – continue the formula established by Ben Popplewell when he bought it in 1925. Under him, and, after his death in 1950, his sons Eric and Leslie, the Gaiety was transformed from a struggling cinema into the premier variety theatre in Scotland.

Below *Gaiety Theatre, 1920s.*
Bottom *Clydesdale Bank*

Q **Tam o' Shanter**, repaired in 1808 (*above*)
Sole survivor of the pre-1800 High Street and a poignant reminder of different materials – thatch, harl – and a vastly different scale. Now a museum, currently (1992) undergoing restoration and re-appraisal of its role in telling the stories of Ayr and Burns. The eastern side of High Street, from Mill Street to Kyle Street, the Tam o' Shanter apart, is the least rewarding stretch architecturally.

Carrick Street
This street has been much battered: its major survival is the **Gaiety Theatre**, 1902, J McHardy Young, its stunning rococo interior, rebuilt by Alex Cullen after a fire in 1903, not hinted at by the plain cream-tiled façade of the 1930s. The mass of the **Caledonian Hotel**, 1970, Leach Rhodes & Walker, dominates but does not inspire. **17-25 Dalblair Road**, 1880, Allan Stevenson, have neo-Greek details, notably the chimney pots, reminiscent of Alexander Thomson; **27-37** are earlier, plainer, early Victorian. These numbers are local grey, probably Townhead, stone, but **75**, 1902, Allan Stevenson, and **85**, 1896, James K Hunter, use dark red Mauchline stone, creating a dark cavern of the street, which here narrows appreciably. Each is an individual interpretation of Renaissance motifs; **85** is baroque in tone, **75**, turn-of-the-century, particularly in the fine detailing of the entrances. In **Alloway Street** the highlights are Allan Stevenson's free Palladian department store, of 1894 and 1910, and Cowie Torry & Partner's **Clydesdale Bank**, 1987, excellently composed post-Modern, though perhaps too tricksy, too Mackintoshy.

R **Burns Statue Square**
A tawdry ill-sorted space, in no sense a square,
containing George Lawson's exceptionally well-
executed **Statue of Burns**, 1892, and Thomas
Brock's moving, if rather neglected, **South
African War Memorial**, 1902. Morris &
Hunter's pedestal for the Burns Statue won
generous praise from the *Builder*: *the designing
of pedestals for sculpture is so much neglected
in this country that it is gratifying to find an
example carefully studied by an architect.* **1-7**,
1901, James A Morris, in a brilliantly
individual Edwardian free style, boldly
sculpted, and **9-15**, 1900, William Cowie (then
with J & H V Eaglesham), equally stylish,
equally forthright, Renaissance-detailed, are
the best: a stunning pair bringing quality to
this corner. The **Odeon**, 1937, Andrew Mather,
with its streamlined tower is one of only three
original Odeons in Scotland; it has been
tripled, and the original interiors lost. With the
Royal Bank of Scotland, 7 Killoch Place,
1936, Thomson Sandilands & Macleod, very
mannered and unadorned until the 1990
refronting in bright blue metalwork, the
cinema adds some inter-war pep to Burns
Statue Square. In Smith Street stands **Shaw's**,
1891, a classy free-form baroque bar, opposite
67 Kyle Street, 1883, James A Morris, a
former bonded store of simple charm, turning
the corner with skill.

S **Ayr Station** and **Station Hotel**, 1886,
Andrew Galloway
Dramatic and surprisingly competent
(Galloway was the chief engineer with the
GSWR: this is his only recorded major
building) in a French Renaissance manner. In
1883, John Mercer, the burgh surveyor, wrote
to Galloway about the plans: *I was very much
pleased with them and have been sounding
their praises so much since that the Provost,
Magistrates &c are quite on the qui vive to see
them ... they cannot believe from my description
that it is of such magnitude.* The hotel block
captures the essence of the chosen style well,
and encapsulates it into something new,
undeniably Scottish and undeniably of railway
origin. The long wing containing the former
railway offices lacks sufficient articulation.

Holmston House, 1857-60,
William Lambie Moffat
Former Kyle Union Poorhouse, excellent crisply

Top *Burns Statue.* Middle *1-7
Burns Statue Square.* Above
9-15 Burns Statue Square

detailed long Jacobean front set back from the road, almost like a lairdly home, its excellence underscored by first-class restoration by Strathclyde Regional Council, and kept company by matching Governor's House (now Volunteer Service Centre) and lodge. The **County Hospital**, 1880, John Murdoch, is a mixture of Queen Anne and French Renaissance detail, upon which the burgh arms and the Good Samaritan are the only purely ornamental work. The **Cemetery Gates**, 1862, also by John Murdoch, comprise an enjoyably over-scaled Tudor archway, with buttresses, squat pinnacles, crenellations and armorials.

T **Fort**, 1652, Hans Ewald Tessin
Cromwell's Citadel is a six-sided structure with bartizans at the angles, much of which still survives, including a blocked arched gateway in a lane off Citadel Place. *Baron* John Miller bought it in 1854, feuing almost immediately to a plan by Clarke & Bell. The odd **turret** which overlooks South Harbour Street is Miller's own addition. The stout stone walls of the Citadel can be seen to advantage alongside the turret, and also below Arran Terrace.

Citadel Place
Some attempt to create a formal entrance to the Fort with pleasing terraces – raised quoins, consoled or pilastered doorpieces, often lying-pane glazing – to either side, which date from Miller's time, and **4-6**, 1883, James A Morris which lend new grace to the vicinity. Bruce Crescent contains some of the earliest and most elaborate villas of the Fort, mostly with finely drawn faintly Jacobean details:
Eglinton Terrace, *c.*1864, is the centrepiece of Miller's feu plan: a long neoclassical ashlar-faced terrace, attractive and competent.

Top Ayr County Hospital. Above *Miller's Folly*

The **Citadel** was acquired in 1663 by the Montgomeries of Eglinton, and it was given the status of a Burgh of Barony – Montgomerieston. In the 18th century, traders from Montgomerieston – particularly brewers – used its burgh status to challenge the right of Ayr to charge milling and other taxes. Ownership of the Citadel passed from the Montgomeries to the Kennedys of Culzean. In 1854 it was acquired by John Miller, out-manoeuvring the Town Council. He was thus Baron Miller of Montgomerieston.

1799 feuing plan for Citadel

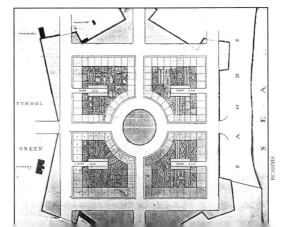

St John's Tower, *c*.1300

All that remains of Ayr's original parish
church, commandeered by Cromwell's troops
and now isolated within its stone-walled
enclosure. The five-stage square tower, which
had been attached to the earlier west gable of
the church, is of local ashlar stone, and has a
corbelled parapet, rounded at the angles, a
caphouse and belfry lancets. Other than the
rose window which dominates the east wall,
the other openings are plain and square-
headed. During the Commonwealth occupation
it appears to have been used as storehouse and
watch-tower: the church is still substantially
intact in Slezer's view of 1693, but must have
been demolished soon thereafter. The tower, an
important sea mark, was allowed to remain.
After acquiring the Fort lands, Miller
converted the tower into a house, Fort Castle,
for himself, using John Murdoch as executant
architect. After his death in 1910, the 3rd
Marquess of Bute commissioned J K Hunter to
restore the tower, Hunter's restoration being
based substantially on Slezer.

St John's Tower

Arran Terrace
Commands a fine view to the sea over a good
stretch of the Citadel wall; **1-8** are elaborately
detailed cottages of *c*.1860. **Cassillis Street**,
connects with the burgh's feuing of the
Washing Green; **2**, an attractive single-storey
double villa of painted stone and rock-faced
quoins, was feued by Miller in 1857; **6-14**,
c.1820, a terrace in the Wellington Square
mould is on burgh land.

∪ Wellington Square
The palace-fronted square proposed by John
Robertson was not pursued; instead individual
feuars were allowed to build within an overall
design. The pattern is a two-storey painted
stone front, usually of three bays, over a
basement, with fanlighted main doors
approached by straight flights of steps. The
terraces are protected from the roads by
wrought-iron railings. The result is reasonably
successful: the east end is patchy, and the
terraces are slightly too squat to enclose the
space, denying the sense of enclosure of the
contemporary squares in Edinburgh and
Glasgow. The gaps between the north and
south terraces and the County Buildings are
especially unsatisfactory. Nor was take-up of

On 26 April 1315, a meeting of
the nobility and Parliament in
Scotland, the first after the
victory at Bannockburn, was
convened in St John's Kirk: at
this meeting the crown was
officially given to Robert Bruce
and his line.
*And after Bannockburn, the
pomp and panoply of Bruce's
Parliament actually held in the
church! On that fine spring
day, St John's had its most
magnificent congregation ever.
Royal personages, eight bishops,
thirteen abbots, and a motley of
priors, deans, earls, barons and
knights appeared to swear
allegiance to the line of Bruce,
and rode off leaving the finest
collection of seals that ever
graced an Ayrshire document.*

the feus particularly swift. Only the central section of **1-14**, the north terrace, with its regular windows, cornice and blocking course, and much variety within, was built by 1818. **1-2**, *c*.1824, by Thomas King and Robert Andrew, wright and mason respectively. The south terrace was complete by 1818, **16**, built in 1808 by Robert McLauchlan, and **21** possibly by Robert Johnstone.

25 Wellington Square, *c*.1803
A taller, Doric doored, classical mansion which completes the south terrace in the style of David Hamilton. Three good statues: the ***Earl of Eglinton***, 1865, and ***Brigadier Neill***, 1859 – Neill *as he might be supposed to have looked when stopping the railway train at Calcutta* – both by Matthew Noble and ***Sir James Fergusson***, 1910, Goscombe John. J K Hunter's rather flaccid **Cenotaph** dates from 1920.

Top *Wellington Square*. Above & right *County Buildings*

The **County Buildings** (with the Town Hall of the next decade) forms built evidence that Ayr, as elsewhere in Scotland, had come of age following the period of national insecurity that followed the defeat of the '45. The building of a relief church, and the new Academy of 1799-1800 – replaced by the present building – are further evidence of a new-found confidence. The new streets north and south of Wellington Square were largely peopled by wealthier townsfolk leaving the increasingly insanitary town centre. Wellington Square, though, was largely the domain of County families, especially from Carrick.

∨ **County Buildings**, 1818-22, Robert Wallace
A dramatic classical court-house, with its huge eleven-bay frontispiece, and scowling four-columned Ionic portico, brings the full majesty of the law to bear on the Square: Alex Mair's 1931 extension is worthy of especial note, matching Wallace's work without any slavish copying, but with just sufficient freshness of detail and composition to give the new building a modern and individual character. Excellent interiors echo the two major building phases. Wallace's court-house has a spectacular stair hall, the stair winding round a Doric peristyle, the Ionic-columned original court-room, and the former County Hall, now also used for court purposes. Mair's extension is notable for the extensive use of dark wood panelling and furnishings, in a typically contemporary mannered classical style. County Buildings are flanked by the Tudor villa **14-16 Bath Place**, 1846, and by James K Hunter's idiosyncratic

Pavilion (*right*), 1911, built by the Town Council as an entertainment centre, aimed especially at the town's increasing summer visitor trade, and still used for those purposes. It is a vaguely Italianate confection incorporating balusters from the first New Bridge. Behind County Buildings are the delightful cast-iron **Steven Memorial Fountain**, 1892 and Pilkington Jackson's 1960 **Royal Scottish Fusiliers Memorial**, coy and of a mannered sentimentality.

1 Barns Street, 1803
The forerunner of development in this district has a stunning quality, enriching the classical box with an Ionic-porched pedimented centre bay and a steep vaguely French roof. The north side of **Barns Street**, completed by c.1818, was the first regular terrace in Ayr, houses and details similar to Wellington Square, without basements and stairs. **3-5** were completed by 1816, but **7-29** not until the early 1850s. As elsewhere in this area (Barns Terrace, Alloway Place) developers and feuars appeared to be happy with anachronistic design.

Charlotte Street, c.1818
The familiar pattern of broad Georgian terraces, with the occasional later addition, e.g. **39**, formerly Green Lodge, 1865, a plain villa enlivened by James Morris's alterations, especially the semicircular window on the side elevation. **1-17 Queen's Terrace**, from 1844, a delightful terrace of single-storey cottages over raised basements, matched by **19-33**, c.1861, Robert Paton.

The **Pavilion**, though splendid in its way, cannot be considered as representative of James Kennedy Hunter's work. Born in 1863, the son of a local plumber and councillor, Hunter trained with John Mercer and James Morris, before becoming Morris' partner and ultimately setting up on his own. By his death in 1929, he had established himself as the foremost architect in the town. His commercial work is exemplified by the Carnegie Library in Maybole; his domestic work is untramelled by the past, and tends towards a harled idiom, without obvious reference to a Scottish architectural past. Black Clauchrie and High Greenan identify the manner: in Wigtownshire the Portpatrick Hotel inflates it considerably.

W **Alloway Place**
Three similar blocks of classical detailed Regency terraces, with sturdy Greek Doric doorpieces; not fully complete until c.1845, only the rustication showing any development of design. Mason and wright for the first blocks appear to be Robert Andrew and Thomas King.

Above *1 Barns Street.* Left *Alloway Place*

Barns Terrace

X **Barns Terrace**
It has a very tasteful appearance and, when finished with dressed ground in front, will form a decided embellishment to our most fashionable public promenade. **1-14** comprise a long terrace with centre and end pavilions, sheltering behind private open space. It was begun *c.*1845, and not completed until *c.*1860, under the supervision of Robert Paton. **Dereel**, *c.*1874, is a chunkily detailed red stone Italianate villa quite at odds with its discreet neighbours. **Barns Park**, *c.*1856, picks up the terrace and the Doric of Alloway Place, but in unpainted ashlar, with entrances arranged in pairs.

Barns House

Y **Barns House**, *c.*1800
An earlier house, of perhaps *c.*1690, is preserved in the low side wing. The new villa is an excellent composition, enlivened by Doric porch and pretty fanlight, and rendered particular by the excellent quality of work. Lovingly looked after, Barns presides regally over the surrounding terraces and cottages.

30 Miller Road

Miller Road, from 1853
Laid out in a dead straight line to improve communication between the Racecourse Road/Barns area and the station. Bounded by late classical villas and terraces, of which the best villas are **3-5** (**Gleniffer Place**), *c.*1860, **7-9** (**Weston Place**), *c.*1860, **25-27** (Windsor Villas), 1870, by John Murdoch, and **30** (Ellerslie), an exquisite villa of *c.*1865 with unusual details. **6-24**, **Havelock Terrace**, *c.*1858 by J I McDerment is workmanlike, with a heavy Greek porch at **6**; **33-43**, **Kensington Terrace**, *c.*1865, is further evidence of Ayr's innate stylistic conservatism. **29 Park Circus**, 1895, H V Eaglesham, detailed villa with Ionic columns and frieze. **St Andrews Church**, 1893, John B Wilson, is rubbly red Perpendicular.

FIRST WARD
Racecourse Road

5, **Meteor Hotel**, 1856, is a good Roman Doric classical villa, while **7**, **Elmsley**, is a simpler, stylish villa. **Kensal Tower (65 Bellevue Crescent)**, c.1887, is a notable improvisation on the Italianate pattern, with a full, canted bay and an entrance raised on balustraded steps; the **Pickwick Hotel (19)**, c.1865, is vaguely baronial with hood-moulded doorpiece including an armorial panel. Hidden from view by a nursing home of unsympathetic design **South Lodge**, 1841, a large Ionic villa, forms the centrepiece of a sheltered housing complex, 1987, by McLean Gibson & Associates. **34**, c.1825, is an attractive Jacobean cottage orné with bargeboards on cantilevered brackets. **Cumberland Lodge**, c.1825, a near-symmetrical Tudor villa, is enlivened by a fanciful porch of neo-Greek ironwork. **Blair Lodge**, c.1828, is similar, with Doric porch and pretty fanlight, whereas **Gartferry**, 1867, by Andrew MacLachlan, is stunningly Italianate and dominant. **Seatower**, c.1860, a tall Scottish baronial villa with crowsteps and strapwork, is reminiscent of architecture by David MacGibbon, while **52**, **Chestnuts Hotel**, is a conventional classical villa of 1846, enlarged in 1893 by J K Hunter.

Seatower

Ayr's premier residential quarter since the 1840s, Racecourse Road and the streets on either side have no convenient all-embracing name. Racecourse Road gives the general impression: street and house names record feuars: Nicholson of Barns, Arthur Lang of Bellevue, Campbell of Blackburn, McLelland at Southpark, Boyle at Ronaldshaw, Carson at Victoria Park. Through most of this period of pre-eminence, it was the First Ward, a term which carries socio-economic overtones in addition to the logistical needs of local government administration.

Gargowan, c.1820

Now the Ayrshire Hospice, this was one of the first villas of Racecourse Road. A quality Regency house with a Greek Doric porch, and matching outbuildings, truly *rus in urbe*. The Italianate villas in **Victoria Park**, c.1848, may be by Clarke & Bell who prepared the feuing plan. The **Old Racecourse Hotel**, c.1876, with its Jacobean details, may have been designed by the architectural historians MacGibbon & Ross.

Left *Chestnuts Hotel.* Below *Ayrshire Hospice*

Above *Savoy Croft*. Right *Savoy Park Hotel*

James A Morris, 1857-1942, is easily the best architect to have worked in the county. The son of a china merchant in Ayr, Morris trained with the Glasgow/Cambuslang architect Lindsay Miller, before establishing himself in Ayr. For a period he was in partnership with James K Hunter, during much of which time Morris lived in London running a second office in Westminster, before returning to Ayr in 1896. Some of his work shows awareness of Mackintosh (for example, the north elevation of his extension to Ayr Academy), but the majority is anchored firmly in a love for traditional Scottish architecture, and the need for high standards of craftsmanship. With family money behind him (he was for many years chairman of the Kilmarnock engineering firm Glenfield & Kennedy Ltd or 'The Glen'), Morris was able to devote his time to other issues: founding the Scottish Society of Art Workers and campaigning to save the Auld Brig. He wrote on a variety of subjects, notably on Burns, the Auld Brig, and *A Romance of Industrial Engineering*, a rosy-visioned history of 'The Glen'. After the First World War, in which his son George was killed serving with the RFC, his practice virtually dried up. A few war memorial commissions provided the last outlets for a craft-based architecture.

Savoy Park, from 1896, James A Morris This spreading, brooding hotel is an introduction to a little Morrisian retreat, itself a chunky interpretation of baronial, complete with re-entrant turret and tower. **Savoy Croft**, 1894, Morris's own house, is a subtly blended mixture of Arts & Crafts and vernacular features in his favoured Mauchline stone: remarkably unchanged inside, and a wonderful evocation of the life and interests of this talented and scholarly architect. **Wellsbourne**, 1905, also by Morris, is equally carefully articulated deploying lush Renaissance details. **Wheatfield House**, *c.*1795, a standard Georgian box harled with a slightly advanced central bay, may be by Hugh Cairncross. **Sheninghurst**, Wheatfield Road, 1888, is an unusually deep-eaved villa in the manner of W J Anderson. At the foot of **Blackburn Road**, a powerful group of forbidding Scottish baronial villas: **Carlton Turrets**, Ayr Youth Hostel (formerly **Craigweil**) and **Westfield**, all of 1879, to designs of John Murdoch.

Right *Westfield*. Far right *Dolphin House*

Midton Road

A road which bends and twists enjoyably, a legacy of its origins as a road through the grassy sandy knolls of the burgh common lands on which much of the First Ward houses were built, and giving ever-changing vistas of its architecture: the rubbly perpendicular

BB **St Columba's Church**, 1898, John B Wilson, with its cultured octagonal pencil tower; **Dolphin House**, c.1807, a pleasant rubbly box with a little round window in the pediment; **Melling**, c.1850, a single-attic villa in the manner of Alexander Thomson's Seymour Lodge, and the Gothic **Edendarroch**, 1883, by Hippolyte J Blanc, planned with some complexity. Good houses in **Racecourse View**, overlooking Belleisle Park: **Hartfield House**, 1850, is a sophisticated house with elaborate classical details and a richly drawn frieze below the main cornice; **3**, **Inverdon**, 1845, by Clarke & Bell, similar to its neighbour, neo-Jacobean; **The Knowe**, c.1845, a mansion of considerable distinction, extended congruently in 1894 by Robert Thomson, and flatted in 1962 by Robert Bluck. **14** Racecourse View, 1965, by Norman McLean – Ayr's Villa Savoie – is almost deliberate in its provocation, all the rooms in a first-floor view-commanding glazed box. **Shalimar**, 1868, is rogue Scottish baronial with Jacobean details, whereas **Hartley House**, 1869, mixes Alexander Thomson-style details with mild Italianate.

CC **Bellevue House**, Marchmont Road, c.1810 Ashlar-fronted rectangular villa with pedimented slightly advanced centre, flatted in 1958 by Edward Darley. **1-7 Carrick Avenue**, 1882, is an eclectic little terrace. The half-timbered **16**, c.1905, by John A Campbell was the gatehouse for the demolished Carrick House. Note the Glasgow Style overtones of **2 Corsehill Road**, 1905, by J K Hunter. **St Leonard's Church**, 1886, John Murdoch, plain rubble geometric, with a 1910 chancel and hall by P MacGregor Chalmers. **Rosebank House**, c.1822, is ennobled by its semi-elliptical central projection and good Doric porch.

Chapel Park, 16 Ewenfield Road, 1916, H E Clifford & Lunan

Fine harled villa whose strong horizontals pulling against the undressed tower, presage the inter-war Modern Movement in Scotland,

Pressure of space prevents a full survey of Ayr's Victorian villa architecture. More can be found in the streets which link Midton Road and Racecourse Road – Southpark Road, Ronaldshaw Park – and to the landward side of Midton Road, such as Broomfield Road. The architects are mostly local, including John Murdoch and James A Morris.

Top *The Knowe*. Above *14 Racecourse View*

Belleisle

At the sale in 1754 of the **Burgh Lands of Alloway**, the lands on which Belleisle was built were bought by John Campbell of Wellwood, but in 1784 they were acquired by Hugh Hamilton, and it is with the Hamiltons that the house is most closely associated. The work by Burn was done for Alexander West Hamilton. The house was acquired in 1926 by the Town Council, the lands merged with the adjoining Council-owned old racecourse, the last surviving part of the Town Common. (In 1788 Alexander Stevens built a dyke 5ft high around the Town Common.) Racing seems to have taken place here since the mid-18th century, and continued until the new racecourse was opened in 1907.

Below *Rozelle*. Bottom *Maclaurin Art Gallery*

emphasising how the latter's roots lay within the Scottish tradition. **39-47 Maybole Road**, 1964, by Norman McLean for William Cowie & Torry, are unashamedly aggressive and monopitched, seemingly all wall and no windows.

Belleisle, 1787 onwards
At first glance, Belleisle appears to be a largely Scots Jacobean mansion, marked by thin towers with conical caps and an odd corbie-stepped entrance with a baroque doorcase. It is an 1829 recasting by William Burn in his Falkland manner (see the *Kingdom of Fife* in this series) of the house built for Hugh Hamilton, *c*.1787. The original, visible from the garden, has a simple configuration and central bow submerged by corbie-stepped gables and balustrading. Elaborate Jacobean plasterwork within, dating from *c*.1830. **The Stables**, *c*.1830, and **lodges** in similar thin neo-Jacobean suggest Burn. The Belleisle golf courses incorporate the old racecourse, whose former Viewhouse, 1867, J I McDerment, survives in **Doonfoot Road**. **Seafield**, now a hospital, is by Clarke & Bell and R A Bryden's impressively large individually designed Italianate house of 1888-92 for Sir William Arrol replaced an earlier house, whose courtyard stable block of *c*.1820 survives as Nightingale House.

Rozelle, *c*.1754
Rozelle, with Belleisle and the Alloway estates (Cambusdoon, Mount Charles) was built on burgh common land sold by Ayr Town Council in 1754. Rozelle, probably the first, was begun for Robert Hamilton, a returned West Indian nabob. A simple harled block with raised quoins, stepped entrance, and sunken quadrant links, something of the manner of John Adam, is in the mainstream of native Scots classical. The main block was fattened up by David Bryce in 1830. The matching stables were elegantly converted into the award-winning **Maclaurin Art Gallery** (see pp.C2, C3), 1976, by Cowie Torry & Partners. A Henry Moore nude reclines in the courtyard. A moving series of sculptures; *The Tragic Sacrifice of Christ*, 1978-9, by Ronnie Rae can be found in the delightful gardens; excellent at rhododendron time.

Main Street, Newton

NEWTON on AYR

Newton had become a Burgh of Barony by 1446, possibly as early as the mid 14th century, Main Street marking its core. Riding on the back of Ayr's growing trade, but free of the restrictions imposed by Royal Burgh regulations, Newton grew steadily, especially during the late 18th century and early 19th century, when exploitation of coal gave added economic impetus. The increasing archaism of the Royal Burgh's restrictions on trade drove industrial and commercial development over to the far side of the river. Newton was further developed during the early 19th century to a grid pattern laid on the burgh green, marked by Green Street and York Street; first feued *c*.1820, and extended a generation later. The houses were generally plain, often single-storey cottages: almost nothing beyond the street pattern survives.

Main Street

Since Newton lines up with Sandgate, it must pre-date Ayr Auld Brig, linked to Ayr by the ford (eventually replaced by the first New Bridge, but which proved too intractable for the builders of the Auld Brig). The **Borderline Theatre** (former **Darlington Place Church**), 1860, by Clarke & Bell, stands sentinel at the bridge, heavily buttressed, and thinly Gothic, converted to its new use by J Wetton Brown in 1986.

Royal Freedoms were awarded to forty-eight men of Newton who performed heroically at Bannockburn. The Freedom Lands of Newton stretched west and north and east of the little town. During the 19th century, they were, at various stages, apportioned out, and distributed among the freedom-holders by lot. First, forty-eight plots were laid off along the east side of the turnpike to Prestwick: thereafter the Newton Green was disposed off in two separate tranches, *for a designed new town* and finally the remaining lands were disposed off from 1834. Houses such as Woodfield (Dalblair Motors, Prestwick Road) and Falkland (demolished) appeared soon after 1834, while local entrepreneurs (such as Oswald of Auchincruive and the foundry-owner Alexander Weir) began to develop land holdings. It was only from the 1880s onwards that the final rump of Newton Lands was developed primarily for housing.

Borderline Theatre

Carnegie Public Library

DD**Carnegie Public Library**, 1893,
Campbell Douglas & Morrison
A dramatic Renaissance titan whose recessed
centre bays suck in the public; it has a
dramatic tiled entrance hall and a powerful
full-height stained glass window by Stephen
Adam & Co lighting the stair hall. The **Orient
Cinema**, 1932, Albert V Gardner, is a joyful
confection, though it has lost its Moorish
interiors.

EE**Newton Tower**, 1795
The woeful remnant of Newton's Tolbooth:
*severely chaste in its simplicity, very
insignificant in its littleness and awfully plain
in its ugliness.* **Newton Church**, 1862, William
Clarke, a simple Gothic Free Church ennobled
by its stylish octagonal tower, was insensitively
obscured by the Church Hall, 1791.

Right *Newton Steeple.* Far right
Unionist Club

1-3 New Road, *c*.1830
A pretty little gusset building with original
pilastered shopfront opposite the former
Unionist Club, 1891, by James A Morris &
Hunter, excellent treatment of older,
vernacular work of the 18th century, and the
faintly Glasgow Style **Salvation Army
Citadel**, 1905, by Arthur Hamilton. **Newton
Academy**, 1911, William Cowie, is a large
forthright school with baronial details.

Ayr Harbour (see pp.C1, C6)
FF The **Ratton Quays** on either side of the river
were rebuilt in 1713, and again in 1724-30, and
much restored subsequently. The Wet Dock,
1873, by J I McDerment, and the smaller Slip
Dock, 1883, by John Strain, were added to the
north and south sides. Berths on the south side
are used by the PS *Waverley* and the fishing

The paddle-steamer **Waverley**,
a much-loved summer visitor to
the Ayrshire coast, first sailed
on 16 June 1947: her
predecessor having been lost at
Dunkirk. Coal-fired, she was
built by A & J Inglis at
Pointhouse, with three-cylinder
triple-expansion machinery by
Rankin & Blackmore of
Greenock, the very last of the
Clyde paddle-steamers.

fleet serviced by the functional fish market. The north harbour handles coal and freight traffic; here there was an attractive, two-storey harbourmaster's office, 1883, with a corner pepperpot turret by John Mercer, and there is still a bonny little lighthouse, 1841, by Robert Paton, with cottage added in *c*.1850.

North Newton and **New Prestwick** – the Freedom Lands of Newton, parcelled out and feued off to the Freemen during the 1830s, contemporary with ribbon development along the Prestwick Road – fill the gap between Ayr and Prestwick. Only **Woodfield**, *c*.1833, suffering with dignity the workshops of a large garage-cum-filling station, survives of the original smaller villas. From about *c*.1875 the area filled up quickly: road upon road between Prestwick Road and Oswald Road: more complex on the landward. The first council housing schemes of Ayr Town Council completed the task, the very first being **3-25** and **6-28** George's Avenue, 1920, by J K Hunter. There are few architectural highlights. The brooding soot-blackened **St James Church**, 1883, John Murdoch, is one: Early English with a good neoclassical hall by Alex Mair, 1933. **100-108 Prestwick Road**, 1896-8, by H E Clifford, are crisply finished tenements with some Glasgow Style scribblings in the door arches, while **149B Prestwick Road**, 1935, Percy Hogarth, is a single-storey flat-roofed bungalow of horizontal steel-framed windows and white harl (now much altered).

Robert Adam's perspective of the proposed first new Ayr Bridge and Quays, c. 1713

John Murdoch, *c*.1826-1907, was the most ambitious of the architects of Ayr in the late 19th century. Trained as a civil engineer, he set up in practice in 1850, and quickly established a considerable clientele. To Murdoch fell most of the important commissions in the town: over a period of thirty years he designed the Cemetery, the Hospital, the Boys' Industrial School, St Leonard's Church, and numerous police stations throughout the county. His style is robust and generally baronial and sombre especially in his domestic commissions.

William Cowie, 1867-1949, came to Ayr about 1900 as chief draughtsman to J & H V Eaglesham. He had trained with A & W Reid, Sydney Mitchell and Clarke & Bell. He set up in 1904: his first work the studio at 2 Dalblair Road, and he and his successors have never looked back. **Fred Torry**, c.1910-80, was taken into partnership in 1947: both Torry and his successor as senior partner, **Ian McGill**, contributed largely to the continuing success of Cowie & Torry. The firm's work includes almost all of Ayr's council housing, and the architectural input into the Galloway Hydro Power Scheme.

WALLACETOWN
The history of Wallacetown resembles that of Newton. It belonged to the Wallaces of Craigie, who were quick to appreciate the advantages of the 18th-century growth in trade and in coal exploration. Their village grew on a field known as the Park of Newton on Ayr, basically a cross-roads – Cross Street (now King Street) and Wallace Street/Allison Street – backing on to the turnpike road to Mauchline (George Street, running up from the bridge), which separated their lands from the adjacent Blackhouse estate. Under the Gordons of Blackhouse, this estate, too, was quick to exploit the opportunities, and the bulk of this area, known as **Content**, based on John Street, Elba Street, Content Street, was developed piecemeal during the 19th century. The name Content has been largely absorbed into Wallacetown, and the whole area radically redeveloped from 1964.

George Street
Begins at Auld Brig, with the pleasing **2-16 George Street** and **2-4 River Terrace**, of c.1830, and the simple pedimented **Free Church**, 1832, eyeing warily **Asda**, 1987, Cowie Torry & Partners' glazed monolith.

Below *Ayr Free Church*. Bottom *St Margaret's Church*. Right *Riverside House*

GG **Riverside House**, 1975, by Cowie Torry & Partners, a dramatic hard-edged office block, is a welcome addition to the riverfront. On the far side of the inner ring road, George Street continues with the former **Morrison Church**, 1779, detailing by J K Hunter, 1901. This little neuk best exemplifies pre-redevelopment Wallacetown and Content. **John Street**, sacrificed to the car, has **St Margaret's RC Church**, 1826, by James Dempster (*an artist of some promise*) in a prickly buttressed Decorated Gothic clearly influenced by J Gillespie Graham. **Wallacetown Parish**

Church, 1834, by John Kay, is notably similar to St Augustine's Gateway, Canterbury, with a Tudor gloss (its twin towers were reduced in height in 1949). Allan Stevenson's simple Gothic Robertson Memorial Church, 1901, has become the **Civic Theatre**, the necessary additions tacked on in 1950-4.

Fire Station

Ayr Fire Station, 1963, J & J A Carrick
A pleasing concrete structure with applied synthetic granite blocks, and stone from Content House, which it replaced, used to create the southern retaining wall. Redevelopment of Wallacetown began in the 1930s, when Ayr Town Council erected a number of monolithic, faintly baronial blocks of flats, such as **50 Elba Street**, 1933, William Cowie, which respected existing street lines, and survived the wholesale demolitions of the early 1960s. Modern Wallacetown is an area of pedestrian/car separation, of linked blocks of flats, all harl and glass and plentiful exposed woodwork for textural variation, well laid out about spacious grassy areas; there is a sculptural quality, and an appropriate respect for scale, which extends even to the three tower blocks, 1969-70, in

Riverside Place

HH **Riverside Place**. Ayr Town Council, with William Cowie & Torry as architects, worked closely to outline proposals by Jack Holmes and Alfred Wood: nine-storey-high flats, maisonettes and one-storey houses built *Roman-style* around a patio as a means of reducing noise nuisance. Wallacetown, a credit to all, is an example of successful redevelopment. **Wallacetown Cemetery** survives in Russell Street, its most notable adornment being the **John Taylor Monument**, 1858.

Craigie House, 18th century
Seat of the Wallaces of Craigie, successor to Newton Castle, in itself a successor to Craigie Castle, whose central block may be as early as

John Taylor, 1805-42, physician, Chartist and reformer, was a Taylor of Blackhouse, born to the *immense affluence* of coal mines and stone quarries. The tribute on the pedestal reads: *Professionally he was alike the Poor Man's generous friend and physician; politically, he was the eloquent and unflinching advocate of the People's cause, freely sacrificing health, means, social status and even personal liberty to the advancement of measures then considered extreme, but now acknowledged to be essential to the well-being of the State.*

C

Craigie House

c.1730. It passed to William Campbell in 1783, after which a palatial seven-bay Georgian house was erected, flanked by pavilions and curving screen walls of c.1770, with an impressive bow projecting to the garden majestically visible across the river from Holmston Road. The entrance front is almost totally obscured by a vast Greek Doric porch, c.1837, usually attributed to W H Playfair. **Craigie College of Education**, begun in 1964, has a meticulous spreading teaching block by A Buchanan Campbell, joined in 1967 by Boswell Mitchell & Johnston's bolder Halls of Residence. Craigie's lodges – the 18th-century pavilion with superarch and Venetian window at 2 Craigie Avenue, and the plainer Victorian ones on Craigie Road – mark the boundaries.

Ayr Racecourse, from 1907
The course and the functional Sanquhar brick steel-framed stands were designed by Allan Stevenson in association with the Newmarket architects W C & A S Manning. From 1964 a phased process of renewal and extension has taken place under J & J A Carrick, of which the Eglinton Rooms, opened in 1967, are the most successful architecturally. Very much of its time, boxy, relying heavily on glazing to give depth and articulation, and balanced above the main entrance on improbably spindly stilts. Within the complex is Annette Yarrow's 1975 statue of the horse **Red Rum**. **Western House**, 1919, by Harold O Tarbolton, is a sensuously sumptuous clubhouse in thick white harl on the site of Blackhouse.

Western House

Whitletts
A colliers' village developed on Blackhouse land from c.1810. The village was absorbed into the

burgh in 1935, and subsequently almost completely redeveloped. The School was rebuilt in 1910 by A C Thomson to a plain school board pattern with his quirky details. J R Johnstone's **Thistle Inn**, 1937, is an excellent example of an *improved* public house. **Dalmilling Parish Church**, 1953, William Cowie & Torry, is timid, financially constrained brick Gothic.

Thistle Inn

Cathedral of the Good Shepherd, 1955, Fred Torry

Raised to cathedral status in 1961, this long, low, and unambitious brick building has standard metal windows and a low tower capped by a chimneylike turret. Refurbished inside in 1985, with lush fittings from St Robert Bellermine, Glasgow, and equally rich glass from Our Lady & St Margaret, Kinning Park.

PRESTWICK

Until the mid 19th century the priests' village led a humble existence despite its having been raised as a Burgh of Barony *c.*1165. By the time of the first Ordnance Survey, *c.*1857, it was little more than a straggle of cottages along the main road and Kirk Street. The parochial charge had been combined with that of another stagnating village, Monkton, early in the 17th century; a new church was built mid-way between in 1837. Both station and golf green appear, however, on the 1857 map, and it was these, in combination, that brought growth and prosperity. Glasgow merchants took houses in Prestwick, often stabling their families here during the summer, for the golf.

Prestwick's merchants were of a lesser calibre than those of Ayr or Troon: their houses are fewer, generally smaller, plainer and less refined or detailed, and cluster close to the station and clubhouse. Despite townly pretence – a Woolworth's – Prestwick's core never fully developed, and remains an unsatisfactory juxtaposition of commercial and domestic, decent cottages cheek-by-jowl with commercial palaces. Large-scale 20th-century speculative suburban growth left Prestwick as a dormitory suburb.

Prestick [sic] Mercat Cross, 1777

Square shaft and ball finial. It has led a peripatetic existence, usually finding itself a hindrance to traffic and is now kept company by the 1921 War Memorial, by James A Morris, a cross-topped shaft. **21-37 Main Street**, 1898, James A Morris, the former Unionist Club and later Town Hall, has Morris's sure touch, notably in the bold hood-moulded hall windows and the tactile doorway. The **Bank of Scotland**, a plain villa of *c.*1860 – at one time burgh offices – around which the burgh intended to build a striking Scandinavian suite of offices, won in competition by Mervyn Noad in 1934. Timidity and events elsewhere ensured that this never happened: a major blow to Scottish architecture.

Prestick Mercat Cross

Broadway

Broadway, 26 Main Street, 1934,
Alister MacDonald
Easily Prestwick's best building: so many cubic
building blocks piled on one another, coated in
white harl, and the edges slightly rounded,
wearing its age easily. MacDonald, an artist
and specialist cinema architect, was son of
Ramsay MacDonald, the Prime Minister.

Freemen's Hall, 1844
Lightweight Gothic hall, with an artisan
strapworked tower, signals the corner of Kirk
Street, which retains a few 18th-century
cottages, the ruin of 13th-century **St Nicholas
Church**, plain with inserted square-headed
windows of post-Reformation date, and **Old St
Cuthbert's**, 1908, J Gibb Morton, an exquisite
little Arts & Crafts former clubhouse by this
much-neglected architect, and now amid
speculative housing which takes its design cue
from it.

*Old St Cuthbert's, former
Airport Club*

Prestwick hosted the first
twelve Open Championships
from 1860, played over the
twelve holes of the original
course of 1851, of which five
still exist in more-or-less
unaltered form. Horace
Hutchinson wrote of the
original twelve holes in 1890:
*They lay in deep dells among
these sandhills, and you lofted
over the intervening mountain
of sand; and there was all the
fascinating excitement, as you
climbed to the top of it, of seeing
how near to the hole your ball
might have happened to roll.*

Prestwick Golf Club

North Church, 1874, James Salmon & Son
Customary plain box with a clumsy belltower
in 1896 by John Keppie and arcaded halls by
Alex Mair, 1932. **38-48 Monkton Road** is a
good run of red sandstone villas, 1894-1903,
all formally presented on a low knoll without
much softening vegetation but with
considerable panache; **40-42** appears to be by
John Keppie; **44-46**, with fawn stone frieze, by
Thomas Dykes & Robertson.

Prestwick Golf Club, 1866
The original clubhouse was nothing more than
a normal late classical villa until
aggrandisement by Morris & Hunter in 1893,
the emphasis on utility rather than
architectural display. Villas in Links Road and
The Esplanade are mostly severe,
unornamented and deeply conventional with
variety provided by **Stonegarth** (RAFA Club),
1908, J K Hunter, in the cottagey manner that

Links Nursing Home

Hunter quarried assiduously; the thoughtful Scottish revival **Greystones**, 23 Links Road, 1897, possibly by A N Paterson, and by the Scots vernacular **Links Nursing Home**, 1901, James A Morris, with its passing nod to Mackintosh.

South Church, 1882-4, James A Morris Morris's first church commission: adept, light handling of Gothic forms, mixed here with judiciously chosen carving in a Glasgow Style manner. Carefully chosen interior fittings include glass by Oscar Paterson, a long-time associate of Morris. Grey Craiksland (Troon) stone, unusual for Morris. **St Nicholas Church**, 1908, typically Peter MacGregor Chalmers, scholarly correct, competent but ultimately not very lovable. Excellent array of stained glass, mainly by the Abbey Studio and by Gordon Webster. A few villas in **Ayr Road**, the best being the stately idiosyncratic **St Ninian's**, **29**, 1912, William Cowie. Others, in a fluid, unclassifiable style, include **2** and **4**. **Sandgate Cottage**, **22**, is an attractive Gothick cottage of *c.*1840.

Kingcase
The origins of Kingcase lie in the lazaretto founded here by Robert Bruce in gratitude for his recovery from sickness after drinking the waters of the well here; Bruce's sickness was leprosy. **St Ninian's Episcopal Church**, 1926, James Hay, displays an elegiac handling of 14th-century detail.

Salt Pan Houses, Maryborough, *c.*1760 (see p.C6) Probably the best survivals of their type in Scotland. Two rubbly two-storey houses linked by a wall. Salt panning took place in the ground-floor brick vault and the salters lived above. The salt pans have been superseded by

Below *South Church*. Bottom *St Nicholas Church*

Salt Pan Houses, Maryborough

The salt-boiling works at Maryborough is the principal survivor of an industry which once flourished on the Ayrshire coast. Reference to *salt pan hous* is found in Prestwick burgh records in 1480. At Maryborough, preliminary evaporation was carried out in shallow ponds between the two buildings, before the finished product was produced over fires in the brick-lined vaults.

St Nicholas Golf Course; the **clubhouse**, 1892, by John Mercer, in a rubbly Italianate style with oriels and projections. Note the fine bas-relief of a golfer by W G Stevenson.

New Life Christian Centre, 1837, David Bryce
The former Monkton & Prestwick Parish Church stands aloof alongside a main road now truncated by a rapacious airport. Similar to Bryce's church at Coylton (see p.43): little pinnacles to a tall tower, large Gothic windows, it is more convincing than Coylton: gargoyles and other details giving it an air of solidity. It was strikingly redecorated during the 1920s and 1930s, the chancel of 1925 by the craft architect Jeffrey Waddell, the neoclassical hall range of *c*.1932 by Alex Mair. The **Towans Hotel**, *c*.1897, Alexander N Paterson, is a sensuous creamy harled Arts & Crafts villa, with bespoke interior decoration: lush rich panelling and couthy mottoes in the Lorimer manner.

New Life Christian Centre

Prestwick Airport

PRESTWICK AIRPORT
The area between Prestwick and Monkton, used as an aerodrome for many years, developed into an airport during the Second World War to maximise distance from German airfields and to minimise the distance from North American ones. T B Wilson of TWA described it in 1945 as the first practical international airport. The **Terminal**, 1964, Joseph L Gleave, of concrete-encased steel-frame construction, is dramatic, an unbroken run of glass, without articulation or contrast, mannered and authoritarian. The vast aircraft works of Scottish Aviation Industries include the **Palace of Engineering**, 1938, Thomas

Gladstone

Tait, re-erected here from the Empire Exhibition in 1941: functional exhibition architecture at its best. The entrance, strongly marked by six square columns, is now replaced by huge sliding doors. No nonsense within: it provided the Air Ministry with four and a half acres of covered floor space.

MONKTON
Pleasant sequestered little village with a few single-storey weavers' cottages, e.g. **1-11 Tarbolton Road**.

St Cuthbert's Church, 13th century
Originally the Kirk of Prestwick Monachorum this plain rectangle was given a north wing, probably in the 17th century, in an attempt to create a T-plan preaching box and a fine round-arched doorway in the south wall. Finally abandoned in 1837. The Weirs of Adamton have a dramatic Doric **Mausoleum** in the churchyard, and the adjacent former manse, 1822, has a curious splayed porch. The **Carvick Walker Hall**, 1929, W R Watson, is a rather gauche Arts & Crafts survival. The ridge behind the village has the stump of a windmill, 18th century, and the **Macrae Monument**, *c.*1750, by John Swan, a naïve Corinthian erection with urns, obelisk and alcove.

Townhead, *c.*1800
An unflinching farm of customary size and pattern, with a good ginhouse, adjoined by the lodge for **Monktonhead**, 1910: a superlative very English Elizabethan house by James Miller which employs the full apparatus of half-timbering, tall brick chimneys and hanging tiles.

Adamton House, 1888
Built for the iron and coal master J G A Baird in swaggering Jacobean taste with ornate carved gables, it is large and impressive with particularly sumptuous interiors. Conversion

Palace of Engineering

A leading role in developing the Prestwick site from a grassy strip into an important wartime base, and then into an international airport was played by **David McIntyre** who, with the **Marquess of Clydesdale**, had been the first to fly over Everest in 1933. They founded Scottish Aviation Ltd in 1935 which ran a flying school from land between Monkton and Prestwick.

Close

Monkton Church

James Macrae, Cartsdyke-born herdboy who died in 1746, made his fortune in India, ultimately becoming Governor of Madras. Returning to Scotland, he built Orangefield House, and presented the statue of William III, now in Cathedral Square, to the City of Glasgow. Orangefield stood in the path of the airport and was eventually demolished after suffering the indignity of having the control tower pushed through its roof by Alex Mair.

Above *Adamton House.* Below
St Quivox Church. Bottom
Campbell Mausoleum

for the British Aerospace Flying College has
involved the erection of additional blocks,
1987-9, Dunlop & Paige.

ST QUIVOX
Small kirktoun of much charm though little
more than church, manse and a few cottages,
dwarfed by the agricultural college and
research institute established here in 1930.

St Quivox Church, 1767
Medieval core extended in 1767 by the Oswalds
of Auchincruive to create the T-shaped building
that contemporary worship required. Interior
fittings date largely from the late 18th century,
including a good pulpit. In the kirkyard,
mausoleum, 1822, of the Campbells of
Craigie, well-executed work of W H Playfair.
Cottar House is a sympathetic modernisation
of a row of traditional cottages. The former
manse, 1823, chunky pink ashlar, given
movement by the tall flat bays and box
parapet. **Mount Hamilton**, *c.*1790,
incorporating older work, is dominated by the
elliptical bow which engulfs the entire façade of
this former Auchincruive factor's house.

**Auchincruive (Scottish Agricultural
College)**
The Auchincruive estate has been developed into
one of the most delightful campuses in Scotland.
The pre-existing buildings, the necessary modern
additions, and the plentiful planting, controlled
by the College's Horticultural Department,
blend together in a joyful, urbane manner.

Auchincruive House (now **Oswald Hall**),
from 1767
Possibly a modification of plans made by the
Adam brothers for James Murray of
Broughton, who had sold the estate to Richard

Oswald in 1764. Enlarged in congruent manner in the late 19th century. Some superb interiors, designed by Robert Adam in 1766, restored recently after years of rough usage. **Hanging gardens**, believed to be a work-creation project of *c.*1840, use fully this deeply cut part of the Ayr valley. The home farm, **Gibbsyard**, *c.*1780, is an excellent courtyard with elliptical pend guarded by a clock tower which transforms itself behind into a doocot. The **Temple** or **Tea-house**, 1778, by Robert Adam, a folly or summerhouse in Adam's castle style, a freestanding version of the round towers at Culzean and Dalquharran, and based closely on Theodoric's Mausoleum at Ravenna.

Top *Auchincruive.* Above *Hanging Gardens.* Left *Tea-house*

The college buildings, especially the early ones – all by Alex Mair – are equally enjoyable, in an unsophisticated neoclassicism which could adapt easily to the various functional requirements: **Apiary** (the first to be completed), **Poultry School**, **Dairy School**, all of 1931. **Wilson Hall**, 1956, by D S McPhail, is an unheralded masterpiece, an X-plan building of dignity and simplicity, a later flowering of the style and manner of Lorimer, using Scots motifs sparingly and to great effect.

Hannah Research Institute, Kirkhill, 1931, A G Ingham
Quiet institutional style, a faintly classical heavily harled isolation hospital effect, but very effective on its low hill with Arran and the

The **Auchincruive Estate** was gifted to the Secretary of State by John M Hannah of Girvan Mains. The greater part was given over to the West of Scotland Agricultural College, transferred from suburban Kilmarnock. The remainder was given for the establishment of a scientific institute to research and promote improvements in dairying which had long been an aim of the Board of Agriculture. The Institute, named in honour of the benefactor, opened in 1931.

Firth of Clyde as a backcloth. Denys Mitchell's bronze, *The Milkmaid*, 1980, is a notable piece of publicly commissioned sculpture.

Ailsa Hospital, 1865-8, Charles Edward
The County Lunatic Asylum, won in competition by Edward (see *Dundee* in this series) in a thin Jacobean style almost engulfed by subsequent additions on the site. **South Ayrshire District General Hospital**, 1988-91, Keppie Henderson Architects, fails to disguise its bulk with rather mechanical humanising details.

Ailsa Hospital

Digital Equipment (Scotland) Ltd, 1979, G R M Kennedy & Partners
A large shed in Mosshill Industrial Estate, given a smooth anodised glass façade so characteristic of high-tech identity, and cut into the hillside in an amenity damage-limitation exercise. **Masonhill Crematorium**, 1965, Douglas Hay, has fyfestone facing, roughcast harling finish and dark grey slate roof which are well chosen and contribute to the successful achievement of tranquillity.

Sundrum Castle, 1792
Georgian mansion erected for John Hamilton of Sundrum incorporating an early tower house,

Sundrum Castle

*c.*1360, through whose walls new windows have been slapped. The adjoining office wings, probably late 18th century, but much extended and altered, flank a cobbled yard, with cupola, clock gable, Venetian windows. **The Cushats**, *c.*1880, is a pretty little cottage orné enlarged into a modest country house. Gadgirth House has gone: **Gadgirth Mains**, *c.*1840, survives: an attractive courtyard farm entered through a pend completed by a gable with doocot, and with well-finished details throughout, while **Gadgirth Holm**, 1906, is an attractive, if rather coarse, Arts & Crafts terrace of cottages.

Gadgirth Holm

Coylton

Straggling village without particular character: Low Coylton, the old village with the kirkyard, a bar and little else, Hillhead, with the parish church, and Joppa, where original cottages can be found. The explosion of speculative housing throughout the 1970s and 1980s has brought population but little else to Coylton, and the result is a formless hybrid, too big to be a real village but lacking the facilities of a town. Figuratively, Coylton stands at a crossroads.

Parish Church, 1836, David Bryce Mechanical Gothic, a tall tower flanked by aisles, all disappointingly thin, and similar to Bryce's former Monkton and Prestwick Parish Church (see p.38). The **Claud Hamilton Memorial Hall**, 1909, by A C Thomson, is faintly Arts & Crafts. **Low Coylton House**, the former manse, 1839, is well built, and slightly French in feel with its steeply pitched hipped roof. At Low Coylton, the old kirk, medieval, fragmentary, repaired in 1776, and the couthy Coylton Arms, *c.*1800. **Joppa** has a pleasant if much altered range of one- and two-storey vernacular dwellings, *c.*1810.

TROON

Now synonymous with golf, Troon was first and foremost a railway town; perhaps *the* first railway town. In 1812 the Duke of Portland opened a railway to bring coal from his Kilmarnock collieries to Troon, where he had begun to create a harbour on the Troon (headland) in 1808, for trans-shipment generally to Ireland. Before then there had been only some fishermen's hovels. Portland begat the harbour and laid out a small town to service it: west of Troon Cross, a grid pattern curves to fit the headland, east of the Cross it

Robert Bryden, *c.*1865-1939, was Coylton born. After a period in the office of James A Morris & Hunter, he became an accomplished modeller of bronze portrait busts, such as those of Wallace and Bruce in Ayr Town Hall, and of naturalistic wooden figures, many of which are gathered together at Rozelle. The War Memorial at Coylton is a rare example of his work transferred to an outdoor stage.

Below Coylton Church. Bottom *Claud Hamilton Memorial Hall*

is more rectilinear, although South Beach Road, with the better villas, curves slightly with the coast. No public buildings: the scheme solely a commercial enterprise. The late 19th-century and early 20th-century churches, impressive in themselves, do not fit the bill. Thus Troon's vistas tend to run on towards vanishing point, emphasising a pleasant, spry feeling of homeliness. Seen from the hills behind, Troon's landmarks are the huge shed of the Ailsa-Perth Shipyard, and the gleaming cuprous dome of Marr College.

Templehill derives its name from a *folly* which used to stand here. Known as Fullarton's Folly, it was a small classical summerhouse, inscribed *Bacho laetitiae datori, amacis et olio sacrum* [Erected to Bacchus, the giver of happiness, for friends and for leisure], built by Colonel William Fullarton in the late 18th century.

Templehill curves down to the harbour beginning with **10-20**, a turreted and battlemented group, heavily cleaned, and dated 1894. **93-95**, *c.*1900, George Washington Browne, are a swagger Tudor Bank, now government offices, while the **Anchorage Hotel**, *c.*1815, is a competent late Georgian villa with long- and short-work dressings, built of Pans Rock dolerite, and **Bank House**, *c.*1815, is equally competent but more flash in its finishes, with porch and pilasters and ground-floor windows in super-arches reminiscent of Robert Adam. The **Harbour Bar** is similar to the Anchorage and Bank House, a villa with single-storey pavilions, but more knocked about. The **Mineworkers' Convalescent Home**, **Wood Road**, is a better class villa of *c.*1840, with typical Troon details such as the long-and-short work quoins and the door entablature. The Roman Doric porch is outgunned by the chunky entrance porch which is the chief glory of Alex Mair's otherwise well-mannered extension of 1936. **Garden Place** has two good blocks of inter-war council houses. At the harbour, a couthy range of ten grey coarse

Anchorage Hotel

1883 Feuing plan of Troon

rubble cottages with red stone margins and prominent chimney stacks, on an L-plan, put up *c.*1883, contains the Harbour Office. The **Ballast Bank**, composed of earth and shingle ballast from sailing colliers, acts as a shield from the prevailing wind. The Ailsa-Perth shipyard boasts a busily windowed stone-dressed office block of *c.*1900 and a long 34-bay two-storey front to the engineering sheds, both in blood-red Sanquhar brick.

Troon Old Parish Church, 1894,
Hippolyte J Blanc
Huge red sandstone pile fronting Ayr Street with a nook-shafted entrance under an impressive traceried window, all overshadowed by the stump of the unbuilt tower. This would have been the soaring landmark that Troon needs, though the congregation is perhaps thankful that their predecessors never had the necessary funds. Equally impressive interior, with barrel-vaulted timber roof, and glass by Gordon Webster and Morris & Co. The church is linked to the former church, now the Church Hall, 1837, a dour towered classical church, very proper, quite uneasy with Troon's general uncorseted image. The commercial development in **Ayr Street**, *c.*1900, James Hay, is the handsomest in Troon, while the **Post Office**, 1932, in Church Street, is chunky neoclassical, almost neo-Gibbsian, by J Wilson Paterson. **20-46 Church Street**, 1934, by J B McInnes, is a jolly multi-gabled composition. **82-86 Portland Street**, is an assured commercial development of *c.*1906, while **129-131**, *c.*1840, are an attractive pair of cottages, 131 given extra class by its Doric door and round-headed dormers.

Below *Troon Old Parish Church*. Middle *Ayr Street*. Bottom *Church Street*

Top *St Meddan's Church*. Above
Our Lady of the Assumption

Marr College is a grant-aided
co-educational school, formally
in the control of the C K Marr
Educational Trust, but totally
integrated within the state
education system, providing
secondary education in the
Troon area. It is John Arthur's
major work. Arthur, *c.*1866-
1936 was the son of a Barr
farmer, and trained with Ayr's
John Mercer, John Burnet and
John A Campbell. He was the
injured party in the Newton
Park School (Ayr) competition
scandal, where his plans were
placed first by the assessor, and
the commission awarded to the
highest-placed Ayr architect,
J & H V Eaglesham.

Marr College

St Meddan's Church, 1888-9, J B Wilson
The tallest of Troon's churches in rock-faced
Mauchline stone: muscular Gothic given grace
and power by the well-composed tower and
spire. **12 St Meddan's Street** is an impressive
pair of red stone villas with corner tower,
*c.*1898. Note the pretty bargeboarding on **85**,
1850. **Portland Church**, 1914, H E Clifford &
Lunan, uses Perpendicular with control and
delicacy: note the tracery of the great north
window, repeated in the nave windows. **Troon
Station**, 1892, by James Miller, is a
picturesque composition with striking platform
buildings with harled finish and imitation
wood framing, linked by a covered footbridge.

Our Lady of the Assumption, 1911,
Reginald Fairlie
Highly impressive church, one of Fairlie's best:
short and stocky with a powerful stance – broad
shouldered and immutable. Fairlie favoured
late 15th-century Scottish architecture. Details
were derived, in part, from the Church of the
Holy Rude in Stirling; thus there are crowsteps
on the chancel roof, squat little buttress finials
and various splays on the buttresses
themselves. Finally, just as the solidity of the
church seems to become a little overpowering,
up pops an endearing little timber spire,
delicate and much crocketed, sitting pertly atop
the staircase adjacent to the west tower.

Marr College, 1919, John Arthur
Arthur's masterwork: a vast classical school,
laid out symmetrically about the copper dome
atop its octagonal entrance block, which leads
into a circular Doric-columned entrance hall.
Subsidiary buildings include the Lutyens-
inspired **Lodge**, *c.*1919, with steeply pitched
roof and deep eaves, elements which recur in
the **Janitor's House**, *c.*1919. Work did not
begin until the late 1920s, and was completed,
after Arthur's death, by A G McNaughtan.

Muirhead, late 1930s, John A W Grant
Troon's major council housing scheme, laid out
on Garden Village principles with wide streets,
plentiful open space, and a vaguely Scots
cottage architecture. Grant was a craft
architect who had won the Saltire Society's
first award for housing in 1937 for a similar
scheme in Westquarter, Falkirk.

Town Hall, 1932, James Miller
Red brick neo-Georgian, elegantly composed,
respectfully extended by Noad & Wallace,
c.1954. Behind is the **War Memorial**, 1924,
Alfred Gilbert, a moving bronze Liberty on a
granite plinth.

South Beach, c.1840
The central stretch of South Beach
demonstrates mid-century values, one-storey
cottages and two-storey pavilion villas, mostly
built before 1857. **36** is single-storey, painted
stone, with Tudor-Gothic details such as the
window in the main stable. **46**, again single
storey, has coursed stonework and hipped
pavilions, while **50** has a spider's-web fanlight
and lying-pane glazing. Such glazing is
frequent here and occurs again at **Elmslie, 56**,
again stone margins to coursed stonework with
hipped-roof pavilions, and the best-preserved of
these villas. Its neighbour, **Alton Lodge, 58**,
has 12-pane glazing, ashlar, and one pavilion
altered. **62** is similar, but altered, **64-68** are
single-storey cottages, while **70-76** return to
the motif of two storeys and pavilions: **72** has
full-height wings, while **74** and **76** almost
match one another, **76** taking elegance a little
further with consoled triangular pediments to
its ground-floor windows.

Top *Town Hall*. Middle *56
South Beach*. Above *36 South
Beach*

Crosbie Tower, c.1890
The earlier Victorian houses generally sit
between the road and the sea – further on the
red stone late-Victorian villas sit on the
landward side and look across the road to the
sea. Crosbie Tower, which is joyously Italianate
and makes free use of the ironwork, is the most
imposing. **117-119** is later, c.1900, and makes
effective use of white harl and tile-hanging.

121 Bentinck Drive, c.1910,
possibly J R Johnstone
A delightful Arts & Crafts villa which can
stand as a synecdoche for much of Johnstone's

John Rutherford Johnstone,
1880-1961, specialised, like so
many other Ayrshire architects
of his period, in big harled
villas. Based in Troon, he was
able to capitalise on the wealth
that existed in the town. His
houses are often distinguished
by a slight free-style tinge,
perhaps best expressed in a
fondness for heavily battered
walls. His few commercial
buildings – as in the former
Liberal Club in Sandgate, Ayr –
are formally composed in
Edwardian stone baroque.

Welbeck House

Below *St Ninian's Episcopal
Church.* Middle *Piersland
Lodge.* Bottom *Marine
Highland Hotel*

work in this part of town. **133-135**, 1905, were
extended in 1919 in the same crisp white
harled manner by Johnstone. **139-145**, 1901-2,
by William Leiper, were the stables for
Piersland Lodge: asymmetrical front of red
stone, half-timbering and tiling, with a pretty
round tower. **Welbeck House**, *c.*1911, is
another stunning, heavily buttressed Arts &
Crafts house with a strong feel of horizontality.
St Ninian's Episcopal Church, 1912-13, by
James A Morris, in long low numinous Arts &
Crafts, in Morris's favoured Mauchline stone
contrasting with the abundant white harling
elsewhere. **134**, 1911, is notable for some fine
Glasgow Style ironwork.

Piersland Lodge, 1898-99, William Leiper
Fine example of his English-derived houses: a
carefully composed and skillfully handled
combination of Ayrshire red stone and half-
timbering. Details are equally sumptuous:
garden terrace, pyramidal summer houses, and
Jacobean wood-panelled interiors. The **Royal
Troon Golf Club**, 1885, H E Clifford, is a
simple, undemonstrative, gabled house
substantially extended, most particularly in
1926 when J R Johnstone added the effective
colonnaded porch. The **Marine Highland
Hotel**, 1897, Salmon Son & Gillespie, (see
p.C2) dominates its landscape in a serviceable,
stripped domestic style writ large: a *fin de
siècle* feature being a cycle house. **Ardery**,
*c.*1902, is a fine free-style villa by John C
McKellar, **Mokoia** is a huge white and red tile
villa of 1904, while the **Sun Court Hotel**,
*c.*1905, Fryers & Penman, is a large domestic
composition dominated by its Real Tennis
Court, one of only two in Scotland. Seemingly
abandoned in the middle of the course,
Blackrock House is a stunning Arts &
Crafts-influenced harl and slate house of
*c.*1913-14.

Fullarton Stables, 1792, Robert Adam
Fullarton House was demolished in 1966: these
stables were converted into flats by Hay Steel
MacFarlane & Partners in 1974. Symmetrical
about the castellated drum-towered entrance,
linked to three-storey pavilions by means of
lower, narrow-windowed ranges, on the south
side. The west range has super-arches, dummy
turrets and crowsteps. All has been totally
rebuilt behind the façades. Two classical
pediments remain from the quadrant screen of
Fullarton House. **Crosbie Church** is a
medieval, roofless rectangle set in a high-
walled kirkyard entered through a broken-
pedimented gateway.

SOUTHWOOD

Bosky and exclusive, Southwood attracted
wealthy Edwardian feuars: the true capital of
Millionayrshire, and an ideal spot to examine
the lush, often English-influenced houses,
which synthesised a romanticised view of the
past, to which the wealthy mercantile classes
sought escape for comfort.

North and east of Southwood Road are
Silverglades (originally Deasholm), 1912, by
T Andrew Millar, Old Scots revival with a
slightly contrived round tower corner;
Lochgreen, 1905, Gardner & Millar, is long,
grey and harled; while **Auchenkyle**, c.1905, is
Queen Anne in influence and strongly English;
Frognal, 1909, James Hay, gleams in its golden
sandstone, an impressive tower dominating the
massing of the garden front: it has a vast
English lodge; **Monktonhall** (formerly
Glenholm), c.1912, H E Clifford & Lunan, also
uses English manorial forms; **South Park**,
c.1910, is redbrick, flint dappled and English;
Dunalton, 1908, by James Hay, English
manorial with a dominating tower similar to
Frognal and a lodge which nods towards
Lorimer; **Crosbie House**, 1908, H E Clifford,
mixes English and Scottish vernacular to great
effect; **Grey Gables**, 1908, has exquisite
English slate hanging; and **Southwood**, 1905,
John A Campbell, is a synthesis of Scottish and
English influences; **Sandhill**, c.1890, a dower
house for the Dowager Duchess of Portland, sits
at the edge of Southwood. Brick with crisp red
sandstone dressings, interspersed with half-
timbering on the gables, it is alleged to have
been the work of a prominent (but elusive)
French architect.

Fullarton had been built in
1745 for William Fullarton of
Fullarton, altered by the Adam
brothers in the 1790s for the
last of the Fullartons, before
the house and lands passed to
the Portlands in 1805, as they
consolidated and protected
their investment in the
Kilmarnock & Troon Railway.
At the time of demolition, Troon
Town Council's intention was to
erect multi-storey flats on the
site.

Below *Fullarton House.* Middle
Lochgreen. Bottom *Crosbie
House*

Tower Hotel

BARASSIE

An alternative name, New Kilmarnock, gives a clue to Barassie's history: a small settlement of weekend and summer houses for Kilmarnock merchants, begun in about 1830. Growth was slow until the 20th century, when the Barassie Garden Village scheme gave it a small fillip. The last twenty-five years have seen its transformation into a vast dormitory suburb. The **Tower Hotel**, *c*.1832-6, is the best original house of New Kilmarnock: a simple single-storey cottage extended in a conventional Italianate manner, *c*.1859. Work on the **Garden Suburb** began in 1911, to a simple saltire-like layout by James Chalmers, whose house plans effectively merged romantic details with modern needs. The First World War put a brutal end to the project with only a few houses such as **49 Beach Road** built. In the interwar period the area filled up to a less spacious plan, with bungalows.

Right *House in Barassie Garden Suburb*. Below *Dundonald Parish Church*

DUNDONALD

Single-street village, workmanlike mixture of weavers' cottages and later infill and extension overpowered by the threatening bulk of Dundonald Castle.

Dundonald Parish Church, 1803
Straightforward T-plan preaching box with a good, attenuated steeple. The former manse, **Glenfoot House**, *c*.1795, is solid, harled with stone dressings. Opposite the church, a good row of cottages including **37-41 Main Street**, the **Castle Hotel**, and the **Dundonald Inn**, all mixing colour-washed harl or plaster with stone dressings.

Dundonald Castle, 14th century
The favourite residence of King Robert II. The castle consists of a very large oblong tower house, distinctive in itself and for the way in which it incorporates the remains of a 13th-century gatehouse. Most of this tower, and much of the barmkin wall survives.

Auchans, 1644
Ruin of the magnificent mock-military country home erected by Sir William Cochrane. L-plan with a square, balustraded stair-tower in re-entrant angle; the western wing has been

Above *Great Hall of Dundonald Castle*. Left *Auchans*

lengthened, but the whole building appears to be of the same period. Principal apartments are chambers opening into each other on the first and second floors. The entrance doorway is a good example of the Jacobean court style: string-courses, crowsteps, corbels and magnificent dormers.

In 1890 it was said of **Auchans** *it is a pity that so interesting and so fine a building should have suffered under the neglect of a whole century; it is so strongly built that it looks as if it could, at no excessive expense, be once more made habitable.* A further century has now passed, the quality of the building has not lessened, though the cost of restoration may have increased. The last permanent resident was Susannah, Countess of Eglinton, who died in 1780, having been a great beauty and artistic patron in her youth. Johnson and Boswell had dined with her here in 1773. According to tradition, she trained rats in her old age which she would summon to dine with her.

Fairlie House, *c*.1803
Pleasant rectangular Regency mansion whose slight central projection contains a recessed columned porch. Plain external walls are given articulation by a low parapet over a moulded cornice, and panelled end pilasters, which imply the hand of David Hamilton. The impressive **Fairlie Mains** has a pedimented entrance topped by an octagonal tower and spire. **Dankeith** is a rambling pile whose many Victorian extensions have swamped totally the original 1790 house. **Coodham** (*see over*), *c*.1831, whose severe front elevation and Doric porch implies David Hamilton, has a sombre little chapel of 1874 by Waterhouse and a recently restored striking late 18th-century courtyard **stable block**.

Above *Coodham*. Below
Symington Church, interior.
Middle *Symington Church,
exterior*. Bottom *Townend
House*

SYMINGTON

Attractive former weavers' village, close to, yet
far from, the bustle of the A77; the focal point
is the little church, from which rows of cottages
radiate.

Symington Parish Church, 12th century
Easily the oldest in Ayrshire still in ecclesiastic
use, Symington's numinous little church is a
delight, most notably the richly decorated dog-
toothed three-light window, the finest of its
kind in any Scottish parish church. The 18th-
century extension is almost a north transept.
Scholarly restoration was carried out in 1919
by P MacGregor Chalmers, whose selection to
carry out the task was surely divinely inspired:
the Norman work was then undreamt of,
hidden beneath 18th-century alterations. In
Chalmers, the church had appointed the
architect most likely to appreciate what he
found, and most likely to press for its
restoration. Excellent glasswork by Gordon
Webster, Douglas Strachan and others.

Wheatsheaf Inn, 18th century
Village inn with widely spaced windows is a
suitable introduction to the cottages which give
Symington its character. The best are in Main
Street, beginning with **The Knowe**. **2-14** form
the most complete range, curving in and out
with the line of the road; **33-35** are slightly
more sophisticated with Corinthian pilasters
and a geometric fanlight to 35. **Townend
Cottage**, *c.*1810, is an excellent dower house
with a charming elliptical porch. **Townend
House**, early 19th century, has grown a rather
pompous if commodious Victorian Italianate
wing. Once the offices of Hay Steel &
MacFarlane, Townend is now a nursing home.

Symington House, Kerrix Road, c.1786
Former solid, harled manse with thin pilasters
at the corners and, introducing some light
relief, rolled skews. Traditional cottages in
Brewlands Road, notably **Lindisfarne**, with its
rustic porch, the **Old School House**, 1805,
stucco incised as mock stonework, the **Old Post
Office**, narrowest of three-bayed façades, its
central door approached by steps, and **Kirkhill**,
well-restored rubble with finials to screen walls.
Brewlands is an attractive courtyard and
Craigowan is a rambling aggrandisement of
an 1849 Tudor dormered confection.

Halfway House Hotel, c.1937
Road-house Tudor, which replaced the old inn
which burnt down in 1935. **Hansel Village**, a
residential centre for the disadvantaged, is
based on the opulent **Broadmeadows**, 1931-4,
by Noad & Wallace, one of the final Arts &
Crafts houses in Scotland. Conscious of its lack
of an authentic past, it makes up for it with
inscriptions and gargoyles. For all its erudition
Broadmeadows demonstrates a sense of fun, a
gentle self-mockery that is a sign of the end of
a tradition. Buildings from 1966, to suit its
present purpose, are of Norwegian log
construction, supervised by Michael Laird.

Craigie Parish Church, 1776
T-plan kirk with a bellcote. This was poor
country, and the church represents a
compromise between the need for a new kirk,
i.e. a grand galleried preaching box as at
Riccarton or Tarbolton, and financial
constraint. The result is little more than an
improved medieval kirk. **17-21 Main Street**,
the most characterful cottages, remain
relatively unspoilt. **House of Craigie**, former
manse of 1808, harled but for the rubble
stonework front elevation, giving great presence
to this conventionally boxy display. **Carnell**
incorporates a well-preserved tower house of
c.1500 within additions by William Burn, 1843.

Craigie Castle, 15th century (*right*)
Sadly ruined remains of one of the finest
specimens of a vaulted hall in Scotland. The
vault was groined and, to judge by the large
blocks of ashlar, a match for anything similar in
the country. Rebuilt for the Wallaces of Craigie,
it was doubtless abandoned c.1600 when they
removed themselves to Newton on Ayr.

Top *Symington Village*. Above
Broadmeadows

Of Ayrshire's churches,
Aiton in 1811 said *Those of
Kirkoswald, Daily, Newton,
Ochiltree, Craigie, Saltcoats
and Kilwinning are convenient
and substantial buildings, but
some of them have more the
appearance of cotton factories,
than of churches.*

*I must confess my own
particular love for the charm
and simplicity of some of the
tiny windows set in splayed
Norman arches, such as
Symington in Ayrshire and
St Margaret's Chapel on the
Castle Rock* [Edinburgh] *so
perfect are they in their setting.
The architectural relationship is
as complete as the windows in
Chartres.*
William Wilson RSA RSW

Above *Wallace Monument.*
Below *Neilshill House*

A local folk-rhyme suggests that the monks at Fail were not held in great esteem by the villagers of Tarbolton:
The Friars of Fail drank berry-
brown ale
The best that ere was tasted ...
And they never wanted gear
enough
As long as their neighbours'
lasted.

One of the many stories surrounding William Wallace is that of the raid on the Barns of Ayr, and the English troops billetted in them. Legend records that he watched the barns blazing from this vantage point, and commented that 'the Barns of Ayr burn weel'. The name Barnweill is said to derive from this remark.

Barnweill
Remote, timeless area of narrow lanes, tall hedges and tight vistas. The **Wallace Monument**, 1855, Robert Snodgrass, is a spiky Gothic tower visible for miles, commemorating Wallace's association with the area. Barnweill Church is ruinous, field-girt, and largely 17th century. **Barnweill House**, 18th century, is a sober-sided better quality farmhouse well restored by Ronald Alexander. **Underwood**, *c.*1790, has a conventional three-bay façade with a slight centre projection, topped out by an urn-capped pediment. Of **Fail Abbey** there remains but an uninformative fragment.

Neilshill House, *c.*1880
A distinctive design in blood-red Mauchline stone: an Italianate campaniled villa, given improbable, totally inauthentic Moorish windows. Equally Byzantine interior and a lodge in the same cod-Moorish manner.

Ladykirk, 1903, by Robert Ingram, lies heavy on the earth: a retrograde quasi-Dutch Renaissance block; a fragment of the Lady Kirk in the grounds.

IRVINE
The confluence of the Irvine and the Garnock long provided one of the few sheltered anchorages on the lower Firth of Clyde as shipping was able to ride the Irvine as far up as **Seagatefoot**. The status of Royal Burgh was conferred on Irvine in 1372 by Robert II, burghal rights having been first granted during the reign of Alexander II in the previous century. Beyond the names of **Seagate** and **Bridgegate**, however, only the plan survives of the 14th-century burgh, the long narrow burgage plots to either side of the curving main street, those to seaward running down to the river. Much has been obliterated by 20th-century development.

A period of great prosperity opened in the 16th century, as trade between Irvine, Ireland and further afield increased, and it became a convenient entrepôt for wares to and from Glasgow, avoiding the Tail o' the Bank and the other vagaries of upper Clyde. During this period, **Seagate Castle** received its present High Renaissance garb. The port's prosperity continued well into the 19th century, surviving

Scottish National Portrait Gallery

the Earl of Eglinton's attempts to create a new dock at Ardrossan. Outside the burgh, across the Irvine, **Fullarton** developed as an industrial, shipbuilding suburb, taking an increasing share of the harbour duties as the sea receded and shipping grew, nullifying Seagatefoot's position. An increasing trade in coal shipping allowed Irvine to weather the changes wrought by transport improvements and the consequent loss of the Glasgow trade, but by the 20th century the port of Irvine was in decline. A progressive Town Council sought successfully to attract new industry to the town after the Second World War and it was tacit recognition of the initiative that led to Irvine's selection as a **New Town**. The Plan for the New Town, extending to **Kilwinning** and **Dreghorn** (dealt with separately) was prepared by Hugh Wilson and Lewis Womersley and based on the well-tried concept of neighbourhoods founded largely on the existing infrastructure. New shopping developments were to be based on existing facilities. One can thus compare Irvine, where **Bridgegate House** successfully bludgeons the new ethos into the heart of the Royal Burgh, irrevocably linking the two cultures, with other New Towns where the (old) **Village** is marginalised, becoming a smart residential enclave denying the existence of the contemporary world. The New Town was forged under IDC's first architect, David

Irvine in the 19th century

Irvine, although existing as a town as early as the 12th century, was granted its first burgh charter, probably by Alexander II, only in about 1240. The burghal privileges were confirmed in a charter of Robert I of 1322. In 1372, it was raised to the status of a Royal Burgh with a charter from Robert II. In the late 16th century it was *in peple, in riches and commodiousness of the sey port ... nocht mekle inferior to Air*, though by the Commonwealth it was, to Thomas Tucker, a *pretty small port but at present clogged and choked up with sand, which the western sea beats into it, so as it wrestles for life to maintain a small trade with France, Norway and Ireland with herring and other goods, brought on horseback from Glasgow for the purchasing of timber, wine, etc.* In 1665 the new harbour was begun, and by 1723 Irvine could be described as a *tolerable seaport* with *upon the key, a good face of business especially the coal trade to Dublin,* and while trade exceeded that of Ayr, Defoe in 1753 noted that ships of no great size could be stuck in the harbour for months.

Seagate Castle

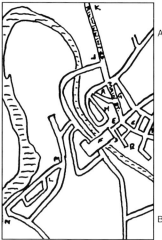

Public sculpture is commoner throughout **Irvine New Town** than perhaps anywhere else in Scotland. Since 1979 the Development Corporation has funded five artists-in-residence – John Upton, Susan Bradbury, Nigel Lloyd, Roy Fitzsimmons and Mary Burne – and each has left their mark on the housing schemes and commercial centres; the work of the most recent, Mary Burne, includes *Two Seabirds* at Cheviot Court Sheltered Housing, and a sculpted birdbath at Heatherstane. Irvine Development Corporation's *Visual Arts in Irvine New Town*, 1991, is an excellent illustrated guide to the subject.

Gosling, and honed by his successors. The characteristics are bold use of colour, wide stone margins against fields of harl, steeply canted monopitch roofs and careful attention to layout. Recent work has refined IDC's distinctive architectural hallmark of blockwork, timber, double-height atria, an increased use of glass, and greater ornament: **Bourtreehill**, **High Street** and **Harbourside** infill, the *Bookends*, and **Caley House** (in Kilwinning) are particularly successful examples. The town has been fortunate in some of its privately commissioned architecture, most notably Connolly & Niven's **St John Ogilvy Church** and Page & Park's **Sea World Centre**; and there is widespread and effective use of strongly shaped sculpture.

A **Seagate Castle**, 1562-85
Substantial ruins of a palatial town house of the Montgomeries of Eglinton which commanded the old harbour area at Seagatefoot, finally abandoned by the family in the 1740s. Built as a showpiece (there is no hint of defensive requirements) with particularly noteworthy enriched window mouldings and the entrance. This pend bisects a long, narrow irregular entowered range, now somewhat reduced in size. Much more could be made of this fine building, an oasis of quiet a few seconds from the bustle of the town.

B **Irvine Parish Church**, 1772-4, David Muir
In February 1772 the Heritors approved a plan of a new church comparable to that of the High Church, Paisley, 1756, John White (see *South Clyde Estuary*). The demurely Georgian steeple alone acknowledges architectural change in the intervening twenty years. The church, on a slight eminence guarding the southern entry into the burgh, looks down on **Kirk Green**, a sequestered corner with a pleasing mix of polite 19th-century houses, earlier humbler, cottages, and the Italian Renaissance **Mission Hall**, 1896, John Armour. Hill Street is generally two-storey and 19th century, intermixed with subservient but comparable modern reconstruction. To debouche from Hill Street into Bridgegate is to be fully aware of the impact of the New Town. Kirkgate spills out on to the High Street, opposite the fanciful
C Italianate **Town House**, 1859, James Ingram, bedecked with a graceful octagonal lantern.

Trinity is now a community
centre, providing coffee,
aerobics, crêches, and the other
accoutrements of such a role.
Redundant, vandalised and
threatened with demolition,
this imaginative church,
amongst the very best works of
F T Pilkington (for whom
Goodhart-Rendel's term, rogue
architect, seems inescapable),
was saved by a vigorous
campaign spearheaded by Knut
Campbell of the Saltire Society.

Far left *Irvine Parish Church
spire.* Left *Irvine Town House.*
Below *Trinity Centre.* Bottom
Rivergate Centre

D **Trinity Centre**, 1863, Frederick T Pilkington
With Parish Church and Town House, Trinity,
built on another slight hill, forms the third
element in the distant view of Irvine (the tower
flats in Fullarton excluded). It is a phenomenal
Ruskinian landmark, and an important staging
post in the Gothic Revival in Scotland.
Pilkington's jumping-off point is Venetian
Gothic, evident in the polychrome stonework
and the round arches: the final vision is his
alone. No longer used as a church, delays in
securing its future ensured that much of
Pilkington's masterly interior was lost.

E **Bridgegate House**, 1973,
Irvine Development Corporation
F Irvine's new focus with the **Rivergate Centre**.
The bold stroke was to replace Herbertson's
Victorian Irvine Bridge, and replace it with an
enclosed shopping mall leaping the river:
surely a transatlantic rather than European
conceit. Internally, the vista, the river beneath,
enlivens and mollifies the rather
claustrophobic main mall. Externally, the
building just fails to meet the challenge; on the
townward side the **Forum**, 1987, private
development shopping with no architectural
pretension, compromises the view from across
the river. **Cunninghame House**, *c.*1976, IDC,
beyond, a crisply detailed office block, suits

Top *Cunninghame House.*
Above *57-59 High Street*

The **Burns Club** has an extensive museum and library, including an extensive collection of Scots poetry and Irvine records. Founded in 1826, Irvine Burns Club claims to be the oldest in continuous existence (see Greenock): its first President was John Mackenzie, doctor in Irvine and husband of Helen Miller, one of the Mauchline Belles, its first Vice-President, David Sillar (*Dainty Davie*).

8 West Road

well its isolated site. Fullarton's churches eke out an uneasy existence in this ungodly world: **Fullarton Parish Church**, 1837, James Ingram, large and coarse, with big Tudor Gothic windows sits amid grassy swards and endless roads, and the dull **Wilson Memorial Free Church**, 1873, now a parish centre.

High Street
The High Street, the heart of the old burgh, acts as the conduit by which the disparate facets of the town are pulled into a cohesive unit. It curves gently northwards from the Town House, revealing new compositions at each step. **57-59**, early 18th century, is particularly impressive, its curly wallhead gable facing the Town House, a fitting introduction to the tighter scale of the urban core. This block continues with Peddie & Kinnear's austere **Royal Bank of Scotland**, 1856, and a fine group of 1979 infill buildings at **85-93** by IDC architects in a legitimate development of the vernacular idiom. The two principal inns, the **Eglinton Arms** and the **King's Arms** glower across at one another: both similarly stuccoed, three-storeyed of the early 1800s: the Eglinton is the better building, with grotesques over the half-dormers. Beyond Bridgegate House's intrusive elbow, the street straightens slightly, and climbs slowly to a backcloth of early 18th-century politesse: additions include the brash Mauchline red **Burns House**, the restrained 1930s moderne of **Woolworths** and, beyond Seagate, a delightful block of neo-vernacular flats, 1987-8, by James Sim & Associates. High Street, now Eglinton Street, soon becomes Kilwinning Road and Irvine's villa suburb.

8 West Road, 1990-1,
Irvine Development Corporation
Lively and assured recreation of a Georgian town house. West Road retains much of the original character of Irvine, its ridge between the High Street and the river has attracted churches, such as the **Roman Catholic Church**, 1882, Robert S Ingram, and urbane villas.

Heathfield, *c.*1830
The best of the villas, now restored and extended by IDC as an award-winning old people's home, a particularly delightful courtyard to the rear in crisp masonry blockwork and warm orange timber. The

bright-red classical **Royal Irvine Academy**, 1902, by John Armour replaced the **Academy**, 1816, by David Hamilton.

κ **Central Ayrshire Hospital**,

Kilwinning Road, 1941 (see p.C7)

Gleaming white flat roofs, arranged around a courtyard, with the centrally located entrance accented by a raised decorative structure. The quality of its composition has been compromised by subsequent building behind.
Redburn Hotel, a former Eglinton dower house, its trim 19th-century propriety compromised by a rash of extensions. Alexander Dunlop has made a commendable effort to transform a decaying army camp into **Volvo [GB] Ltd's Centre**, 1978, the company's crisp image reflected by imported Swedish steel sheeting and aluminium cladding on a brown brick base. **Ravenspark Hospital**, 1856-8, former Cunninghame Combination Poorhouse, is solidly Jacobean, seemingly designed to inculcate a desire not to finish up there.

Scottish Maritime Museum

Fullarton, Irvine-across-the-water, is an industrial suburb untramelled by the rules and regulations of the Royal Burgh, aided by the

Top *Heathfield.* Middle *Central Ayrshire Hospital.* Above *Ravenspark Hospital.* Left *Scottish Maritime Museum, Linthouse Building*

The **Scottish Maritime Museum** has a growing collection of sea-going craft. Some have little style, the working life of tugs and puffers allows little scope for such things. The ocean-going and racing yachts are different – stylish, streamlined vessels which are a potent reminder of the role that Ayrshire played in the development of yachting: builders such as the Fife family at Fairlie, owners such as Thomas Lipton, and others, notably, the Marquess of Ailsa who combined them both, racing yachts and building them at Culzean. The shipyard at Troon is a direct descendent of this enterprise.

Above *The **Bookends***. Below *Harbour Street*. Bottom *Automatic Tide Marker Station*

seaward shift in the harbour facilities. Of the industries which flourished here, little remains. The Museum is based in the unassuming late Victorian office buildings of **Laird's Forge**. The **Winch House** and the **Pontoons** are by Irvine Development Corporation. In 1989 the Museum embarked on the re-erection of the **Engine Shop**, 1872, William Spencer, a gargantuan iron-framed structure originally at Stephen's of Linthouse yard at Govan. A restored shipworker's flat at **122A Montgomerie Street**, forms part of the solemn, but well-articulated tenements, 1907, which link town and harbour.

78 & 101 Montgomerie Street, 1984, Irvine Development Corporation
Known locally as the *Bookends*, these flats act as a formal entrance to the harbourside in a refreshingly different interpretation of vernacular form with exposed concrete block and much glazing, their triangular form underlining the gatehouse idiom. The **Harbourside** is a successful mix of traditional cottages with modern infill, 1983-5, handled with skill and panache, though there is a tendency to rely too heavily on the quainter aspects of this reinterpreted vernacular: variable window size and corner chamfering: old and new are clearly distinguishable. The restored 1754 coat of the **Ship Inn** conceals the older core – an ostlery and stables said to have been built in 1597. The **Harbour Master's Office, 174 Harbour Street**, is a simple stuccoed early 19th-century cottage, which may have begun life as a farmhouse, while beyond is the **Automatic Tide Marker Station** of 1906.

Irvine Beach Park
Large-scale re-landscaping and redevelopment of Irvine's seaward side – paths, marram grass, lochs and *wet-weather* facilities. The most obvious of these is the enormous **Magnum Centre**, 1976, IDC. With no neighbours to respect, the exterior is very basic – just a large shed, with a sinuous curving concrete ramp and bridge to the upper-floor entrance. Successful from the outset, the Magnum was among the first of the present generation of huge sports and leisure complexes. The **Sea World Centre**, 1985, Page & Park, with its deep-eaved hipped roof over external timbering is a pleasing foil to the Magnum's bulk. The helical **Maintenance**

Irvine Development Corporation

Close

Close

Left above *Beach Park Maintenance Department.* Left below *Dragon, Beach Park*

Irvine, in the late 18th century, still retained important links with Glasgow, and Glasgow Vennel was still the main eastward and northward route to Glasgow. The young Robert Burns lodged at **4** for two years while learning the flax trade at **10** (The Heckling Shop). A little museum illustrated this period in the poet's life, while the Ayrshire Writers & Artists Society continues an artistic connection with a small gallery.

In Irwin toon whaur leeved the Bard,
A place we haud wi' high regard
The very grun oan which he stood
Tae be preserved,
The fact, tho' late, maun make us prood.
An' weel deserved.
The chiels wha' thocht o' conservation
An' saved this place fur oor ain nation,
Wur blesst tae mak the rich decision,
As weel they should,
Lord, grant them some o' Rabbie's vision,
Fur common guid.

Thomas M Wark

Department and red sandstone **Dragon** are both exactly the sort of lightheaded architecture that the park and the sea demand.

P **Glasgow Vennel**

The main road to Glasgow, once lined by simple vernacular cottages. The impetus for their award-winning restoration was the Vennel's links with Burns; **4**, simple black stuccoed cottage, was Burns's lodging house from 1781 to 1783. Together with its heckling shop behind, it has been converted to an artists' centre and small Burns-flavoured museum. **Townhead** is an impressively wide street with a number of good 19th-century houses: note **45** with its double-flight entrance stair. **Red Cross House**, 1990-2, IDC, is a recent example of the high quality of their work.

Below *Red Cross House.* Left *Glasgow Vennel*

Irvine Development Corporation

Close

Stanecastle gates

Perceton House

Stanecastle, 16th century
Small rectangular tower-house, a minor seat of the Montgomeries, made safe by IDC after attempts to market it for restoration failed. Its best features are two rows of detached corbels between continuous moulded courses. Gothick windows were slapped through c.1750, so that it would form an interesting object when seen from the Stanecastle drive to Eglinton Castle. The **Stanecastle Gates**, c.1800, an attractive pair of lodges linked by an arch, have been restored as part of the Corporation's typically bright and cheerful **Braehead Housing**, 1977-9, (see p.C5) with roughcast like icing. More in similar style at **Girdle Toll**, with *Flying Fish* kinetic sculpture, 1981, by Candice Girling.

Perceton House, c.1770 (see p.C5)
One of a number of strikingly similar houses in Ayrshire (like Skeldon and Belleisle) that take their cue from John Adam's Dumfries House. Odd front elevation; into its four-bay, harled, unpedimented façade a fifth, half-bay entrance bay is squeezed. When the house became the IDC headquarters in 1968, it was extended in contemporary design. Remains of a medieval church in the grounds: the parish of Perceton was conjoined to Dreghorn in 1668.

Oldhall East Industrial Estate, 1974-5, Irvine Development Corporation
Irvine's factories maintain a high design standard. Block A with its fully glazed gable office, displays excellent use of colour, and has a crisp and impressive appearance. **SUN Newspapers** at South Newmoor, 1978, IDC, maintains these high standards, with its orange logo and black steel cladding above white roughcast walls. **Paper Mill** at Meadowhead, 1986-9, James Cunning, Young & Partners, has, by sheer bulk alone, been able to defeat the resourcefulness of the architects. In its multi-toned steely grey-and-blue cladding, it dominates and cows the surrounding landscape; function is all.

The paper mill is huge: this £215m structure dominates many vistas, and has become an instant landmark from the Firth, supplanting the shipyard at Troon.

DREGHORN

An undemanding crossroads village, at the heart of the Eglinton estates, its current appearance primarily the result of industrially led growth in the late 19th century, and growth as part of the Irvine New Town area. The industries were primarily coal and bricks, though relicts of the industry have all but vanished, along with masters' houses such as Bourtreehill and Warwickhill; the New Town impetus in the village is primarily private housing development, though Bourtreehill is close at hand.

Parish Church, 1780
The plan is octagonal: a feature it shares with another Eglinton estate church: Eaglesham, 1788. There is evidence to suggest that Archibald, 11th Earl of Eglinton, played a prominent role in the design of Eaglesham, and his involvement cannot therefore be ruled out here. There is a central steeple, rather weak and an inadequate foil to the building, whose details are conventional enough: aedicular porch and Gothick windows. The wedding-cake interior has a fine stained-glass window by Susan Bradbury. The **Session House** is a plain schoolhouse, 1774, at the kirkgate converted to its present use c.1890, while opposite the church is the **Parish Hall**, 1903, John Armour & Sons, an energetic eclectic mix of Gothic and Scots baronial details given increased muscularity by the harsh red Mauchline stone.

Leggat Farm, much altered, presents a rural image close to the core of the village, while, opposite, the **J B Dunlop Memorial Hall** introduces a bland, bowling clubhouse style which is at odds with the inherent grittiness of the village. **Holmsford Bridge**, 1880, Charles Reid, carries the Dundonald Road over the Irvine. Nearby **Holms Farm**, very functional, has a small window high in the seaward gable which is alleged to have been illuminated as a beacon for smugglers.

Bourtreehill, 1973-80
The apogee of Irvine Development Corporation's residential design. Great lengths were taken to vary the effects to create an interesting, virile, changing environment; consequently much use is made of bright colours (even the occasional truly dramatic black house), of window surrounds, of varied

Kyle and Carrick Libraries

Parish Church

Dreghorn is generally regarded as the model for Dalmailing in John Galt's entertaining *Annals of the Parish*, the yearly jottings of the worldly-wise village minister, Micah Balwhidder. Galt interweaves the lives and loves, hopes and fears of the minister and his parishioners in a narrative which carries the reader into the very heart of this ordinary Scottish parish at a time, 1760-1810, of great change.

John Boyd Dunlop, 1840-1921, the son of a Dreghorn farmer, became a vet in Belfast. His interest in the late-Victorian craze for cycling, and the need to find a smoother rise than that offered by solid tyres, led him to develop a pneumatic rubber tyre, which he patented in 1888. The invention was taken up and developed further by others, and Dunlop, who lived out his life in Dublin, had no financial involvement in the company that has taken his name to every corner of the world.

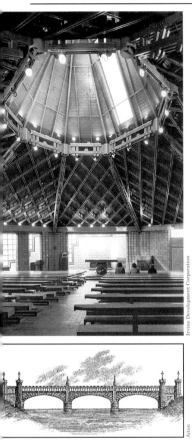

roof shapes, and of differing house types. The commendable **Church of Scotland**, *c.*1976, Hay Steel & MacFarlane, and the dramatic RC **St John Ogilvy** (see p.C8), 1982, by Douglas Niven & Gerard Connolly, with Clunie Rowell, the latter enhanced by Susan Bradbury's imaginative *Light* which uses cast-glass prisms to produce dazzling illumination and constantly changing rainbows, add to the character. The **Towerlands Centre**, 1982, Irvine Development Corporation, is the admirable restoration and extension of a courtyard farm to provide flats, clubhouse, and holiday homes for paraplegics.

Eglinton Castle, John Paterson, 1796-1802 (see p.C2) This huge castellated mansion, the home of the Montgomeries, Earls of Eglinton, one of the most powerful families in Ayrshire, was unroofed in 1925. After use for gunnery target practice, the ruinous shell was finally demolished in 1973, leaving only a single corner tower and some low walls. Also within the much-reduced and much-abused policies – the requirements of a New Town road network have left lodges and gates in improbable positions – are the **Tournament Bridge**, David Hamilton's attractive airy iron Gothick bridge *new building* in 1811, and the **Stables**, of *c.*1800, a large pedimented courtyard range with battlemented corners and a clock tower on the rear elevation, now conscientiously converted into a meat-canning factory! The Home Farm has been transformed into a Visitor Centre for the **Eglinton Country Park**, while **Eglinton House** is the former gardener's cottage of 1798, with a polygonal main block and in style slightly reminiscent of Paterson's Montgomerie House (see p.145).

Top *St John Ogilvy Church.*
Above *Tournament Bridge.*
Right *Eglinton Castle drawn by J C Nattes*

This magnificent seat of Eglinton, *with all its woods, its gardens, its waters and its approach roads, is ... equalled by few places in Scotland: perhaps surpassed by none.* Thus George Robertson could write in 1808 shortly after the house was completed. This was probably Eglinton's zenith: the increasing costs of the proposed canal and harbour at Ardrossan, coupled with the expense of the Eglinton Tournament, severely circumscribed the family's potential to play upon the national stage.

KILWINNING

The New Town absorbed two burghs: Kilwinning was the other. Incorporation in the New Town has manifested itself more gradually: the commercial heart of the town was redeveloped, unfortunately, before the establishment of Irvine Development Corporation. Pedestrianisation, judicious new-build and careful restoration have regained for central Kilwinning a vitality that it had lost. The burgh remains proudly independent, though architecturally it does not aspire to the promise held out by the distant spectacular view of the abbey ruins and David Hamilton's Tower.

Kilwinning Abbey, from 1187 (*right*)
One of the finest of Scotland's ecclesiastical buildings, and unusual in its design: the nearest in manner is the other major Tironensian foundation, Kelso, while the ultimate source is among the cathedrals of Charlemagne. Its nave and transepts, nearly 100 ft across, were broader than Paisley Abbey or Glasgow Cathedral – broader even than our largest medieval church building, the Cathedral of St Andrews – yet it was not especially long, being about 225 ft. What makes it unique among Scottish abbeys is that it had twin towers at the western end which did not rise from the mass of the buildings, but rose alongside, as independent units, opening into the church by great arches 20 ft high. In consequence of this structural abnormality, amounting almost to weakness, the towers had to be built on massive piers, which are larger than the ones supporting the main tower of Westminster Abbey. One of the towers, that to the south-west, was destroyed very early in its history. The other remained until 1814, though standing as a gaunt ruin since 1809, when it was struck by lightning.

Today the most prominent feature is the gable of the south transept. It is excellent 13th-century work, with three tall lancets beneath a wheel window and a final, narrow, round-headed window high in the gable. At the junction of nave and south transept walls there is the particularly fine east processional door. It is excellently proportioned, with an arch of four orders, and great detail variation. One capital bears a badly weathered representation of two figures, said to be Adam and Eve, which is reminiscent of Norman work and is unique

The **Eglinton Tournament** of 1839 was a magnificent display. The Government had decided to scale down the pomp of Victoria's Coronation; one role abolished was that of Queen's Champion, and his ritual challenge in full armour. This role would have fallen to the Knight Marshal of the Royal Household, Sir Charles Lamb of Beaufort, the stepfather of the 13th Earl of Eglinton. Encouraged by Lamb, and recognising a growing public interest in a more chivalrous, honourable past, Eglinton set about organising a medieval tournament, attracting thousands of visitors to see the combatants and the ladies in their finery. Excursion trains – amongst the first ever were run from Ayr (predating the formal opening of the line in 1840); an ironic contrast between old and new. The only thing that Eglinton had no power over was the weather: it rained for the best part of three consecutive days. The show went ahead: champions were crowned, Queens of Beauty enthroned, and Lamb's honour assuaged. Within 100 years, Eglinton was deserted. The Tournament perhaps marked a turning point, being a severe drain on the family fortune which, with bottomless expenditure on the Ardrossan Harbour and the Glasgow, Paisley & Ardrossan Canal, undermined a family who had been among the great families of Ayrshire.

Close

Kilwinning Abbey

in Scotland. The surviving 13th-century work is concluded by the south transept aisle arch, a very fine example of the pointed Early English, and a chapter house of considerable distinction.

Abbey Church, *c.*1774, John Swan
The chancel remained in use as the parish church until it was torn down and the Abbey Church erected. This is a dark-harled, simple, plain, T-plan preaching box: although built some 200 years after the stirring events of the 16th century, its severity can be seen as a continuing expression of contempt for the Abbey and what it stood for. Inside, things are a little less grim: there is a particularly attractive Eglinton loft supported on slender Corinthian columns, and an effective window, 1903, by Stephen Adam, in memory of the Revd Lee Ker. Much more humane is the detached **Tower**, 1815, David Hamilton, on the site of the north-west tower which finally fell in 1814. Though inferior in size and grandeur to the ancient tower, it has an elegance and lightness of appearance much superior to it. Its graceful Gothic charm is in marked contrast to the austerity of the church. Those most affected by the fall of the old tower were not the Church, but the Kilwinning Archers, denied a venue for the annual papingo shoot, and it was undoubtedly secular, not religious, necessity which ensured that a new tower was erected.

Abbey Church Tower

Mother Lodge, 1883, John Armour
The Masonic movement carries the name of
Kilwinning across the world. This is Lodge
No 0, the Mother Lodge. The dark red
Collegiate Gothic façade is suitably severe and
reverential, though at odds with the remainder
of the street and the church complex behind.
The street itself rises and falls, curving
slightly, in a particularly pleasing way, its
unplanned response to landforms far more
satisfying spatially than the planned approach
of the 1970s; Robert Allan & Partners'
Shopping Centre displays a contemporary lack
of awareness of the wider townscape needs.
There are some unalloyed pleasures: the hybrid
Mercat Cross with a wooden cross, a rare
survival. **24-28 Main Street**, including the
Masons Howff, is a particularly fine group of
vernacular buildings, 1714, stuccoed, with
rusticated quoins and a central pediment.
These buildings were restored in 1985-6, by
IDC along with the adjoining Victorian
tenement, which was given a new extension,
with a cut-away entrance at the corner,
bringing a sense of purpose back to this main
entrance to the core of Kilwinning. Otherwise,
the highlights are two fore-gabled properties –
one, **150 Main Street**, single-storey, the other
110, double-storey, – the gaudy Victorian
display of the **Lemon Tree**, **91**, and the spruce
harl of the **Belfry**, which boasts one corbie-step
gable, the surviving c.1840 glazing at **65** and a
few late Victorian commercial blocks, mostly
belong to the Co-operative.

Caley House, 1984,
Irvine Development Corporation
The site of the Caledonian Railway station had
been derelict for many years, yet lay close to
the town centre. The project – self-catering
accommodation for single young people –
allowed a particularly unique answer: this
blocky, aggressive building, its rough diamond
edges softened by much use of glass to create
an internal street and the conservatory-styled
meeting place at the hinge between residential
and communal wings. **Dalry Road** boasts most
of Kilwinning's villas, the majority of these on
the east side, such as the compact **52**, and the
red rock-faced **54**, both of 1896. Protected by
the McGavin Park, bought by the Burgh in
fulfilment of a will condition of John McGavin,
1806-81. **58** is John Armour's heavy classical

Top *Mother Lodge*. Above *24-28
Main Street*

The origins of freemasonry
in Scotland are believed to lie in
the bands of skilled masons,
travelling the country and
producing the detailed work
that local masons could not
aspire to. The pre-Reformation
abbeys, such as Kilwinning,
would require such itinerant
labourers, and it is said that it
was at Kilwinning that these
masons first codified a mutual
help and protection society.
Hence the importance to the
Scottish Masonic movement of
Mother Lodge (Lodge No 0 after
another lodge took the number
1 during the Victorian
reorganisation of the
movement), and the frequent
occurrence of Kilwinning in the
title of other lodges.

Caley House

Irvine Development Corporation

High Church

Close

manse of 1888. Beyond is **Melvin House**, built as Ledcameroch, 1898-1901, by J J Burnet for Kilwinning solicitor, R C King. It is a large, harled, Arts & Crafts villa.

STEVENSTON

A straggling town with no effective focus or dominant style, it is an old settlement, and parish centre (much of Saltcoats being in Stevenston parish), yet despite abundant coal seams, which were near the surface and exploited relatively early, failed to grow rapidly during the 19th century, being eclipsed by the burgeoning Saltcoats. Critical to its subsequent development was the establishment of Nobel's explosives factory in 1873: the dynamite stick on the town's arms, and the former Dynamite Road are indicative of this importance. Stevenston achieved burgh status in 1958, the penultimate burgh to be created in Scotland.

High Church, 1832, Thomas Garven
On a prominent site, looking across the little town towards the Firth. Straightforward oblong preaching box, not especially large; the fancy work restricted to the Gothic arcading on the tall tower. The equally conventional interior is enlivened by seasonal wall paintings and two windows of *c.*1900 by Oscar Paterson.

In the churchyard is the ornate Gibbsian monument to Revd David Landsborough and the 1933 centenary gates. This little religious community, somehow remote from the town, is completed by the **Manse**, 1787, with an earlier rear wing dated 1700, and 1885 addition by John Burnet, its core a plain, solid, harled Georgian box, the pretty **21 Schoolwell Street** at the manse gates; and the neat **Champion Shell Inn**.

Boglemart Street

The main east/west road: **6-14** are workmanlike houses of *c*.1870, well restored, and **58** a Gothicky tenement, while the rest is a higgledy-piggledy assortment of nondescript development and gap sites. That charge can be levelled at the other arms of the cross: in **Townhead Street** only the post office, 1939, neatly crowstepped baronial, but notably *retardataire*, and **9-13**, a 20th-century bar with Glasgow Style details have any pretension. **New Street**, with a chunky brick Shopping Centre, James Hay Steel & Partners, and the vaguely Scandinavian Masonic Hall, *c*.1958, of impossibly spindly columns, leads to Ardeer and The Works. In **Station Road**, the Trust Bar, 1906, Hugh Thomson, was a Gothenburg-principled public house; its Brewers' Tudor architecture has no similarly Swedish derivation.

Top *9-13 Townhead Street.* Above *Trust Bar*

Ardeer

This is a wonderful sand desert where the wind always blows, and often howls, filling the ears with sand which also drifts about the room like a fine drizzle. There, like a huge village, lies the factory. A few yards away the ocean begins, a sea whose mighty waves are always raging and foaming. Now you will have some idea of the place where I am living ... without work it would be intolerable. Thus wrote Nobel of Ardeer, where he had begun to build his explosives factory in 1870. It was designed by Alarik Liedbeck, but has since hugely outgrown the original buildings. Among the buildings on the huge site is **Africa House**, the reconstructed South African Pavilion from the 1938 Glasgow Exhibition; the architect was George Millar, the style Dutch Reformed Church. **Nobel House** is a vast, well-composed, office block, 1966, Sir Basil Spence, Glover & Ferguson.

Africa House

Mayville

*O saw ye **bonnie Lesley***
As she gaed o'er the border?
She's gane, like Alexander,
To spread her conquests farther.

To see her, is to love her,
And love but her for ever;
For Nature made her what she is,
And ne'er made sic anither!

Mayville, 1720

Now absorbed into the town, this exceptionally attractive house, with its stonework of pleasing hue and texture, still cultivates an atmosphere of *rus in urbe*. Built for a sea captain, Robert Baillie, at some period in the later 18th century it acquired a porch, pediment and ornamental urns. It has a sundial of 1773, and, formerly in the grounds but now in Glencairn Street, an obelisk of 1784, repaired in 1929 as a memorial to Burns's Bonnie Lesley.

Kerelaw Castle, 15th century

A seat of the Earls of Glencairn, now a massive ivy-mantled ruin, renovated to retard its decay and increase its picturesqueness. This occurred *c.*1830 when it was turned into a garden folly for the now vanished Kerelaw House, the Gothick windows slapped through, and workers' cottages made in the courtyard.

Right *Kerelaw Castle.* Below *Auchenharvie Engine House*

Auchenharvie

A Cunninghame seat lying equidistant to Stevenston and Saltcoats. The house has gone, its site used by Auchenharvie Academy, very conventional sub-Brutalist brick-clad structure, which dominates the area. Seaward is the ruinous **Auchenharvie Engine House**, *c.*1720, a purely functional structure which housed the second Newcomen pumping engine to be installed in Scotland. It was designed to pump water from a coal-pit, but failed to do so. On the hill above the school the very minimal remains of Nelson's Tower, a folly-cum-lookout tower of uncertain history.

SALTCOATS

An intricate, multi-faceted town which keeps much of its charm and character well hidden, but rewards the perseverer. Developed around

Saltcoats seen from Ardrossan Castle

a small harbour and salt-panning community, it has been coal port, bathing resort, shopping centre: Saltcoats blends these past and present activities well, though the first is long gone, the second suffering badly from competition from the Mediterranean, and the third from competition from Irvine. The built consequence of all this is primarily 19th century, the period of greatest growth, under the tutelage of Robert Reid Cunninghame of Auchenharvie. The tight, well-defined shopping streets – **Nineyards Street**, **Dockhead Street**, **Hamilton Street** – have a true urban feel, compact, busy, enhanced by recent partial pedestrianisation. The harbour area is messier, less sure of its future. Saltcoats, like Stevenston and Ardrossan, spreads inland; no tower or spire gives any distant focus for the town.

The town is partly in Ardrossan parish, partly in Stevenston parish, which further complicates its ecclesiastical history, and helps to explain the lack of a visual landmark.

North Ayrshire Museum, 1744

From 1744 to 1908 its role was as Ardrossan Parish Church. With all ornament subsumed to the strictly Calvinist views of the 18th-century Church, the result is a severe rubble-built church, with a rather gauche pedimental projection and bellcote. The adjacent **Erskine Church**, 1866, William Stewart, at the end of Station Road, has spire and pinnacles atop a polychrome Venetian Gothic façade.

Saltcoats in 1792 enjoyed unprecedented growth and prosperity: *Upwards of forty vessels belong to this port; some of them are fishing vessels, but most of them are employed in the coal trade to Ireland, the making of salt also, from which the town takes its name, is another branch of trade, which the abundance of coal enables the inhabitants to carry on with success. Since 1775 they have done much in the article of shipbuilding. They have a rope works, and three ship carpenter yards, employing a number of hands. The place is favourable to manufacturers in general.* Much credit rests with the Cunninghames of Auchenharvie who actively exploited coal from their land. They also ran a brewery, and would have benefited greatly if Eglinton's Ardrossan & Glasgow Canal had materialised.

North Ayrshire Museum

Betsy Miller, 1792-1864, is the best-known of Saltcoats' sea captains. Daughter of a shipowner, and of strong will, she became master of the brig *Clitus*, successfully pursuing the coal trade with Ireland. This proto-feminist was the only female sea captain registered in the United Kingdom. *She was a sonsy woman, weel favor't, neither wee nor tall, an' wi' as much sense o' humour as made life aboard gang pleasantly.*
Quoted in Carragher, 1908

Below *Town Hall*. Bottom *Station*

St Cuthbert's South Beach Church, 1907, Peter MacGregor Chalmers (*left*)
A scholarly design, characteristic of this architect: the text is Romanesque and the resultant rubble-built church, with tall clerestory, aisles and delicate tower, has his usual crisp detailing and sharply defined elements. Adjacent is the **Argyle Primary School**, 1876, Alexander Adamson: stunning red sandstone range of School Board buildings in a flamboyant French Gothic manner.

This is the hub of suburban Saltcoats: a vast area developed during the final quarter of the 19th century. The major thoroughfares are **Argyle Street**, **South Beach Road** and **Caledonia Road**. There is a clear hierarchy, but the typical house is a semi-detached villa or dormered cottage, slated over the local grey stone. Occasional detached villa, such as the Jacobethan **81** Caledonia Road; some terraces, such as **Springvale Street**, no more than a few pilastered doorways, a correct sense of scale and relationships; and the odd outbreak of red stone, as at **79** Caledonia Road, a baleful Arts & Crafts villa near the seamless border with Ardrossan.

Town Hall, Countess Street, 1825, Peter King; 1892, Howie & Walton
King's original structure has a tower of middling height, flanked by low wings, done in a provincial, classical manner; the swags and medallions of its addition picked out in an honestly cheerful paint scheme. The Town Hall dominates a small group of houses of *c.*1810: **26-32**, plain, honest fare. **1-3** are earlier, *c.*1750, but extensively altered: the true age revealed by the steeply pitched roof, crowsteps and skews. The **Station**, 1894, is an attractive group of buildings, tall Renaissance office and low similarly styled down-platform group, with glazed canopy, restored in 1986-7. **Dockhead Street** is the dog-legged main shopping street, its 19th-century buildings (one dated 1833) lost in a welter of modern signs, with one good corniced banking palazzo, **87-89**, free Venetian, 1931, A Balfour & Stewart. In **Nineyards Street**, the **Mission Coast Home**, 1888 onwards, H & D Barclay, baronial, a striking feature being an octagon tower, about 65 ft high, on which are carved in panels the monograms of the founders of the Home; the quirky **Windy Ha'**, a bar of *c.*1900, with corner tower and spirelet; and the spreading Dutch-gabled **Free Church**, David Cousin, 1843.

Hamilton Street

Begins with **Metro**, one of Harry Kemp's cinemas with stylised sunburst pediment, and **Halifax Building Society**, **1-3**, 1986, J & J A Carrick, a refreshing post-Modern block which turns the corner with surprising ease; its light airy feel in pointed contrast to the traditions of Saltcoats. The pattern for Hamilton Street is two-storey, usually dormered, houses of two or three bays, built *c*.1810-20. **6** establishes the pattern, though the despoliation of shopfronts lessens as one moves westward, and concludes with the 1930s **Café Melbourne**, the tall column and alert squaddie of the **War Memorial** and the **Catholic Church**, 1856, by Baird of Airdrie. The **Congregational Church**, 1863, Lewis Fullarton, on the more variable north-east side, is a Gothic counterpoint to this minimalist classicism. In **Windmill Street** the heavily chamfered corner of Eglinton Court, well-composed brick neo-vernacular housing development of *c*.1982.

Halifax Building Society

Harbour, 1686 onwards

The old pierhead may incorporate masonry from the harbour works constructed by Robert Cuninghame in 1686; it certainly incorporates the Custom House, 1805. The present structures date largely from the reconstruction in 1914 and 1988: the latter distinguished by post-Modern ball finials and a giant sundial. Winton Circus and Montgomerie Crescent follow the coast towards Ardrossan: villas and semi-villas such as **20-21 Montgomerie Crescent**, with grey stone margins and a red ashlar minimally crowstepped triple-gabled front.

Old Saltcoats Harbour

Lord Cockburn was in Ardrossan in 1842: *It is above, or about, thirty years since I last saw it. It was then a sort of poor fishing village, with no harbour, and no fashion as a bathing place. The late Earl of Eglinton was just beginning the attempt to realise his vision of glorifying and enriching his family, by carrying a canal from Glasgow, by Paisley, to this part of his property, and thus making Ardrossan Tyre and Saltcoats Sidon. The canal, after being bankrupt, reached Johnstone, and now, with its railway rival, it will certainly never advance an inch further. But his lordship succeeded in compelling the sea to submit to be a small port, and in alluring genteel invalids, by a large bad inn, and small bad baths, to resort there in the summer ... The summer population consists mostly of strangers, few of whom have what, in Scottish Irish, are called self-contained houses, most of them cramming into the small, but clean, upper flats, which are let for bathers by the poorer people below. The whole place is respectably clean.*

Nicholson's Plan for Ardrossan

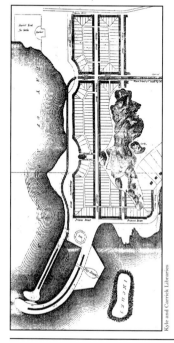

Kyle and Carrick Libraries

Close

ARDROSSAN

Interesting town, its character – now sadly eroded – largely created through its planned development by the Earl of Eglinton, with Peter Nicholson as his architect, in the first years of the 19th century. The plan is very simple, the most facile of grid, but none the less effective. Eglinton also began the development of the harbour, partly for coal shipment and partly as the seaward end of his proposed canal hence to Glasgow, and also encouraged the development of expensive residential and resort areas, such as **South Crescent**, in what seems, to modern sensibilities, over-close proximity to the port areas. Death, and the costs of the Eglinton Tournament (see p.65), caused abandonment of the canal project, and it was only in the mid-19th century that the harbour was completed.

Ardrossan Castle, 15th century
Only a few fragments remain of this once powerful fortress of the Montgomeries. The castle is said to have been destroyed by Cromwell and the stone taken to Ayr to build the Citadel there. Only a portion of the tower, a vaulted kitchen and two cellars remain. The tower retains a few corbels of the parapet and the jambs of a fireplace, and a single loop-hole. These scant ruins are kept company on the **Castlehill** by the **Obelisk**, 1849, in memory of Dr Alexander MacFadzean who originated the proposal to form the town into a burgh, and the even scantier foundations of the first Parish Church in its old burial ground.

Princes Street
The centre of the town is the junction between **Glasgow Street** and **Princes Street**. The latter is the short arm of the cross, running between the mobile cranes of the harbour and

the **Bath Villa**, 90 Princes Street. This building, *c*.1870, was the lodging house attached to the baths, now gone, and its sternly plain late Georgian mien is important in the townscape. The architect was James Cleland: restoration, 1988-9, by E C Riach for the Three Towns Housing Association. The **Eglinton Arms Hotel**, 1806-7, Peter Nicholson, was the main inn for Eglinton's new town. It is a striking symmetrically faced block of painted ashlar. Opposite are the **Library Headquarters** of Cunninghame District Council, 1985, a well-planned group in the ubiquitous neo-vernacular, not especially mindful of the importance of Ardrossan's grid pattern to its character. The rest of Princes Street demonstrates the piecemeal manner by which the grid filled up. **41-69** date probably from the first years of development, that is, built according to Nicholson's plans; battered but unbowed, their severe minimal classicism seems to thrive on neglect and indifference. **10** is dated 1839, and **46-78** date from *c*.1850: there is a little more scope for detailing and individualism, but they are still controlled by the tyranny of Nicholson's master plan. Later still are **44**, dated 1858, and **89-93**, *c*.1860, all continuing the pattern, as do **59-61**, *c*.1880.

Top *Ardrossan from Saltcoats.*
Above *Eglinton Arms Hotel*

Galt's Ayrshire Legatees
stopped briefly at Ardrossan *en route* for Glasgow and London: *The weather was cold, bleak and boisterous, and the waves came rolling in majestic fury towards the shore, when we arrived at the Tontine Inn of Ardrossan. What a monument has the late Earl of Eglinton left there of his public spirit! It should embalm his memory in the hearts of future ages, as I doubt not but in time Ardrossan will become a grand emporium; but the people of Saltcoats, a sordid race, complaint that it will be their ruin; and the Paisley subscribers to his lordship's canal grow pale when they think of profit.*

Congregational Church, Arran Place, 1905, John B Wilson
This is an undemanding simple rectangle, Perpendicularly detailed, from this prolific church architect, turning the corner into **Arran Place**. This is a mixed terrace of *c*.1850, a cheerful mixture of colours, finishes, styles, Ardrossan's continuing tenuous link with the Glasgow Fair trade. At either end of Arran Place are two churches: **Barony Parish Church**, 1844, Black & Salmon, another plain Gothic rectangular preaching box, enlivened by

Top *St Peter-ad-Vincula.* Middle *Harbour Office.* Above *Power House*

its elaborately detailed tower and spire, with clasping buttresses and a lively silhouette; and **St Peter-ad-Vincula**, 1938, Jack Coia and T Warnett Kennedy (Gillespie Kidd & Coia), a stunningly direct design in red and yellow brick, showing clearly the Scandinavian influence; a brilliant light-filled interior adds to the charms of one of Ayrshire's best churches.

South Crescent

A development of large villas, houses for the well-to-do, and always an integral part of Eglinton's and Nicholson's plans for the development of Ardrossan. The result is patchy, due chiefly to the long period over which it was developed, and not helped by the current stagnation into which the area has fallen. It runs from **St Peter's** to **St Andrew's Episcopal Church**, 1875, David Thomson, an exercise in Early English design, lacking the planned tower. Between are a number of gaunt 19th-century villas, creating a rather down-at-heel guide to provincial architectural taste.

Harbour, 1806 onwards

Work was carried out for the 12th and 13th Earls of Eglinton, greatly improving the existing natural harbour, and planned as one end of a proposed canal to Glasgow, circumventing the Tail of the Bank, its tides and shallows. Plans for the canal and harbour were prepared in 1800 by John Rennie, and amended plans prepared by Thomas Telford in 1805. The pier was completed by 1813, with David Henry as contractor. The attractive Italianate **Power House** was opened in 1892, while the **Harbour Office** is an enjoyably robust exercise in 1930s streamlining.

Glasgow Street, 1806 onwards, Peter Nicholson

The long arm of the cross. Much of the original housing has been demolished, and little of any merit put in its place. The Town Hall is a Tudor Gothic private house, **Castle Craigs**, in pink and white masonry, compromised by the 1960s additions, while the **Church of the Nazarene**, 1857, Thomas Wallace, is a further simple church, its most notable feature the onion-domed pinnacles which top the tall pilasters that flank the central bay. **30-56**, **66-72** and **86-98** are original houses, part of the original Eglinton/Nicholson plan; similarly

Winton Primary School, overdoor detail

severe to the houses in Princes Street, but well restored in the 1980s by McMillan & Cronin. In **Anderson Terrace**, **Winton Primary School**, 1899, John Armour, is a particularly fine Arts & Crafts structure.

Seafield, 1820; 1858, Thomas Gildard Gildard is better known as a historian and architectural hagiographer. This prominent house is a particularly ornate and fancy variant of Scots baronial, with a great deal of carved Jacobethan strapwork detail, and a steeply pitched French-influenced tower roof, rising amid the crowstepped gables and turrets. Off the coast here is **Horse Island** which has a slender pyramidal seamark of probably early 18th century date.

Horse Island is said to have got its name from its use as grazing for such beasts, either as a quarantine station for livestock coming into Ardrossan Harbour, or by local farmers.

Seafield

CUNNINGHAME COAST

On the narrow strip of flatter ground between the Clyde and the peaty, inhospitable hills which run from the archaeologically rich **Knock Ewart**, above West Kilbride, to the unfrequented wastes of **Ferret of Keith Moor**, lie a string of towns: **West Kilbride**, **Seamill**, **Fairlie**, **Largs**, **Skelmorlie**. This is Glasgow merchants' *get away from it all* country: an idyllic retreat from the city. The first flowerings of this new economy began in the 1790s, as Gilpin successfully changed our perception of wild places from fearful and awesome to picturesque. The peak of this trade was the years on either side of 1900, though Largs, with its pier, successfully adapted to the needs of the charabanc and steamer tripper of the inter-war period, and provided some exciting architecture.

WEST KILBRIDE

Sedate, lace-curtained village nestling under the lee of **Law Hill**. It still retains much pre-tripper dignity, and a well-composed main street which speaks, above the traffic, of a quieter, slower age. It merges seamlessly with its brasher suburb, Seamill, where are to be found the golf course, the beach, the hotels: West Kilbride does its best to ignore such vulgarities. The two most notable beacons pinpointing the town seem almost an irrelevance.

Below Law Castle. Bottom Simson Monument drawn by F T Pilkington

Law Castle, *c.*1468
Local lore says that Law Castle was built for Princess Mary, on her marriage to Thomas, Master of Boyd. It is a simple rectangular block, probably given its final appearance *c.*1510. It has, as everyone from MacGibbon & Ross onward has noted, strong similarities to other Firth of Clyde castles, notably **Fairlie**, **Skelmorlie** and **Little Cumbrae**. It is currently being restored, under the benign eye of Ian Begg.

Simson Monument, 1865, F T Pilkington
In the middle of West Kilbride's otherwise undistinguished cemetery, and visible over a wide area, is this bizarre monument: a huge Egyptian-detailed structure, typical of the excesses of which Pilkington was well capable. Robert Simson, was the *Restorer of Greek Geometry*.

Kirktonhall, 1791 onwards
This is the birthplace of Robert Simson. The chief glory of Main Street, to which it shows its rear elevation. The front façade, with its double-height porch and Gothic Venetian window was rebuilt in 1791, Frank Ritchie, and the battlemented parapet added in 1807. The core is undoubtedly earlier, and the final effect, with a **sundial** of 1717, alleged to have been designed by Simson is a slightly whimsical, inelegant but comforting house. Now used as Council offices. The churches of the little town are late 19th century: **Barony** (now Boys Brigade Hall), 1873, Henry Blair, rather dumpy Early English; **St Bride's**, 1881, James Ritchie, in a bellicose Frenchified style, compounded by the bullnosed stonework; and **Overton**, 1883, Hippolyte J Blanc, a boldly detailed original composition. The **Station**, c.1900, is a delightful Arts & Crafts composition by James Miller, while the **Public Institute**, 1900, Alexander Paterson, is a charming little design.

Kirktonhall

Robert Simson, 1687-1768, studied with Edmund Halley in London before becoming Professor of Mathematics at Glasgow University in 1712. Halley introduced Simson to the works of Euclid and other Greek geometricians, then known only in various fragmentary forms. Simson devoted much of his life to restoring and editing these texts, and is hence known as the *Restorer of Greek Geometry*.

The village grew especially rapidly in the inter-war period: roads such as **Caldwell Road** and **Corsehill Drive** have an impressive range of bungalows in a bewildering variety of styles. The architects most often responsible are Fryers & Penman of Largs and J Austin Laird.

Seamill
Picturesque group of mill and cottages, c.1790, now completely given over to residential use. Looming over the villa propriety of Ardrossan Road is **Seamill Hydro**, extensively extended in the 1920s by Thomas Marwick and in the 1960s by Hay Steel & MacFarlane.

Crosbie Tower, 1676
This typical vernacular house occupies an impressive defensive site, two sides rising from

Left *Station*. Above *Public Institute*

Top *Crosbie Tower*. Middle *Portencross Castle*. Above *Hillhome*

the deep ravine of the burn beneath. The original T-plan house has been partially swamped by the rich red sandstone additions made *c*.1896, which make no concessions to the character or needs of the original house, and for which, oddly, the architects appear to be those great Victorian cataloguers, MacGibbon & Ross.

Portencross Castle, 14th century (see p.C4) This Boyd seat is a fine example of a stronghold of this period, providing, on its rocky seagirt site, a conspicuous landmark to voyagers. It has an unusual plan, a variant on the L-plan with the wing to one end and not to the side, though it is unclear whether this is the result of subsequent addition. It still stands to almost its full height, and has vaults on both ground and first floors, and entrance doors in the re-entrant to both these levels, juxtaposed one on one face, one on the other. The hamlet – no more than the castle, a farm and a few cottages – is much frequented on halcyon days: its end-of-the-road atmosphere and the castle appear to be the main attractions, though **West Cottage** and **Castle Cottage**, both *c*.1860, are consciously picturesque. **Hillhome** is a flat-roofed house of 1937 by J Austin Laird.

HUNTERSTON (see p.C8) A name which conjures many disparate images. The Power Stations cannot be denied: the glazed mass of **Hunterston A**, 1957-64, Howard V Lobb & Partners, compares with **Hunterston B**, 1967-76, Robert Matthew Johnson-Marshall & Partners, more boxy, inaccessible and inward-looking. Between them are the rail, road and sea facilities associated with the **Ore Terminal**, 1979, Frank Mears & Partners, a heavy-duty barn, unavoidably functional, with administration centralised in a huge grey '1'. Heavy expenditure on effective, massively scaled landscaping by Scottish Landscaping Ltd renders most of this invisible from the main coast road, though the conveyors and rail links bring a sinister urban menace to this rural corner. The effect is more jarring seen from the sea or the hills above Largs.

Hunterston Castle, 16th/17th century Standing aloof from the world of reactors and steel mills, this small four-storey tower, with a single vault, was sensitively adapted by Robert Lorimer in 1913; much of the internal decoration is his. The ranges of farm buildings

Left *Hunterston Castle*. Above
Hunterston House

which enfilade the castle appear to have been
added *c.*1847 in a congruous style; they create a
quaint group against the dark mass of the
tower, as was presumably the intention. Close
by is **Hunterston House**, *c.*1799, a pink-harled
unflustered house of the period, enlivened by its
Doric-columned porch. Internally, the tone
changes from restrained Georgian to a freer
manorial feel, brought about by exceptionally
attractive panel- and plaster-work, inserted
*c.*1920 by Robert Lorimer.

FAIRLIE

A village halved: the southern portion is almost
exclusively inter-war bungalows, looking across
Fence Bay to Hunterston; further north is the
older village, tucked in between road and
shore, the church and the castle secreted up
Fairlie Glen. *Fairlie is the best village of the
wealthy in Scotland. Excellent houses, capital
gardens, umbrageous trees, the glorious Clyde,
backed by Arran and its dependencies stretched
out before them, a gravelly solid, and a mild
western climate.* That was Lord Cockburn's
verdict in 1842.

Fairlie Castle, early 16th century
Another of the group of similar structures, with
Skelmorlie, **Law** and **Little Cumbrae**, that
dot this particular area. The shell survives
relatively intact, up to and including the ornate
chequerwork corbelling, and although there
has been inevitable weathering of the masonry,
many of the quoins and chamfered window
dressings remain crisp and sharp-edged.
The main road runs through the upper village,
squeezed between the high garden walls of the
seaside villas and the cliffs which press in from
the landward side. Almost the only building
tucked in on the landward side is the **Church**

Fairlie was renowned for
many years for the quality of
the yachts produced by the Fife
family over four generations.
The company was founded by
William Fife, 1785-1865, in
1812, and lasted until the
1980s. From the slip in Bay
Street, now replaced by new
housing, William Fife & Sons
launched a succession of
famous racing yachts, such as
the Marquess of Ailsa's
Bloodhound (1864) and
Shamrock (1899) and *Shamrock
III* (1903) for Sir Thomas
Lipton.

Fairlie Castle

Kelburn has been the seat of the Boyles since the 12th century. The family became Earls of Glasgow in 1703 but suffered badly in the collapse of the City of Glasgow Bank. Since 1977, the castle has been at the heart of a lively and energetic Country Centre where the emphasis is distinctly on letting off steam: adventure trail, assault course. The centre is run from the 18th-century South Offices. Antipodean exotica in the museum recall the 7th Earl's Governorship of New Zealand, a link continued in the New Zealand Garden of gunnera, bamboo and New Zealand flax.

Below *Kelburn Castle in 1875.* Bottom *Monument at Kelburn*

Hall, 1879, formerly the Free Church. The **Parish Church**, 1883, J J Stevenson, incorporates the original 1834 structure into a powerful freeform structure. Excellent collection of stained glass includes work by Morris & Co and Heaton Butler and Bayne. By Stevenson also is the delicate little Village Hall of 1892. Of the secluded villas, **Fairlieburn House**, *c*.1845, is a well-composed, if a trifle pretentious, essay in the manner of David Bryce.

KELBURN, 1581; 1692-1722; 1879-80 (see p.C1) The house and grounds form a delightful sylvan arcady between Largs and Fairlie, and find estimable use as golf course and very vigorous, dynamic Country Park, finding, incidentally, new uses for the 18th-century farm buildings. The estate also calls a halt to the southward spread of Largs: o! for a Kelburn north of Largs. It would be too much to expect another house of such interest and complexity, and much of the story still requires to be unravelled. The Z-plan tower house, which incorporates earlier fabric, was built for the Boyle family, and was later extended by the addition of the long symmetrical block attached at an oblique angle but substantially a new house in its own right; the mason seems to have been Thomas Caldwell. A 19th-century wing contains a dining room and billiard room.

Internally, the basement rooms of the original tower are vaulted yet, although the floor above has been altered at various times, it was obviously the great hall, and some original features, such as wall presses, survive. The wing completed in 1722 contains a drawing room with magnificent plasterwork of *c*.1700 in classical taste but clearly applied without the mechanical precision of the Regency-style ceiling of the Victorian dining-room.

There are in the grounds two **sundials** contemporary with the 1692 wing, one dated 1707, and a **monument** to the 3rd Lord Glasgow, dated 1775, and designed by Robert Adam.

The approach to Largs is marked by **The Pencil**, 1912, James Kay's singular monument to the Battle of Largs. **Largs Cemetery**, laid out in 1886, is a gem of its kind, superbly well planted. The family tombstone, 1899, designed by **Herbert MacNair**, Mackintosh's friend, should be sought out; above the void is visible the MacNair crest, a mermaid.

Kelburn Country Park open to visitors: Kelburn House open annually, usually in April/May

LARGS

Largs is wonderfully blowsy, with the icons of the pre-Torremolinos tripper trade perkily pitched between the sober-sided corner-stones of an earlier generation of seasiders, the churches and the hotels, both models of respectability. Post-Torremolinos Largs is rapidly becoming one large retirement home; nonetheless, Largs retains its rather brash image and, on a busy July Saturday, queuing for gelati outside **Nardini's**, one can pretend that time has not moved on.

The **Pierhead** was dominated by two buildings: the **Moorings**, 1936, James Houston, quirky, nautical and brilliant, and the **Cumbraen**, which is none of those things. The *new* Moorings, 1990, McMillan & Cronin, is a commercial block which takes some of its cues from its predecessor. **Bath Street** is dominated by the **Clark Memorial Church**, 1890-2, T G Abercrombie, a huge red stone edifice detailed in a particularly successful Early English manner, reeking of munificent endowment. It has a particularly rich interior with a hammerbeam roof of East Anglian character and excellent contemporary stained glass, and overwhelms the adjacent **St John's**, 1886, A J Graham, in a peculiarly idiosyncratic Romanesque, which is not unlikeable, but is clearly ill at ease with the imagery across the road, and it is no surprise to discover that it began life as a Free Church. Opposite are the former **Baths**, 1816, in a suitably jaunty round-headed classicism. Across the **Gogo Water** is the **New Town** of Largs, laid out for

View of Largs painted by John Fleming

In 1782, a Glasgow merchant of means **John Reid**, and his family, decided to summer in Largs. The journey took two days and involved hiring farm carts to cover the final eight miles of roadless moorland from Kilbirnie. The Reids are the first recorded summer visitors to Largs.

Clark Memorial Church

Top *Former Baths*. Middle *Elderslie*. Above *72-74 Main Street*

The Battle of Largs, fought on 2nd October 1263 between the forces of Alexander III and Haakon of Norway, was a decisive turning point in the history of Scotland, marking the end of Norse attempts to increase their power and influence in western Scotland. Thereafter, the Scots steadily gained control of Norse possessions along the western and northern seaboards, culminating with the acquisition of Orkney and Shetland in 1468.

Thomas Brisbane of Brisbane House from 1810, to plans by Alexander May. In **Broomfield Place**, the **Elderslie Hotel**, 1829-30, David and James Hamilton, displays delicate Tudoresque with delightful ironwork, and in **Broomfield Crescent**, stands the unassuming but alluring **Little Raith**, *c.*1830. **Warriston**, *c.*1830, echoes the Elderslie closely, and must also be by David Hamilton. All that remains of the **Curling Hall** is the **Lodge**, *c.*1850, restored by G D Lodge & Partners, 1988.

Main Street

Main Street is generally early 19th-century two-storey houses, usually with late 20th-century shopfronts. The bustle, and its completeness, saves it, though the sense of space becomes ragged in the broader space in front of the **Station**, 1936. This was the Market Place, but no longer. **21-29** is the best group of buildings: very different are the banks: **Royal Bank of Scotland**, 1900, florid Dutch Renaissance; **Bank of Scotland**, *c.*1860, the typical banking palazzo; and **72-74**, the former British Linen Bank, 1907, George Washington Browne, the quality of his design carrying off the insertion of this piece of Cotswold Revival.

Skelmorlie Aisle, 1636

Sole remnant of Largs' former Parish Church. The exterior, despite its elaborate details, including thistle and fleur-de-lis finials, is no match for the interior. Beneath the richly **painted timber ceiling**, 1638, signed J S Stalker, with its imitation barrel vault and superlative panels of biblical texts, zodiacal and symbolic images and the four seasons (summer including a view of the town) is an

Skelmorlie Aisle: ceiling

equally superlative Renaissance **canopied tomb** to the Montgomeries of Skelmorlie, dated 1639. Hay felt able to compare it to Colt's Westminster Abbey memorial to Elizabeth. It is notable for the refinement of its Italianate detail; standing over a balustrade above the burial-vault entrance, it takes the form of a triumphal arch surmounted by strapwork, finials and cherubs, but was almost certainly intended to have a recumbent effigy.
Open to the public (Historic Scotland): booklet available

Gallowgate

Gallowgate begins unpromisingly with the side view of the Cumbraen. **St Columba's Church**, 1891-3, Henry Steele & Andrew Balfour, is another richly endowed, richly ornamented red stone church, and, across **Nelson Street**, **Nardini's**, 1936, Charles Davidson, the *sine qua non* of Largs. Creamy white streamlined plastered exterior, its corner tower a prominent landmark, and inside, the true Nardini experience: wicker chairs, **torchères**, gleaming steel ice-cream and coffee machines. *The massive soda fountain is a notable work itself, and it is in charge of an American expert dispenser.* In **Greenock Road**, with **Brooksby**, *c.*1837, David Hamilton, is a sober, but finely executed, yachting residence; **Our Lady of the Sea**, 1962, which has dated well, its Hew Lorimer Madonna giving additional interest; **Moorburn**, 1876, a boldly featured cast-iron decorated Italianate villa; and **Barrfields Pavilion**, 1929, William Barclay, fun architecture, approachable and not designed for serious analysis.

St Columba's Episcopal Church, 1876, Ross & MacBeth

Charming, delicate exercise in the simpler forms of Early English, quite able to withstand the dominating influence of the major town centre churches. **Netherhall**, 1876-92, Campbell Douglas & Sellars, for Lord Kelvin, and approached through a gatehouse which picks up the main elements in the design, is a striking, basically baronial design, but Scots with a strong French accent, while **Northfield**, *c.*1830, shares (with Warriston and Elderslie) David Hamilton's Tudor detailing; and **Danefield**, 1883, its assured handling of polychrome Scots baronial details, is the work of John Douglas of Chester.

Top *Brisbane Aisle.* Middle *Skelmorlie Aisle.* Above *Nardini's*

Alongside the Skelmorlie Aisle is the **Brisbane Aisle**, an attractive miniature burial vault of 1634. The Brisbanes of Brisbane were important landowners around Largs. **Brisbane House** (formerly Kelsoland), a remarkable 17th-century structure, acquired by the Brisbanes in 1671, was demolished in the 1920s. It is illustrated in MacGibbon & Ross.

Above *Halkshill*. Below *Knock*.
Middle *Knock Castle*. Bottom
Manor Park

Halkshill, 1815, another David Hamilton-style villa, began life as a stable block; it has a gay Gothick summerhouse, *c.*1840. Once in the Halkshill policies, but now marooned alongside the public road, are the **Three Sisters**, 1808, three rubble-built square-plan meridian pillars, situated on a motte. When the Brisbane Trustees sold Halkshill to John Scott in 1815, it was stipulated that no buildings were to obscure the line of vision between the pillars and Brisbane House.

Knock

A splendid pair of houses. The **Old Castle** is of 1603-4, a Z-plan tower, still new when Pont wrote of *a prettey duelling seatted one the mane occeane and veil planted.* The subsequent history of alteration and enlargement is complex, and the unravelling not eased by the repair, often with whimsical details, which J T Rochead undertook in 1853, transforming the castle into a large garden folly. Rochead was also responsible for **Knock Castle**, finished in 1852, a truly superb Tudor-castellated pile, grouped in a neat tight composition belying its huge size. Well massed, this is undoubtedly among the most successful 19th-century mansions in Scotland. It has equally impressive interiors, on a Burn-style corridor plan, and respectful 20th-century additions by Fryers & Penman. **Manor Park**, 1843, David and James Hamilton, is a relatively modest A-plan mansion in the Hamilton style which permeates widely in this part of Ayrshire.

Skelmorlie Castle, *c.*1502

This magnificent mansion surveys the Firth of Clyde from a spectacular situation high at the end of a ridge. The core is a tower house (broadly similar to Law and Fairlie), altered, *c.*1600; and in 1636 a particularly beautiful office range was added. In the 1850s further additions were made, probably by William Railton, in an amalgam of Scots baronial and Gothic. After a fire, much of the Victorian work was pulled down, and restoration undertaken by Noad & Wallace. Despite demolition, this is still a substantial pile, the old grey-harled tower blending pleasingly with the fantasy red stone baronial of the surviving Victorian work and the splendour of the 17th-century stable block. Pont described it as *a fair, weill-bult housse and elefantly featted decorated with orchards and voodes.* It still is.

John Graham of Skelmorlie Castle, *c.*1795-1886, was an avid art collector. His fortune was based on the export of cloth from Glasgow. In 1878 it was said that *for years and years – ever, indeed, since the* [Glasgow] *Institute of Fine Arts was formed – has he treated us to an annual glimpse of two or three rarer and more valuable canvasses than by any other chance could we have hoped to light upon in a public gallery.* Indeed, the 'Graham Pictures' have long been looked upon as a main feature of the exhibitions of the Institute.

SKELMORLIE

Attractive little village squeezed between the
sea and the cliff. The weekend and summer
mansions of the Glasgow and Renfrewshire
merchants can be found on the cliff top in
Upper Skelmorlie, far removed from the hustle
of the main road, though the first villas were
built on the limited land available on the
seaward side, the very first being the
Italianate-style **Beach House**, completed in
1844, which was, to Millar, to be considered as
a model for a modern marine villa.

Parish Church, 1895, John Honeyman
Unpretentious church, competent but unmoving.
Its chief glory is the freestanding wrought-iron
lamp outside, probably contemporary, and
undeniably the work of Charles Rennie
Mackintosh (*CRM Society Newsletter no.33*),
with its gorgeous flowing patterns and tactile
quality. The former **Free Church**, 1874, almost
astride the county line, has lost much in the
course of residential conversion.

Skelmorlie Castle

Lower Skelmorlie
South of the churches and beach villa, red
stone villas line the road, crowding into the
cramped space between sea-coast and cliff.
One such is the fancifully bargeboarded and
chimneyed **Thorndale**, 15 Shore Road, *c.*1875.

Upper Skelmorlie
Arrayed in spacious gardens and stretching
inland from the cliff top are a number of
substantial villas. The best are in Montgomerie
Terrace, such as John Honeyman's **Manse**,
1874, and in The Crescent, with **Skelmorlie
House**, 1890s and the excellent, and well-
named, **Tudor House**, 1904, Watson &
Salmond. There is a villagey core, with a harled
and battered **Evangelical Church**, 1904,
H E Clifford, that began life as a village hall.

*Lamp at Skelmorlie Parish
Church*

GARNOCK VALLEY
Montgreenan, 1810-17
Built for Dr Robert Glasgow, who had made his
fortune in the West Indies, Montgreenan is a
magnificent classical mansion in crisp red
ashlar. It has similarities with Montgomerie,
John Paterson's Ayrshire masterwork (see
p.145), most obviously in the semi-elliptical
central rear projection, although the giant
panelled pilasters which control the front
elevation have similarities with the work of

Montgreenan

Davis

The **Garnock Valley** has become almost a late 20th-century synonym for industrial decline and the concomitant disincentives of decay, stagnation and unemployment. The effect on the valley of the closure in the 1970s of the major source of employment, the Glengarnock Steel Works, should not be forgotten by anyone. The scars, physical and emotional, are still there. But the Garnock Valley was not always thus: before the exploitation of iron and coal reserves began, on an industrial scale, in the 1830s and 1840s, the valley had been a pastoral idyll. The south-facing valley, protected by the hills above West Kilbride and Largs, was a place of resort for many. Close to Glasgow, the pattern in the early years of the 19th century was of a number of small estates, from **Montgreenan** and **Monkcastle** close to Kilwinning, to **Ladyland**, **Woodside** and **Caldwell**, close to the Renfrewshire border. These estates were serviced by three small towns: **Beith**, **Dalry**, **Kilbirnie**. Of these, Beith was the most commercially oriented – its particular skills in furniture-making were already well known.

The establishment of an ironworks at Blair in the 1830s changed that. The landscapes of the valley became disfigured by the ironworks, and by the pits which sprang up to feed the voracious monster, and its successors.

David Hamilton. The house is now run as an elegant hotel, a befitting use which has not detracted from its great qualities. The **West Lodge** and **East Lodge** are probably contemporary with the house: they undoubtedly exhibit the same architectural manner, as does the ornate **Mains Farm**, with a grand, impressive front, topped by a cupola. Greater show was allowed by mid-Victorian taste, and the **stables** are allowed more expression, a slightly freakish centre tower appearing to crush the low pediment.

Monkredding, 1602-38
Together with neighbouring Monkcastle, Monkredding dates from the period when the lay abbots of Kilwinning Abbey began to feu the abbey estates. Between 1539 and 1545, Thomas Nevin, the tenant, acquired the lands of East and West Monkredding: thus secured, he is said to have enlarged his wealth through coal exploitation, and the family was able to begin the present house. Turn-of-the-century work is found in the north gable of the west wing and the base of the circular tower, and the remainder of the spreading L-plan house was completed by 1638. Additions were made in the 19th century to create the present entrance, and a porch added in 1905 by Hugh Thomson, who is also probably responsible for the large Edwardian **lodge**. Pulled together by brightly painted white harling, Monkredding is a delight. Nearby **Clonbeith Castle** is less happy, lying among farm buildings; its ornate, slightly baroque doorcase dates from 1607, almost contemporary with Monkredding.

Smithstone, *c*.1791-1804
Very plain late Georgian house of no great architectural pretension, to which has been added a mid-Victorian circular bayed addition

and a rather less fortunate dormer. There is some *Jacobean* geometric plasterwork inside which is probably contemporary with the bay addition. Nearby **Dalgarven Mill** (see pp.C1, C3) is the early 19th-century successor on a site whose importance goes back to the early years of Kilwinning Abbey. The mill lay disused for many years, but meticulous restoration by Robert Ferguson has brought it back to life, and to a new use as the Museum of Ayrshire Life.

Monk Castle, 17th century
Now a full but ruinous shell, Monk has many similarities with another Ayrshire T-plan house, **Crosbie**. Its sound state of repair appears to be due to an early 20th-century scheme of consolidation. The name implies that some form of *retreat* for the Abbots of Kilwinning stood here, prior to the construction of this small laird's house, which is domestic rather than military in scale: the rough-hewn stone laid in courses, the corbie-stepped gables creating a *pretty fair building veill planted*. Close by is **Monkcastle**, the stately but severely classical mansion, possibly by David Hamilton, built between 1802 and 1805 for the Millers, who had acquired the property in 1723.

BLAIR, 17th century (see p.C7)
This vast mansion, set in an extensive well-timbered park, with the **Bombo** stream passing in a steep declivity to the rear, has its origins in a tower which has been integrated in an L-shaped house; this work is situated in the centre of the entrance front where two dates, 1617 and 1668, appear above doors. Behind the entrance and stair tower are several vaulted basements, the thick walling of which clearly represents the ancient *castell and strong dounion veill beautified* that Pont saw. From this early core extend two wings forming a great L-plan: one to the left dated 1668 and one to the right dating from the early 18th century and partly remodelled in 1893 to resemble more closely the 17th-century work. The remodelling was done by Thomas Leadbetter, who also added the similarly respectful rear wing. The great park was laid out in the 1760s by William Blair; within it there are a late 18th-century castellated **stable block** and a delightful little Gothick **garden house**, *c*.1840. **Swinridgemuir**, *c*.1830, a neat box-like mansion with accented corners, is close in spirit and style to David Hamilton's Ladyland.

Dalgarven Mill

The Fergusons had been the last family to mill commercially at Dalgarven. Robert Ferguson, after training as an architect, has returned to the family mill and set about the meticulous restoration of the mill and associated buildings and lands into the Museum of Ayrshire Life, which illustrates not only mills and milling, but also domestic life and costume.

Blair, entrance

The Cross, Dalry

Below *Clydesdale Bank*. Bottom *Dalry Library*

DALRY
St Margaret's, 1871-3, David Thomson
The parish church dominates the central square of the town as effectively as it marks it from afar. In 1870 the heritors had suggested a design based on Eastwood Parish Church, and that its architect, Thomson, be employed. His ultimate source for Dalry was the late 13th century: the result is this powerful, carefully handled composition. The contemporary wealth of Dalry is illustrated in the frequent elaboration of fittings, most notably in the door hinges. The broach spire is inventive, worthy indeed of the many tasks thrust upon it. The interior was almost totally gutted by fire in the 1950s. During restoration the decision was made not to renew the plasterwork; the result is a space of deep solemnity, which is enhanced by the stained glass by Guthrie & Wells.

The Cross
The church forms one side of The Cross, Dalry's village core. The formality of the space is in contrast to the informal unplanned relationships between the various buildings: each is true to itself firstly and the needs of the space a secondary consideration. These stand out from the supporting cast of rude mechanicals: **Trinity Church**, 1857, Robert Snodgrass, coarsely detailed Perpendicular, making a particular contrast with St Margaret's; the **Clydesdale Bank**, late 19th century, a typically muscular banking palazzo, and the **Library**, 1853, its classical pretensions a match for the bank. The whole ensemble has benefited greatly from a Cunninghame District Council and SDA funded facelift project in 1985-6, and especially from the removal of unnecessary clutter and signs.

New Street
New Street, southward extension of The Cross,
is similar in pattern: a generous display of
early 19th-century two-storey houses. The
King's Arms Hotel is part of that pattern,
neatly overseeing the spatial change where The
Cross narrows into New Street. **43-51** are dated
1842; the **Royal Hotel**, another beneficiary of
the Dalry facelift, turns the **Garnock Street**
corner with aplomb; **16-18**, 1877, David
Barclay, is a former banking palazzo; **81** was
the Railway Tavern: a pertinent clue to date
and function of the New Street. Further out,
Bridgend Mills, begun in 1876; are
impressive, assured sixteen-bay bulk, clad in
yellow and red brick, with stone dressings.

North Street
North Street squeezes out from the north-west
corner of The Cross. Early properties, of
perhaps 1800, are in a state of benign
picturesque neglect. At the junction with
James Street, very effective 1980s sheltered
housing. The **War Memorial**, 1927, Kellock
Brown, is in the public park to the north while
Templand is the 1828 Orr's Academy, rubble-
stoned Gothic of pleasing provinciality. Off
North Street is **Main Street**, which, with
North Street, formed the true urban core until
the railway's needs imposed a new order. It is
straight and short, the visual effect the same
shuggled picturesque. The **Auld Hoose Bar**,
*c.*1790, is probably the oldest building in the
street. The adjoining houses of **11-15** are nearly
contemporary and top their rustic detailing
with crowsteps. A final renewal of 1870 at
28-38 can be linked with preparations for the
new church, providing a more fitting entry to
the kirk grounds. **Sharon Street** continues the
theme, updating the motifs. **Courthill Street**
is the final escape from the Cross. Its character
is different, much more spacious, a trip to the
country. The **Mission Halls**, 1876, William
Railton, are a musclebound Tudor Gothic,
competent but not very approachable. **Parkhill
House** is an elegant late 18th- or early 19th-
century house, with wings, incorporating a 1732
lintel, added in 1900 by Leadbetter & Fairley in
their usual self-effacing manner.

Broadlie, 1891, T G Abercrombie
Impressive red sandstone house, the general feel
of which is English Manorial, though
Scottishness breaks through in the dormer

Top *Bridgend Mills*. Above
Templand

The field of the king [Dail
righe] sits above an important
crossing of the Garnock; its
position further determined by
the Rye Water to the north. The
distinguishing feature of Dalry
is the elegant spire of
St Margaret's; viewed from the
Ayr line railway Bridgend Mills
provide a strong foundation for
the spire. From the north the
all-embracing image is of the
Roche Chemical Plant, a
major complex of silos and
pipes, linking functional post-
war buildings. A major product
is Vitamin C: the silos are full of
glucose. Earlier trade, reported
by Heron in 1799, was in the
manufacture of silk and cotton.

Mission Halls

Sir James Cunninghame of Glengarnock was a leading Reformer in Ayrshire, in the party that supported John Knox at a meeting in Ayr on 4 Sept. 1562. More solid evidence of his support for the Church is the Cunninghame or Glengarnock aisle at Kilbirnie Church, completed in 1597.

James Houston, 1893-1966, the Kilbirnie architect, espoused the philosophy of modern architecture expressive of its function, with great panache. His cinemas, especially the much-missed Viking in Largs and Radio Cinema in Kilbirnie, and the recently demolished Moorings Café in Largs, display an ease, his own interest in the burgeoning telecommunications industry, and a delightful sense of fun. Kilbirnie should honour his memory.

Barony Parish Church. Below Exterior, c.1848. Bottom Interior

Kyle and Carrick Libraries

pediments. Commissioned by John Fulton: in 1892 it was reported that Broadlie was fitted up for producing electricity for lighting and that Mr Fulton was leading the way in Ayrshire.
Baidland, nearby, is 17th century and, despite modern accretions, is one of the best early farmhouses in Ayrshire. Three-bay with a single storey between an attic and a raised basement, and with a wing of the succeeding century at right angles.

KILBIRNIE
A mixed bag: one complex church, the battered remains of the Radio City Cinema, a garden suburb and an architectural practice of long standing, which has produced consistently good work over a long period: Houston & Dunlop.

Barony Parish Church, from 1470
The core is a rectangular coursed rubble nave, ashlar dressed. Built in 1470, the two-stage tower was added twenty years later. Aisles were added in 1597 (for the Cunninghames of Glengarnock) and 1642 (for the Crawfords), and finally Charles S S Johnston added a transept and new entrance front in 1903-5. The effect, externally, is barely that of a church, with the low tower failing to mark the site. Internally, the changes wrought by Johnston pull the units together, while the stages in the church's growth are seen to better effect, and the thinking behind the pattern of development better understood. Some magnificent fittings, pride of place going to the elaborately detailed Crawford Loft of c.1705, and to the 17th-century sounding board, all exuberant carving.

Close

Garden City, 1916, J Walker Smith
Early example of a planned urban community.
The 250 houses which make up Kilbirnie
Garden City were built during the First World
War for workers at the Glengarnock Steel
Works. **Central Avenue**, running southward
near the church, connects a circle and an oval.
The scheme is completed by outward-looking
houses on **Dalry Road**, generally semi-
detached bungalows and villas, of a type alien
to Scotland. In Council ownership, Garden City
has maintained a great deal of its character
and other-worldliness, which is being eroded.

Newton Street and **Main Street** connect
the church with the core of the straggling town.
Eastward the view is across the remains of the
Dennyholm Mills, the spinning mill founded
by the Knoxes *c.*1830, pulled down in the late
1970s. Newton Street has precious survivals:
1-7, *c.*1850, are of traditional pattern; the
Eglinton Inn is dated 1835. The **Salvation
Army Citadel**, 1966, Alex Cullen & Co, sits
alongside the **Royal Blue Lodge**, 1904,
cheerfully anachronistic.

The **Knox Institute**, Main Street, 1892, is an
eclectic building with an urbane touch; the
William Walker Statue, 1894, D W Stevenson,
portraying Hygeia with a bust of the good
doctor, battered but unbowed, is an unexpected
treat. The **George Cinema**, the old Radio City,
is the rump of James Houston's ultra-modern
super-cinema opened in 1938. **Stoneyholm
Mills**, from 1831, still produces nets for fishing,
and twine; one block survives as a plain eight-
bayed five-storey wing on the southern flank,
the bulk of the current mill is mid-19th century.

Glengarnock
The community which developed around the
iron-smelting works, founded in 1840, and
Kilbirnie station on the Glasgow/Ayr railway.
Growth has always been patchy, and subsequent
demolition has also taken its toll. The effect is
thus gap-toothed, and the little settlement lacks
any effective focus. The most wholesome tooth is
the Co-operative, 1899, John McLellan, crisply
detailed in Swinridgemuir and Overwood stone.

Moorpark, *c.*1860-70
Opulent mansion which mixes metaphors in a
particularly singular manner. This former Knox
family home has been restored in the 1980s by
Cunninghame District Council using MSC
labour, after years of neglect and destruction.

Top *Memorial to Dr Walker.*
Above *Stoneyholm Mills*

Moorpark

Old Place of Kilbirnie

Kilbirnie is said to take its name from a cell or mission of St Brendan, Abbot of Clonfert, Columba's uncle, who was in Scotland *c.*AD 563.

Old Place of Kilbirnie, *c.*15th century
The tower of the Crawfords of Kilbirnie. Simple rectangular tower extended in *c.*1627, with a narrower, but equally plain wing, with circular staircase tower and, unusually, a projecting porch. This, and the remnant of the grand avenue, suggest that Place of Kilbirnie was in the forefront of mid-17th-century design.

Ladyland

Ladyland, 1817-21, David Hamilton
One of the most picturesque of Hamilton's country houses, recognised as his by the giant pilasters which grab all the corners, and distinguished by the original tartan-checked window-bar pattern. Also by Hamilton are the attractive contemporary **stables**. Nearby is **Redheugh**, a rambling house, of which the most assured element is Clarke & Bell's entrance front in a plain Jacobean style, matched by the internal decoration, much of which survives as a memorial to *fin-de-siècle* taste. There is a pleasantly pompous **lodge**. The scant remains of **Glengarnock Castle**, a Cunninghame house of indefinite date, but probably 15th century, are superbly situated on a neck of land above the infant Garnock.

BEITH
The gentlest of the Garnock Valley towns, dominated by the Parish Church. The ruins of the old church mark the old focus of the town, but rather insensitive new road systems have damaged its integrity, isolating the old church and driving a wedge between the workaday town and the charms of Eglinton Street.

Beith's period of greatest prosperity was the mid 18th century, during which period a considerable part of the town was engaged in cotton spinning, thread making and muslin weaving, together with the service industries of the valley: a brewery, distilleries, a tobacco factory and corn mills. The 19th century saw a switch away from cotton and thread, and the development of an economy based on furniture making.

High Church, 1807-10
Tall five-stage tower at the north end of dominating Gothic T-plan kirk. The entrance front appears almost infinitely wide, and is,

like the near-contemporary Muirkirk, heavily battlemented: truly the church militant. **Townhead Street** has some 19th-century cottages and a pair of better-class houses: **Knockbuckle**, with a dainty Gothic façade, and **Taynish**, Grecian detailed sobriety, both early 19th century.

In **Braehead Street**, the **Clydesdale Bank**, 1902-6, brings an engagingly alien form to its important corner site. Neither the style adopted, a Glasgow Style baronial, nor the colour of stone, blood-red Mauchline, has anything to do with old Beith, yet the building works. The **Strand** is more typically Beithian – restrained, subdued – **5-9** are early 19th-century stuccoed houses; **2** is a handsome, ashlar classical house of the same period, now the Public Library; while **12** is the former Town House, 1817, an undemanding classic hall of pilastered walls and pedimented gables, which marks the entry into Eglinton Street.

Top *High Church.* Above *The Strand*

Eglinton Street
The chief glory of Beith: a long, gently curving run of two-storey houses on both sides. Originally the main concourse of the town, trade has drifted eastwards to Main Street, leaving Eglinton Street relatively unspoiled by 20th-century changes. It has dignity but the rather faded dignity of an old dowager. **25-31**, the old post office, dates from 1897: its gaudily painted Royal Arms enhances rather than detracts from that dignity and gives it a focus. The majority of the other houses play themes on the main tune, which marries two storeys, three bays and ashlar: **13-23** are of c.1800, with contrasted stone dressings, **33-35** is earlier, and rubble built, **39**, c.1800, of Aberdeen-bonded whin rubble. The pattern is repeated on the north side, with the same tune, though the **Saracen's Head** and its neighbour, **14-16**, both of the late 18th century, follow a different path: wider, and with a wallhead gable each. The inn, especially, is a delightful piece of evolved design. Rendering is more frequent on this side, as at **40-42**, but the quality of cut stonework is again evident at **46**, which advances its central bay. Stuccoed is **44**, with ashlar end pilasters. These all date from c.1800, but **32** is later: a late 19th-century insertion, more showy, with rusticated quoins and a display of pattern-book decoration on the door, windows and sills.

In the church, a walltablet, the work of London Scot James Fillans, commemorates **Captain Alexander Wilson**, of the 64th Bengal Native Infantry, *who fell in action while commanding the Regiment in the Khyber Pass, Afghanistan, on the 24th January 1842.*

Eglinton Street

Top *Auld Kirk*. Above
Smugglers' Tavern

Auld Kirk, 16th century
The gable wall of a church, converted into a
mausoleum, trapped amid a wee kirkyard,
containing one notable vault. Far more vital
are the houses of **The Cross**, **20-32**, whose
prominent presence rescues this road-battered
corner. The left and centre blocks date from
c.1750, though substantially altered. The third
dates from *c*.1810, hiding an earlier core.

Main Street
There is another fine crop of early 19th-century
buildings in Main Street, but the ravages of
change have been severer here. The street, too,
is narrower, and has a true sense of enclosure.
The effect here is tighter, taller, with
widespread use of render, often painted, which
gives the street more variety, and the final
effect could hardly be more different from the
formality of Eglinton Street. **26-30** and **35-41**
are earlier, *c*.1790, while the **Smugglers'
Tavern** is a strikingly attractive bar, *c*.1750,
with High Victorian shopfront. **Wilson Street**
continues the pattern, but the sense of
enclosure is wholly lost, and the view
terminated by **Trinity Church**, 1883, Robert
Baldie; the chief external feature is a graceful
octagonal tower about 80 ft high, at the left
side of the principal elevation.

Woodside House, 1759; 1890,
Charles S S Johnston
The original square tower built in 1551 for Hew
Ralston was enlarged *c*.1640, and additions
were again made in 1759, by removing the old
turrets, erecting a new roof and transforming it
into a modern dwelling. Further crowstepped
mimicry of this was added in 1848. In 1890 the
house was given back its baronial image with
the clever formation of a tower, complete with

Woodside House

bartizans and crowsteps, to the left of the entrance front. The manner in which Johnston's tower has been built atop the wallhead can easily be detected, but it is sufficiently convincing to take in the unsuspecting. The Tudorish **lodges** and **Home Farm** must date from shortly after 1848.

The otherwise unexceptional road-hugging village of **Gateside** has a surprising **Village Hall** of 1897, a single-storey double pile, Tudor details beneath crowsteps, which may also be by Charles Johnston.

Drumbuie

MacIntyre

Drumbuie, 18th century
This is a most interesting – indeed, precious – group of picturesque buildings, consisting of two corbie-step gabled dwellings and two barns. **Drumbuie Farm** incorporates an early 18th-century small, two-storey house, originally thatched, and built probably in 1736 for Hugh Patrick, as is stated by the plaque on the 1815 addition. The low range at right angles may be even earlier: it incorporates a lintel of 1723. **Drumbuie House** is said to be 18th-century but has later been altered: it is single storey with Victorian dormers, and is crowstepped yet; a barn in near proximity to the house also has crowsteps, and a roll-moulded door lintel.

Caldwell, 1773, Robert & James Adam
One of the last examples of the Adam brothers' early castle manner, Caldwell, built for the Mures, displays the regular procession of square-headed windows with label mouldings above them, the flatness of the façades and the rectangular, boxy appearance of the overall design common to this type. Caldwell was transformed into a castle late in the design evolution, and is simply a reworking of a

G

Caldwell

Through the inventive and entrepreneurial skills of such men as Andrew Barclay and Thomas Kennedy, the wealth and fame of Kilmarnock in the 100 years after 1850 was assured, and the railway locomotives of Andrew Barclay & Son and the hydraulic systems of Glenfield & Kennedy took the name of Kilmarnock to the far corners of the earth.

Goldberry, incorporated in the arms of Boyd of Kilmarnock, and those of the former Kilmarnock Town Council, refers to Goldberry Hill between Largs and West Kilbride where in 1263, as part of the battle of Largs, a detachment led by Robert Boyd roundly defeated a party of Norsemen, a small victory which was significant in securing the victory won that day by the Scots.

classical scheme submitted two years earlier. The wallhead was crowned with a crenellated parapet supported by a corbel course, carrying small dummy bartizans. The parapet is insufficiently deep to seem acceptable, even as make-believe, and can be seen as little more than a rather bizarre crenellated confection added as an afterthought. By comparison, the walls themselves have a monumental monolithic presence, and the house cannot be denied a certain grandeur. Its most impressive face is the rear, where the grey walls with their absurd climax soar above the huddle of modern huts which have arrived and multiplied since conversion to a hospital in 1927.

KILMARNOCK

The industrial capital of Ayrshire, Kilmarnock superseded Irvine as the focal point for north Ayrshire during the 18th century. The change in character from a small provincial burgh to incipient industrial town can be dated to a single stroke of the axe, 400 miles away in London. On 18 August 1746, William Boyd, Lord Kilmarnock, one of the few Lowland lairds to have backed the 'wrong' side in the '45, went to the block. His death, and the concomitant forfeiture of the Boyd estates, left a power vacuum in Kilmarnock. The opportunity to transform the medieval burgh, to develop new manufactories, in relative freedom from lairdly interference, was seized by the nascent entrepreneurial classes, both from within and outwith the burgh.

Kilmarnock photographed by G W Wilson

Weaving had been the mainstay of the old burgh, and this trade was developed greatly, and two main specialisms arose: bonnets and carpets. Bonnets, the tam-o'-shanters of the 19th century, had been a particular trade of the weavers of Kilmarnock and of Stewarton. Increasing industrialisation allowed this product to capture an expanding share of the British headwear market. The *Kilmarnock* bonnet is the overwhelmingly large version.

Carpet manufacture began in the early 19th century. The spur was the increasingly plentiful local supply of coal, improved machinery, and the rapidly expanding domestic market in Edinburgh and Glasgow. Firms such as Gregory, Thomson & Co were able to harness the local weaving tradition to meet the demand. Almost as an act of contrariness, carpets are still woven in Kilmarnock.

Coal had long been worked in the Kilmarnock area: the early 19th century brought increased demand, and the decision of the Duke of Portland to construct his wagonway from Kilmarnock to Troon. This put Kilmarnock on the earliest railway maps, and indirectly led to its world-wide renown as an engineering centre.

A **Laigh Kirk**, 1802, Robert Johnstone
The 17th-century tower has outlived two churches: its original mate was replaced in 1750, and that church in turn demolished in 1801. Johnstone's replacement follows closely the pattern of the 18th-century structure: a spreading rectangular preaching box, harled

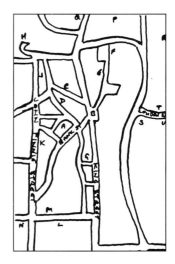

Conspicuous in most views of Kilmarnock is the striking 23 span **Viaduct** of 1848 which leaps across the Marnock Water, between the station and the Kay Park, and forms a definite edge to the northern part of the town centre. This coursed-rubble, ashlar-dressed, structure was built for the Glasgow Paisley Kilmarnock & Ayr Railway.

Laigh Kirk

The present **Laigh Kirk** is well endowed with some thirteen exits. On 18 Oct. 1801, its predecessor was filled with worshippers when, as a result of the fall of some plaster, panic broke out among the congregation, and twenty-nine were killed in the ensuing mêlée. The profligate use of exits in the new design was to ensure that such a tragedy was not repeated.

Kilmarnock Cross in early 19th century drawn by D O Hill

and of subdued classical character, contrasting with the robust vernacular of the tower, which has lost its parapet balustrade and its harling, leaving the coursed rubble stonework exposed. Subsequent additions in 1831, and extensive renovation in 1903-4 by Andrew & Newlands, have helped to pull the kirk together into a unified whole. Inside, there is a horseshoe gallery on cast-iron Doric columns, and the subdued light of plentiful stained glass. The kirk sits well, to one corner of its raised, walled graveyard, which has a memorial to the Covenanters Ross and Shields, and gives a quiet distinction to this corner of the town. There is a refined, sedate air here, reminiscent of a cathedral close. The area about the church lost its pivotal role after 1780 when new, direct roads were slapped through, creating a new centre-point, and divesting streets such as **Bank Street**, **Sandbed Street** and **Cheapside Street** of their function. The new streets had brave new names, **King Street**, **Portland Street**, **Duke Street**, **Titchfield Street**, and the new pivot was **Kilmarnock Cross**.

Kilmarnock Cross

Though the road patterns have changed again, the cross is still the pivot about which Kilmarnock life circles. Jimmy Shaw (see p.113) acted as the centrepiece from 1848 until 1929, when he became an encumbrance to traffic and flitted to London Road. Post-war redevelopment has shied away from the cross, destroying the sense of enclosure, the sense of dignity. Only the Heworth Burn stone *villa*

rotunda, 1937-9, W K Walker Todd, for the **Royal Bank of Scotland** attempts to bring dignity to the area, using to great effect the narrowing site between the former **Fore Street** and **Portland Street**. The interior preserves the original Hoptonwood marble floor, its centrepiece a mosaic 1939 threepenny piece. **2-8**, Cheapside Street, 1980, Boyer & Partners, is a noble attempt to recreate a possibly mythical past.

Portland Street, from 1805
The new main road to Glasgow, replacing the twisting route by **Fore Street** and **High Street**. Plain two-storey houses mingle with grander signs of Victorian and Edwardian prosperity. Grandest of these is Gabriel Andrew's **26-34**, opened in 1905, a striking Ballochmyle red stone modern Renaissance store for **Kilmarnock Equitable Co-operative Society**. It combines plentiful glass and Glasgow Style ironwork with, above the cornice, Corinthian colonnades and allegorical figures in a highly assured design.

C **Wheatsheaf Inn**, Croft Street, 18th century
A rare pre-industrial survival; one of the main coaching inns of the town and allegedly frequented by Burns, this is a corbie-stepped vernacular bar, given in about 1820 a Georgian top-dressing and forewing addition. The
D adjacent **whisky bonds**, 1897, Gabriel Andrew, huge brick and stone behemoths, built for Johnnie Walker's, create a streetscape unequalled in western Scotland. Narrow setted streets wind in deep canyons beneath. Long façades, one with generous use of terracotta, the others in French Renaissance style, all unrelieved by doors or windows. They are a stunning example of how industrial use can be reconciled to beauty and outward display.

E **Foregate**, *c*.1972,
Percy Johnson-Marshall & Partners
Award-winning shopping development, straightforward in execution, relying on cohesion of design, and strong use of concrete for its effect. Fore Street had degenerated badly when it was replaced by this and by the
F **Clydesdale Bank**, *c*.1975, a dramatic stone and glass composition seen from all angles, and able to withstand such openness, and by the **multi-storey carpark**, 1975, which, while it dominates too closely the Johnson-Marshall

Royal Bank of Scotland

Fate has not been kind to **Robert Johnstone**, who died in 1833. He was the first true Kilmarnock architect and is credited with Kilmarnock Town House and King Street Relief Church (both demolished). The spirit of the Relief Church lives on in the other churches *c*.1790 – Tarbolton and Riccarton especially – which may also be by Johnstone.

Below *Wheatsheaf Inn*. Bottom *Whisky Bonds*

Foregate

The major casualty of
Kilmarnock's redevelopment
was Duke Street, *the street of
fairy castles with little turrets*,
opened in 1859 to expedite
communication between the
town and the eastern suburbs.
The architect for this
distinctive street was probably
William Railton.

Duke Street and Corn Exchange

shops across the narrow Foregate, presents to
the world an accomplished, lasting, treatment
for this type of building; no attempt is made to
disguise its bulk, but instead sheer size is made
the prominent feature, and the ploy works.

Burns Shopping Mall, 1974-80,
Hay Steel MacFarlane & Associates
Built in three stages, this attempt to create a
new Kilmarnock Town Centre fails to impose
itself sufficiently on the town. The earlier
stages, the **Bus Station** opened in October
1974 and the **Burns Mall** opened in 1976, with
a red brick finish in a stone town, draw back
from the cross, almost as if embarrassed, and
then, through two sharp – too sharp – right
angles line up with **King Street**. The concrete
colonnade obscures views of Walker Todd's
bank. The final stage, stringing along King
Street, is all façade, with no depth and no
ornamentation. The unavoidable impression is
that of a stage set. Demolitions to make way
for this included **Duke Street**, Robert
Johnstone's **Town House**, and **Wilson's
Printing Works**, natal home of the
Kilmarnock Edition of Burns.

King Street, 1803-4
The first of the new streets to be laid out in the
centre of Kilmarnock, linking up with the 18th-
century development to the south, and now the
main commercial street in Kilmarnock. The
mixture is, as in Portland Street, harmonious
two-storey buildings of *c.*1850 intermixed with

the grander, more competitive notions of
subsequent generations, though it has weathered
the economic climate better, but has paid a price
in some unimaginative post-war replacement
buildings. The eastern side has been largely lost
to the Burns Shopping Mall. Major elements on
G the west side are the former **Lauder's
Emporium**, tentative Moderne of 1923, and
65 King Street, 1901, Thomas Smellie.

Kilmarnock Station

H **Kilmarnock Station**, 1850, Hugh Maclure;
1878
The Troon wagonway excluded, the railway
first arrived in Kilmarnock in 1843. The
austere grey sandstone **Station House** of
seven years later stands yet, neglected and
unloved, but still capable of raising emotion, as
it stands proud and haughty above a landscape
of portakabins and *ad hoc* car-parking. The
present station dates from 1878, crisp red
sandstone with an Italianate tower in the
contemporary manner; it has lost most of its
impressive platform detailing. The pedestrian
approach to the station is via a contemporary
subway, entered through a grim battlemented
façade, more in keeping with prison visiting
than the joys of rail travel.

John Finnie Street, 1864, William Railton,
architect; Robert Blackwood, surveyor
The need for a new street, parallel to King
Street and providing the correct image of the
town to disembarking rail travellers had been
seen as early as 1860. Progress was
expeditious, and the new street, named after
Finnie, a Kilmarnock-born merchant in
Manchester, whose financial support assured
the success of the venture, was opened, with
due ceremony, in October 1864. It never
became the major mercantile street that was
intended, and only slowly were the feus filled
up, but by the 1900s had developed into this
notable red sandstone vision, running straight
for the station tower, though it remains much
on the periphery of Kilmarnock's commercial
core. It is now easily the most architecturally
stimulating street in the town, spoilt only by
some crass shopfronts and its incorporation in
Kilmarnock's one-way system.

J **Nos 6-12 John Finnie Street**, 1874,
James Ingram
The former Opera House, very much in
Ingram's elaborate style, contrasting with the

In 1820, **John Walker** gave up
farming and bought a grocery
business in Kilmarnock. His
brand of whisky, Walker's
Kilmarnock Whisky, thrived,
and, with the entrepreneurial
skills of his grandson, Sir
Alexander Walker, Walker's
whisky in its distinctive square
bottle and skew labels spread to
every corner of the globe, and
continues so to do. The firm
remained on Strand Street
until 1955 when they moved to
the 40-acre Hill Street site.

*Go, Fame, and canter like a filly
Through a' the streets and
neuks o' Killie*
Burns' poems were first
published in Kilmarnock in
1786 from John Wilson's
printing shop. It was to
Kilmarnock that Burns the
Mauchline farmer came to
trade and socialise, with a
group of cronies of whom Tam
Samson the seedsman is best
remembered. The Burns
Federation, the result of an
informal suggestion made at
the unveiling ceremony of
Burns's bust in Westminster
Abbey, was instituted in
Kilmarnock in 1892; its **Burns
Chronicle** is an annual
literary journal wherein ardent
admirer and animadverting
academic find common cause.

KILMARNOCK : John Finnie Street

Top *John Finnie Street seen from Station*. Middle *District Council Offices (1905), John Finnie Street*. Above *72-84 John Finnie Street*. Middle right *30-38 John Finnie Street*. Right *60-62 John Finnie Street*

austerity of the street. The following blocks, **14-28**, 1880, and **30-38**, 1895, are by Ingram's son, Robert. The style is similar – elaborate Renaissance commercial palaces, competently handled – but lacking real feeling for the architecture or the setting. The next block, now **District Council Offices**, originally built for the Co-op, 1879, Gabriel Andrew, is similar in concept to that of the Ingrams, but already displaying the talent which was to blossom in Andrew's later work. Between **John Dickie Street** and **Low Church Lane**, more **District Council Offices**, 1905, James M Pearson, the conception again the same, slotting happily into the format of the street.

K **Nos 60-62 John Finnie Street**, 1889, Gabriel Andrew
Built as an **Oddfellows Hall**, doubtless an influence on the choice of Tudor Gothic details; **72-84**, 1879, William Railton, has, like many of Railton's buildings, details in the manner of Alexander Thomson. The original street-level elevation remains in part. **100-106 Smith's Buildings**, are Italianate of 1876. Late 20th-century additions to this street add to its merit; without attempting to ape or parody, the **Royal Bank of Scotland**, 1976, Henry Dawes & Sons, with its double-height glazed banking hall and oversailing upper storey, and the **Halifax Building Society**, 1968-70, Hay Steel MacFarlane & Associates, conventional, with contemporary emphasis on the vertical elements, both enhance the image of a triumphal way.

L **St Marnock's Church**, 1836, James Ingram
Ingram's first major work in his adopted town, now dwarfed by the 1970s **Police Station**, and **Sheriff Court House**, 1985, PSA, St Marnock's understated, rather scholarly Perpendicular architecture appears tentative against their strong lines and sheer size. In fact, it has a wealth of Gothic Revival decoration from the battlemented tower and the hood-moulded door, to, inside, the pulpit, an expression of the crescendo of Gothic Revival.

M **Procurator Fiscal's Office**,
St Marnock Street, 1852, William Railton
The former Sheriff Court House, newly restored by the PSA and Hay Steel & Partners. Railton's building, a diminutive three-bay classical mansion with single-storey wings, respects the architectural convention, but fails,

Top *Smith's Buildings, John Finnie Street.* Above *6-12 John Finnie Street*

Gabriel Andrew, 1851-1933, is perhaps the most imaginative of a group of architects practising in Kilmarnock in the early 20th century. He trained with William Railton, before setting up in 1875, taking William Newlands into partnership in 1900. Andrew's best work is in a vigorous, almost Glasgow Style, seen to great advantage in the Co-operative Buildings, Newmilns.

Right *Procurator Fiscal's Office.*
Below *Borland's Seed*
Warehouse. Bottom *Holy*
Trinity Episcopal Church

and must always have failed, to impose a sense
of civic dignity on its surroundings.

Borland's Seed Warehouse, 1850

Large ashlar warehouse on rubble-built
basement, unornamented but a powerful
composition alongside the **Marnock Water**,
and still boasting a particularly fine interior,
of wooden beams on cast-iron stanchions.

N Holy Trinity Episcopal Church, 1857, James Wallace

Wallace was a master builder: the chief glory of
his plain Early English building is the chancel,
an addition of 1876 to plans of George Gilbert
Scott, the style is similar to the original,
crisper, sharper, and with the stump of an
unexecuted tower. Internally, the chancel is a
riot of High Victorian colour: stained glass and
mosaic marble from Powell & Sons amongst
wall and wood painting by Burlison & Grylls.
This is mature, high-quality London work and,
while the subjects – evangelists, prophets –
may be conventional, the effect in Presbyterian
Covenanting Ayrshire is devastating.

Holy Trinity occupies the site
of the Kilmarnock terminus of
the Kilmarnock & Troon
Railroad (*The Duke's Railway*),
which has claim to be the first
steam passenger railway in the
world. The impetus for the
railway was the need to get coal
from the coalfields of the Duke
of Portland around Kilmarnock
cheaply and efficiently to the
coast for onward export. A
harbour was created at Troon,
and a plateway wagon road,
using horse power, opened
between Troon and Kilmarnock
in 1812, originally for goods
only. Passenger services were
introduced soon after, and in
1816 a steam locomotive, **The
Duke**, put to work on the line;
a silver model of which is in the
Walker Halls, Troon. The line
was upgraded and incorporated
into the national rail network,
but a new crossing at Gatehead
left the Viaduct (see p.120) as a
major relic.

Alongside is **Winton Place Church**, 1860,
James Ingram, also Early English, far more
adventurous in its treatment of the motifs than
Wallace's work at Holy Trinity, while opposite
Holy Trinity is **Howard St Andrews**, 1970-1
(*below*), white concrete in a sea of pebbles.

Dundonald Road

These churches guard two of the main approaches to the town: Dundonald Road and Portland Road. The former contains a number of wealthy merchants' houses, for example the Scottish baronial **5** Dundonald Road, 1868, and **52** Dundonald Road, *c.*1880, and the Italianate **Westmont**, **78**, of *c.*1860. **Portland Road** is different, earlier: early 19th-century terraces interrupted by small classical lodges, of which **Etruria**, **41**, and **Flowerbank**, **37**, are the best, though surprisingly late, 1870s, for such a formal symmetrical approach. **Portland Terrace** is the best terrace, ashlar facing with intricately carved bargeboards and cornices. **46**, a plain house of the 1870s was given major additions by Thomas Smellie, most notably the first-floor studio. It was restored in 1988 by Nicoll Design.

Below *Annanhill House.* Left *Annanhill House, courtyard housing*

Springhill House, *c.*1840

This standard classical mansion house, of painted ashlar, was probably never the country retreat that the Finnies, Kilmarnock coalmasters, had envisaged. In 1945 it became an eventide home, suitably amended by Gabriel Steel, who also designed the **cottages** in the grounds, which contrast piquantly with the **lodge**, also *c.*1840, but in a controlled Greek Revival style. **Annanhill House**, 1796, is a fine Palladian mansion, long demeaned by use as a golf clubhouse, and now restored by Nicholas Groves-Raines & Partners, who are also architects of the adjacent courtyard housing.

North Hamilton Street

From Portland Road, North Hamilton Street leads northwards to the original industrial heart of the town. **21-29**, 1883, are by Robert Ingram, a row of tenements using white enamelled bricks, unusually and surprisingly effectively, on the front elevation. In **West Langlands Street**, amongst the other forges and machine shops, are the **Caledonia Works** of Andrew Barclay. Begun in 1851, compact

21-29 North Hamilton Street

107

Top *High Church and Soulis Cross*. Above *Kilmarnock Infirmary*

William Railton was a Kilmarnock architect who combined professional practice with a high public profile. He was Secretary to or Director of many institutions in Kilmarnock, not least the Infirmary where he was a Director from 1868. The conflict of interest between his Directorship and his authorship of the building appears not to have troubled him. Railton's best buildings, such as the Infirmary and the commercial block at 72-84 John Finnie Street, are strongly reminiscent of the work of Alexander Thomson.

and essentially functional and plain in appearance, the works are enlivened by one small reminder of Barclay's personal obsessions: the double dormer towards the west end lit his observatory.

High Church, 1732-40

Built at a cost of £850 to cater for an expanding population, the High Church is modelled, in spirit, on St Martin-in-the-Fields; the tower, added in 1740, which, with an octagonal belfry on its square clock stages, is clearly rooted in a knowledge of Gibbs' work: the church is plainer, and there is but the merest hint of a pediment at its gables. A straightforward Presbyterian preaching box, the original harling would have stressed the external antecedents. Internally, there are galleries on stone Doric columns, and a fine collection of stained glass by W & J J Kier, the Irvine-born Glasgow artists, from the 1860s and 1870s.

On the outside face of the east kirkyard wall is the **Soulis Cross**, a monument of mysterious import once; it is a Doric column in a niche, rebuilt in 1825 *in a style more in harmony with modern taste*, said to commemorate the killing here in 1444 of Lord Soulis.

West High Church, 1844, Cousin & Gale

Of a mixed kind of architecture: it uses Gothic elements without recourse to the archaeological strictures of Rickman and Pugin. Alterations from 1881 onwards introduce the equally eclectic work of Gabriel Andrew. The church is overlooked, indeed overwhelmed, by the bulk of the **Kilmarnock Infirmary**, 1867, William Railton. The hill, Mount Pleasant, dominates the northern side of the town, and Railton's fever hospital is a fitting climax to that domination, raised on a terrace to give additional height, enthroned in state and glowering over the West High Church. The large main block, to which Railton added a further wing, which had been envisaged in the original composition, in 1875, borrows largely and successfully from Alexander Thomson, a major influence on Railton's style. Within the strictures of this essentially plain style, he is able to include handsome doorways and controlled but effective use of the caballas of Thomson's style: antifixae, Greek key, etc.

Black's Bar has an attractive 1930s art deco public bar frontage of gleaming white tilework and streamlined lettering.

Dean Castle, *c.*1400 onwards (see p.C3)
There is a raised mound here which may
represent the original wooden pallisaded
structure, but the current buildings begin with
the massive late 14th- or early 15th-century
north tower – one of the larger Ayrshire
towers of that date, reflecting the early
importance of the Boyds of Kilmarnock, and
their national prominence in the 15th century.
Rising from its plinth, the tower is a powerful
physical reminder of that strength. Internally
much dates from the restoration this century,
though original layout and function appears to
have been strictly conventional: barrel-vaulted
basements, with prison pit; great hall rising
through two storeys, with minstrel gallery and
stone benches. Up again, a further large
chamber, then the garrets and the parapet
walk, flush with the wallheads.

About 1460, a major extension: the long
palace range on the west side of the
courtyard. It is detached from the old tower,
and offering on its main floor a hall, and
private rooms. Its external appearance is
varied, with a five-storey tower at one end,
contrasted with the remainder, which is
generally two storeys high, with attics. The
tower has a garret within a boldly corbelled
parapet, and this may have applied throughout
this range. The courtyard walls appear to have
been built, or rebuilt, at this date. Additions
were again made *c.*1645, though Pont had
found, *c.*1608, *a staitly faire ancient building,
arrysing in two grate heigh towers, and bulte
around courtewayes, with fyne low buildings.*

Andrew Barclay, 1814-1900,
who founded the locomotive
building industry in Kilmarnock,
is an excellent example of the
Victorian entrepreneur. Son of a
miller in Dalry, his early
employment was in the carpet
mills of Kilmarnock, before the
completion of an apprenticeship
under a Kilmarnock plumber
called Lawson. Barclay had an
aptitude for machines, and from
1840, was in business on his own,
moving from general engineering
to meet the growing need for
steam locomotives throughout
the world. Barclay appears not to
have been as astute financially –
in the period 1870-1900 he
appears to have lurched from one
crises to another – nonetheless
Andrew Barclay & Co exported
widely to countries such as Chile,
Peru and New Zealand.

Dean was leased to Alexander
Boyd by Queen Margaret in
1508, *and the said princess sall
cause the castell and place of
Kilmernock to be theket and
maid watter ticht incontinent
with all deligence apoun the
expense of the said hie and
mitchtie princess.*

Dean Castle

Davis

Top & above *Dean Castle*

Dean Castle has two particularly fine collections. The Howard de Walden Collection of Arms and Armour includes a large number of German and Italian pieces, while the Charles van Raalte Collection is an extraordinarily fine assemblage of early musical instruments, including many lutes, guitars, spinets and other small keyboard instruments. It is among the most important collections of instruments in Europe.

It is veill planted and almost environed with gardens, orchards and a parke. Decline began in the 18th century, first through a major fire about 1735, and secondly, through the forfeiture of the estates to the Crown after Boyd's execution in 1746.

In 1905 Lord Howard de Walden began a comprehensive system of restoration and addition, first with Ingram and Brown, who also worked for him at Chirk Castle in North Wales, and latterly, and more sensitively, with James Richardson, whose major contributions are the **timber fighting platforms** and the Rowallan-inspired Lorimeresque **gatehouse**.

At times, Howard de Walden's approach – seeming almost archaeological in its reconstruction of the past – contained a strand of imaginative though convincing fantasy: the platforms were *reconstructed* on top of the courtyard wall, although it is unlikely that such a construction, interesting though it is, actually crowned these walls in the past. As he was not actually intending to repel boarders, they emphasise his commitment to something which is, strictly speaking, more than merely architecture. As it now stands, Dean Castle is a marvellous illustration of Scotland's national and nationalist architecture from the 14th to the 20th centuries. Its present function as a museum is perhaps a fitting comment on the nature of its restoration: Lord Howard de Walden appears to have resided mostly in the adjacent incongruous and largely 19th-century villa which he doubtless found more comfortable. His son, the 9th Lord, donated the entire castle to the town of Kilmarnock in 1975. *Museum and country park open to the public*

Burns Monument, Kay Park, 1879, Robert S Ingram
Shortly after the death of his father, Robert Ingram was present at the formal opening of what must count as the crowning moment in his career, this slightly sinister Gothic 'spacecraft' of a memorial, 80 ft of Ballochmyle red sandstone, entombing a museum of Burns artefacts and Grant Stevenson's first-rate statue of the poet. Burns as icon obfuscates reaction to the building: for some it is a huge temple – an Albert Memorial in red sandstone, but a correspondent in the *Ardrossan & Saltcoats Herald* was in no doubt: *the architect must, like Michaelangelo, have looked to posterity for his reward.*

Burns Monument

Kilmarnock, with only one vote for its 13,000 inhabitants, was a ready supporter of the campaign for Parliamentary reform. On 7 Dec. 1816, about 6000 people gathered at a meeting. All speakers called for extension of the franchise and Alexander McLaren, a local merchant, blamed the Government for the prevalent appalling social conditions. The meeting unanimously declared the representation of Scotland in Parliament as *unreasonable, unconstitutional and unjust*. The speeches were published, and 400 copies sold by another merchant, Thomas Baird. McLaren and Baird were arrested and, at the High Court in Edinburgh in March 1817, found guilty of sedition, fined heavily and gaoled for six months.

The **Reformers' Monument**, 1885, Robert S Ingram, is a single Giffnock stone Corinthian column on a tall plinth, in memory of early 19th-century parliamentary reformers in Kilmarnock. Charles Grasby's statue of Liberty was blown off in a storm in 1936 and not replaced.

S **Palace Theatre**, 1862-3, James Ingram
The elder Ingram's *pièce de resistance* is this magnificent large complex of Italianate buildings, fittingly brought together by the tower at the angle, the **Albert Tower**. This, with its motto clearly showing the original function as a Corn Exchange, is a dramatic octagonal tower, finely and boldly detailed. Along **London Road**, the first nine bays belong to the Corn Exchange: the succeeding block, 1886, Robert Ingram, picks up his father's style and details, and was built as a **Corporation Art Gallery**. It has long vased balustrades above the regular Renaissance niches and panels. Substantial alterations were made after 1947, Gabriel Steel, to create the Grand Hall, and again in the 1980s, KLDC Architects, to form the Palace Theatre.

Palace Theatre, Albert Tower

Henderson Church

T Henderson Church, London Road, 1907,
Thomas Smellie
Brilliantly individual Arts & Crafts treatment
of Gothic motifs. Very tall tower above equally
tall church built on rising ground, with halls
below. Smellie, like Maclennan in Paisley (see
South Clyde Estuary), was able to transform
the new messages in architecture – and he has
been clearly influenced by Mackintosh – into a
lucid and free-flowing church ethic.

Masonic Hall, London Road, 1926,
William Valentine
A stripped-down classical design in
Ballochmyle stone, reticent about its function.
The contrast with the overt display of wealth
and position in the houses opposite, including
10, simple but assured late Georgian, and **14**,
an elaborate Victorian Gothic villa, is marked,
and points up a dichotomy between the public
face and the private life of the Kilmarnock
merchant princes.

Thomas Smellie, 1860-1938,
is as well known as a book
illustrator and author as for his
architecture. He illustrated his
own *Sketches of Old
Kilmarnock,* and also a reprint
of Kelso Hunter's *Retrospect of
an Artist's Life.* He finished his
architectural training with
Gabriel Andrew, and may be
seen as the third member of the
triumvirate that includes
Andrew and another erstwhile
assistant, Hay.

James Dick, 1823-1902, the
son of a Kilmarnock spirit
merchant, was in business in
Glasgow with his elder brother
Robert, 1820-91. Following the
appearance of gutta percha, or
rubber, in Britain *c.*1843, the
brothers saw its potential for
creating longer-lasting boot
soles, and were able to develop
this successfully and profitably.
James Dick gifted the
wherewithal for the Dick
Institute to Kilmarnock in
memory of his brother. He had
previously commemorated his
marriage in 1886 with another
act of public benevolence: the
gift of Cathkin Park to the
people of Glasgow.

U Dick Institute, Elmbank Avenue, 1897-1901,
Robert Ingram (see p.C5)
Elmbank, one of the largest villas in London
Road, was bought by the Town Council, but
conversion to house Dick's bequests of books
and museum material was not a feasible
option, and fell short of Kilmarnock's
perceptions of itself. Ingram was brought in to
design a building, and Elmbank cleared away.
His solution was this pleasing classical villa,
with vast Ionic-columned portico and
Corinthian pilasters. The Institute acts as a
focal point for a semi-formal civic piazza.
Opposite are the outstanding **War Memorial**,
1927, James Miller, a Grecian shrine like a
miniaturised Miller bank, and **statue of Sir
James Shaw**, 1848, James Fillans. To the
south is a further grassed space, graced by
three powerful red stone schools: **Kilmarnock
Academy**, 1909, Gabriel Andrew, restrained
Edwardian classicism; **St Columba's
Primary**, 1902, Alan Crombie, plainer and
more conventional; and **Loanhead Primary**,
1905, Robert Ingram, plainer yet gaunt,
intimidating School Board work. Andrew's
building was the original Kilmarnock Technical
School, the contemporary Kilmarnock Academy
building is behind: the architect is Robert
Ingram, the style, Queen Anne, the desired
effect obtained from a bold and striking outline
with no elaborate mouldings.

Above *Kelburn Castle and Gardens, Largs.* Left *Dalgarven Mill.* Below *The Harbour, Ayr*

C1

Above *Marine Highland Hotel, Troon and Arran hills.* Right *Eglinton Castle, Eglinton Park, Kilwinning.* Below *Maclaurin Art Gallery, Rozelle*

Above *Maclaurin Art Gallery, Rozelle*. Top left *Miller's Cottage, Dalgarven Mill*. Left *Engine House, Waterside Ironworks*. Below *Dean Castle, Kilmarnock*

Top *Ayr, 19th century painting*. Middle left *Portencross*. Left *Greenan Castle*. Above *Rowallan Castle*

Left Orchardhill, London Road.
Below 45-47 London Road

London Road

This was, despite its situation on the eastward, or downwind, side of the town, the favoured habitation of the well-to-do in Kilmarnock, and despite the inevitable changes in use, and occasional subdivision, the area still has an aura of wealth; the abundant trees enhance the suspicion that one has strayed into a private demesne. The quality of the individual villas is high, and a variety of styles represented, beginning with conventional classical boxes such as **Orchardhill**, though little is yet known of many of them. **Deanmont, 77**, James Ingram, displays asymmetric classicism, while **42** is grandly detailed Italianate. Others are Gothic, such as **25**. Development continued into the 1890s and 1900s, with villas such as **45-47**, Thomas Smellie, in a convincing reinterpretation of native Scots idiom. Equally fine is the 1920s estate for Kilmarnock Town Council, attractively detailed houses laid out in accordance with Garden City principles, between London Road and Holehouse Avenue.

High Glencairn Street

Glencairn Street and **Titchfield Street** were laid out in 1765: they connect Riccarton with Kilmarnock. **59-65 High Glencairn Street**, two-storey, painted stone, lying panes, are representative of the few survivors. Most plots have been redeveloped, often more than once. In Titchfield Street the mastering elements are 20th century: the **ABC Cinema**, 1904, Alex Cullen, has exactly the right degree of vulgarity: nor should its nods in the direction of Mackintosh be ignored. The block at **90-94**, c.1900, must be by Gabriel Andrew. The **Galleon Centre**, 1986, Crichton Lang Willis & Galloway is another pleasure palace: the front façade, between the unrelieved brickwork, breaks out into a riot of colour and steel. The building tries to shrink back from its size-derived domination of the street. Opposite, its

James Shaw (*above*), 1764-1843, son of a Riccarton farmer, spent the first years of his working life in the United States, but returned to Britain, and to London. A successful merchant, he was elected Lord Mayor in 1805. A generous artistic patron, he helped James Tannock, from whose portrait Fillans' statue is taken, and raised funds for Jean Armour after Burns's death. The Carrara marble statue was moved here, away from the traffic bustle of the Cross, in 1929.

Top *Detail, Fire Station.* Above
Walker Buildings, Hood Street

sobriety betraying a very different function, is
Gabriel Steel's **Fire Station**, 1937, Thirties
classicism with good sculpture. High Glencairn
Street has a number of, often neglected,
inevitably red stone flats of *c.*1900: **20-24** are
dated 1903, **30**, 1904. Others are earlier, for
example **11-15**, **33-37** and **71-75**. Finally,
opposite the last, a 1960s parabolic-roofed
garage, and an early 1970s render and glass
bank.

Low Glencairn Street
The biggest scars of Kilmarnock's post-
industrial trauma are here. This was once
Glenfield & Kennedy – the 'Glen' site is now
occupied by **SDA Advance Factories**, Baxter
Clark & Paul, with effective, jolly use of
prestructured components. **2-4**, former Co-
operative shops and flats, *c.*1895, are virtually
all that is left of the street itself. At **21-31
Hood Street** there is a rare and precious
survival, **Walker Buildings**, a group of
Glasgow Style tenements built in 1904 – there
is nothing quite their like elsewhere in
Scotland. Built for Alexander Walker, of the
whisky business, this superb group displays
subtle variation and sturdy construction.

RICCARTON
Riccarton is a separate entity, totally absorbed
in the growth of Kilmarnock, the original
village buried beneath the spread of council
housing through **Bellfield** and **Shortlees**. The
final indignity came in the 1980s when the
improved A71 was driven through the historic
core, making of it a giant traffic island.

Parish Church, 1823, John Richmond
Built on ground known as *The Seat of
Judgement*, the church looks down on what
was Riccarton. This is a workaday Georgian
preaching box given a faintly oriental feel by
pediments with an unusual concave profile.
The design is very similar to Tarbolton Church
(see p.144), built two years earlier, and it may
be that Robert Johnstone was the architect,
and Richmond, a Riccarton millwright, merely
the executant. Beyond some much-altered
vernacular buildings, and two bridges – the
Old Bridge, 1723, and the **New Bridge**, 1835-8,
both straightforward structures, each very
much of its date, the earlier sturdy and artisan,
the later more polite, prissier in its feel.

Parish Church

Left *Treesbank*. Below *Blacksyke Tower*

Treesbank, 1926, James K Hunter
Designed possibly by James Carrick, who trained with Hunter, it is one of the major inter-war country houses in Ayrshire, built for Gavin Morton, of the carpet manufacturers, BMK. The result is a massy and rustic Tudor manorial with some indication of an interest in contemporary developments in the USA. In the grounds are a rubble-built **stable block**, c.1770, and a brick **doocot**, 1771, survivors of the previous houses on this estate.

Blacksyke Tower, early 19th century
At first glance, this ruin, in the midst of a golf course, appears to be that of some long-abandoned fortalice. Further investigation shows it to be an industrial building, associated with the early coal works and railways here, and disguised as a tower house, as it could be seen from Caprington Castle.

Caprington Castle, 1829, Patrick Wilson
As seen today, Caprington reflects chiefly Wilson's work, with the addition of an odd Victorian cast-iron framed verandah, but his battlemented four-square centrally towered mansion hides a complex pattern of building and adaptation. The design is essentially conservative, advancing little from the plan and style of Morris's work at Inveraray, though Wilson, called in to modernise the existing structure, was perhaps slightly hamstrung. The theatricality of Caprington suggests he was aware of his predicament, and sought, through parody, to carry off the task.

FENWICK

In many ways, Fenwick epitomises everything that is attractive about Ayrshire weaving villages: the low-roofed, single-storey cottages stretching along the main road, by-passed since

Riccarton claims connection with The Wallace. His father, Malcolm, is supposed to have been born in Riccarton Castle, its site marked by a plaque in Fleming Street, while the Bickering Bush recalls the story of the young Wallace's conflict with a band of English soldiers, slain after they attempted to purloin the lad's catch of fish from Irvine.

Fenwick co-operatively claims precedence over Rochdale. The Co-operative founded at the Lancashire mill town in 1844 is generally regarded as the genesis of the co-operative movement. The Fenwick Weavers Society, however, was founded in 1769 to promote and maintain high standards in the craft; and soon became involved in the bulk purchase of oatmeal for resale to its members.

Waterslap

the 1930s, which connects the two parts of the settlement, **High Fenwick** and the older, more sequestered **Laigh Fenwick**. The Laigh village has the best of the cottages, most notably the fine groups at **12-20 Main Street**, one of which is dated 1769, and again at **34-56 Main Street**, where one is dated 1812. The charm of this particular sequence is enhanced by the controlled way in which it follows the line of the road. **Waterslap**, with cottages on one side only, facing open fields, is the epitome of weaving rows. The 18th century, as elsewhere, saw the first major development of Fenwick as a weaving village, the hand-loom weavers here making tweeds, blankets and muslin.

John Fulton, a Fenwick shoemaker, perfected a working scale model of the solar system – an orrery – through the years 1823-33. Built with shoemaker's tools, and inspired by an amateur interest in astronomy, Fulton's orrery was astonishingly accurate, and may be seen in Glasgow Art Gallery & Museum.

Right *Fenwick Parish Church*. Below *Sentry box*

Fenwick Parish Church, 1643 (see p.C7) A Greek cross planned church, similar to Kirkintilloch and Lauder, but much plainer in decoration: no wealthy heritors in this barren parish. The result is severe, white harling and Gothic survival windows beneath corbie-stepped gables and the steeple added in 1660 by John Smith, a Kilmaurs mason. Gutted by fire in 1929, a competent restoration, installing harmonious, if unchallenging, fittings was undertaken by Gabriel Steel. The hexagonal **sentry boxes** in the kirkyard, dated 1828, and possibly by Robert Johnstone, are an uncommon feature, and appear to have doubled as collection points and observation posts to prevent unauthorised leave. The adjacent **manse**, 1783, with a reused lintel of 1645, repeats the theme of poor, plain and honest.

King's Arms, Main Street
At the core of this bar lies the traditional
unassuming coaching inn; it is now coated with
Brewers' Tudor, that unthinking reworking of a
style without historic antecedents in Fenwick.
In Mansheugh Road, two good houses of *c*.1970,
one at least by Hay Steel & Partners, bring a
dramatic presence to this part of the village.

Kingswell, 18th century
Important coaching inn on the Ayrshire/
Glasgow road at the very bleakest stretch of
the Fenwick Moor, which declined into a mere
farm once the improved turnpike pioneered the
existing A77 route. This part of the moor has
its share of Covenanting mementoes; these
simple pillar memorials are best exemplified by
that at **Lochgoin**, erected in 1896 to designs
by Thomas Lyon, adjacent to the **Howie Farm**
of **Lochgoin**, itself rebuilt in 1858. A much
different, and ultimately more satisfying, work
of art is the **monument to Mrs Corbett** near
Kingswell, designed by Robert Lorimer. She
was the wife of Lorimer's client at Rowallan,
and it was her early death which resulted in the
curtailment of the original grander proposals.

**Alice Corbett's simple
memorial** was designed by
Lorimer, and she was buried on
the Windy Moor, *an eerie place,
loud with the whistling curlew,
which the late Lord Rowallan
yet found 'strangely peaceful'.
There heather, rushes, lichen
and coarse grass grow free,
symbolic of the liberated spirit.*

ROWALLAN CASTLE, *c*.1560 (see p.C4)
The unique main east front of Rowallan is best
understood in terms of a palace gatehouse, and
its exquisite round towers flanking the
entrance should be seen more as an echo of the

Rowallan Castle, 19th century

Kyle and Carrick Libraries

regal splendour of Stirling Castle, Falkland Palace and the Gatehouse of Linlithgow, rather than as a return to the aggressive defence of the 13th-century keep-gatehouse. It was a desire for increased accommodation and show, not security, which gave rise to the forework at Rowallan. The roof is brought down to the wallhead, omitting both parapet and battlements, and this may well be the first instance of this convenience on an Ayrshire castle. Behind this show façade, things are simpler – an L-plan main block, and courtyard.

Rowallan, 1901, Robert Lorimer
In many ways the most conventional of Lorimer's major houses, and the one that most consciously echoes the ambitions of the Scots baronialists, especially if the full scheme had been completed, but is able to soften their direct approach with full use of ogee curves and wit. Unfortunately, on the principal garden elevation, the demand on Lorimer, following the death of the client's wife, to substantially reduce the scale of the building, has left a weak climax to the design, though from the south the house appears successfully as an L-plan tower house.

KILMAURS
The form of this former weaving village is its chief charm: the sinuous way in which the rows of cottages wind seemingly first one way and then back the other, dividing at the village centre, with its Tolbooth, and then continuing onwards, where the cottages give way to 19th-century two-storey houses.

Tolbooth
Known locally as the *jougs*, after the iron neck-ring attached to one wall, Kilmaurs' Tolbooth symbolises the village: an unavoidable icon at its heart. The style is the traditional vernacular solution to the needs of such a building: a miniaturised tower house: single courtroom reached up stone steps over vaulted basements.

Place of Kilmaurs, *c*.1620
One of a number of T-plan houses in Ayrshire, representing the move away from defensive to domestic requirements. There is an adjacent structure which can be seen as the remnants of a precursor building, but Place is essentially new build on a new site. Substantially altered subsequently, most obviously by the slapping out of additional windows.

Below *Tolbooth*. Bottom *Place of Kilmaurs*

Kilmaurs Parish Church

Kilmaurs Parish Church, 1888,
Robert Ingram
Despite Ingram's close and careful attention to
existing details, today's church is essentially
his own work, based on the spirit of the old
kirk. The part to escape reconstruction is the
Glencairn Aisle, the 1600 burial aisle of the
Cunninghames of Glencairn. The Aisle holds
the monument to the 8th Earl of Glencairn:
upright figures on either side of a cartouche
with, beneath, their children weeping, the
whole ensemble reminiscent of the family
gathering in their kirkloft. David Scougal of
Crail was the mason. **Tour**, 1841, James
Ingram, is a moderately sized mansion, suited
to its role as a country estate for a Glasgow
merchant. Tudor Gothic, brought to Ayrshire
by William Burn at Blairquhan, consummated
here in a polished and pleasing manner.

CROSSHOUSE
A roadside miners' village, almost completely
reworked as Ayr County Council housing of the
1950s and 1960s. There is a neat, unobtrusive
Early Perpendicular red stone **Church**, 1881,
by Bruce & Sturrock. For most Ayrshire folk
today, Crosshouse means: the Hospital.

North Ayrshire District General Hospital,
1973-82, Boissevain & Osmond
Crosshouse Hospital cannot be ignored; seen
from afar, as from the Kilmarnock by-pass, it
appears as if a set for a film, gleaming white
and slightly unreal. Closer at hand, one finds
that the architects have provided a structure
which works visually: the crisp horizontal lines
of the structure balance perfectly with the
dominant towers to provide a fitting addition
to the Ayrshire landscape.

*North Ayrshire District General
Hospital*

Gatehead Viaduct

Gatehead Viaduct, 1807, William Jessop
Important piece of industrial archaeology, the
oldest railway viaduct in Scotland. It carried
the Duke of Portland's wagonway from mines
at Kilmarnock to the new port at Troon over
the Irvine, but was abandoned in the 1850s
when the Duke's railway was incorporated in
the burgeoning national network, and a
straighter route over the river created. It is
currently (1992) the subject of restoration
proposals.

Craig House

Craig House, *c.*1835, James Ingram
Imposing classical mansion, with Ionic-
columned portico: particularly noteworthy are
the greatly accentuated pediment, giving extra
emphasis to what might otherwise be less
effective, and the exuberance of J J Burnet's
winter garden attached to the house.

**Bonnet manufacture in
Stewarton** dates back to the
16th century. The Bonnet Guild
of Corsehill was established in
1666 to ensure quality control
and effective marketing. In the
19th century, machine knitting
of bonnets replaced hand
knitting, and the industry
evolved from a home-based to
factory-based one. Bonnets are
still made in Stewarton at the
Bridgend Mills.

STEWARTON
Created a Police Burgh in 1868, Stewarton's
increasing size and importance in the 200 or so
years prior to that had been on the back of two
distinctive trades: bonnet-making, for which
records extend back to the 16th century, and,
as machine-work displaced the handworked
bonnets, knitwear. Both industries survive in
town, though the bustling air is attributable to
its current status as a dormitory for Glasgow,
Kilmarnock and Irvine.

St Columba's Church

St Columba's Church, from 1696
The plan suggests a complicated building history.
Today, the kirk is essentially a Greek cross, with
the southern arm, as a double pile, of which the
crowstepped half represents the original 17th-
century structure, while the remainder dates
largely from alterations in 1775 and 1825 to
conform to current preaching practice. Peculiar
off-centre belfry tower, with Cunninghame
shakefork and unique triangular window.

Paton

Paton

Above *Lanfine House, Darvel*.
Left *Dick Institute, Kilmarnock*.
Below *Braehead Housing,
Irvine*. Bottom *Perceton House,
Irvine*

McKean

McKean

Paton

Above *Culzean Castle*. Right
Salt Pan houses, Maryborough.
Below *Watersports Centre,
Cumbrae*. Bottom *The Harbour,
Ayr*

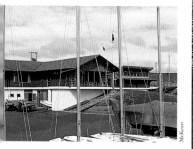

McKean

McKean

Close

C6

Above left *Blair*. Top *Central Ayrshire Hospital*. Above *Burnock Holm*. Left *Fenwick Parish Church*

Top *Interior St John Oglivy
Church, Irvine.* Above
*Administration offices,
Hunterston.* Middle right
*Exterior St John Ogilvy
Church, Irvine.* Right *Painting,
Hunterston Power Station*

Lainshaw Street

The church is tucked into a corner, off Lainshaw Street, the main south road. Here there is the quirkiness of **9-19**, particularly the rusticated, shell-topped pilasters at **9-13**, to which only Amon Wild's ammonite fixation at Brighton seems comparable, and the **Royal Bank of Scotland**, 1860, which has severity and deeply cut lettering. **Vennel Street** leads to the **Kirkford**, where a much-altered group of cottages still exudes some rustic character. **Craigston**, 1902, H E Clifford, is an Arts & Crafts villa in red Mauchline stone.

Woodlands and **Braehead**, both *c.*1840, large asymmetrical houses in their own grounds, identify this part of Stewarton as the home of the masters: Braehead's unobtrusive elegance has been seen as a restrained Roman-inspired triumphal arch. **Old Glasgow Road** has some traditional cottages, Stewarton Town Council's flatted block, and **John Knox Church**, 1841, unornamented builders' work.

Avenue Square

With Avenue Square the real architectural excitement of Stewarton begins. Coupled with **Avenue Street** and **Graham Terrace**, this marks an attempt by Cunningham of Lainshaw to impose some classical order on the town. The **Institute Hall** heads the square, but fails to dominate in any effective way: the off-centre approach to Avenue Street ensures a lack of any sense of procession, and the failure to develop a fitting climax renders the whole a poignant hint of what might have been.

Standalane

An excellent example of an Ayrshire courtyard farm: beside **2 Standalane** is an unobtrusive master's house with wide eaves. It and much of Stewarton is overshadowed by the ten-arch **Annick Water Viaduct**, 1868, George Cunninghame, which carries the railway across the valley with panache and elegance.

Robertland, *c.*1804, David Hamilton
A very sophisticated design, which uses the pilasters to terminate the window bands, much enlivening the surface of what would otherwise have been a standard façade, with slightly advanced and timidly pedimented centrepiece. **High Williamshaw**, 1771, is a handsome, strongly pedimented house rescued in the 1980s from total dereliction by Stuart Ingram.

David Dale, 1739-1806, born in Stewarton, was a journeyman weaver in Paisley. A deeply religious man, he went into business on his own account in Glasgow, on the putting-out system – that is, sending one linen yarn to home-workers and collecting the finished cloth. The business was profitable, and Dale made further use of his skills in banking and development. Recognising the potential of the cotton spinning machinery in the 1780s, he turned his attention to developing mill communities, first at New Lanark, in partnerships with Richard Arkwright and the Utopian socialist Robert Owen, his son-in-law, and subsequently at Catrine, in partnership with Claud Alexander of Ballochmyle, communities where enlightened treatment of the workforce was as important as the financial rewards.

Institute Hall

Close

Thomas Leverton Donaldson, 1795-1885, Professor of Architecture at London University and prodigious author on the subject, was born at Williamshaw. In its obituary the *Kilmarnock Standard* recorded that *he took an interest in Kingsford School and designed the present commodious schoolhouse.*

Lainshaw

Close

Dunlop cheese, a hard keeping cheese, was reputedly first developed at The Hill, near Dunlop, in the years around 1700, by Barbara Gilmour, who had learnt the techniques in her native Ireland. Being a hard cheese, it could withstand transportation to the markets in Glasgow, &c. This, coupled with its long-keeping ability, gave it a distinct edge over the pre-existing soft cheeses, and ensured a saleable end-product for the growing Ayrshire dairy industry. Eventually farm-produced Dunlop cheese was replaced by creamery cheese, and little or no cheese is now produced commercially in Ayrshire, though Dunlop Cheese is still produced on Arran.

Ayrshire suffered a shortage of houses in the 1920s and '30s, especially in the mining areas, where many continued to live in the substandard and insalubrious rows. The county architect, Robert Lindsay, was intrigued by the speedily-erected timber houses sent over by the Swedish government and put up in five weeks in Carntyne Road, Glasgow. Basing his designs on Swedish practice, Lindsay brought timber houses to Ayrshire, and the first, experimental, block was erected in Dunlop in 1937.

Below *Main Street, Dunlop.* Right *Chapeltoun*

Close

Lainshaw, David Dale Avenue, *c.*1800 Straightforward classical mansion to which a major addition in Tudor-Gothic style was made in 1824; the result is a house of great charm. Adjacent are the crumbling contemporary **stables** and, on the hill above, **Lainshaw Mains Farm**, the most astonishing classical estate farm, topped by an enormous octagonal lantern – the effect is distinctly unnerving.

Kennox, *c.*1820; 1911, James A Morris A house of real quality, which incorporates an earlier gabled wing to the rear: this is dated 1762. The Regency house is of conventional pattern, with a central Palladian window above the pedimented, Corinthian-pillared door. Original wooden jalousies are a notable feature. **Chapeltoun**, 1909, Alexander Cullen, like much of his oeuvre, is restrained and harmonious. There is widespread use of harl, which was originally left in an unpainted, artistic, grey state.

RIAS Collection

DUNLOP
The core of the village is off the main road, and the casual motorist will see nothing of especial merit. Connecting the road with the church, **Main Street** is delightful: a crowding-in of single-storey cottages, seemingly anxious to meet one another across the winding street with its oft-changing views. It would be invidious to pick out individual cottages: the

effect is dependent on consonance and good-
neighbourliness, though for sheer effrontery,
the breeze-block crowsteps at **75** should not be
missed. **Kirkland** is a good L-plan house (once
the Manse), unobtrusively and brilliantly
enlarged by James Chalmers in 1910. The
result is one of the finest compositions in
Ayrshire, a house which is clearly one with and
evolved from the ground on which it sits.

Parish Church, 1835
The previous church on this site was built in
1641, and details from it are incorporated in
the north aisle: these include Jacobean
elements, notably strapwork, and can be
compared with similar work at Skelmorlie
Aisle, Largs. In 1835 the church was largely
rebuilt to give the present form with its
battlemented west tower. There are two
notable buildings in the churchyard: **Hans
Hamilton's Tomb** is early 17th century, a
rough-hewn ashlar box, with a steeply pitched
flagged roof; primitive, no doubt, but expressive
and moving. Alongside is **Clandeboye School**,
equally rustic, corbie-stepped, two-storey
schoolhouse of 1641, with polite addition of
1925. This is a particularly fine pair of unspoilt
vernacular buildings of great importance.

Dunlop House, 1834, David Hamilton
Prodigious work in Scots Jacobean style.
Hamilton's notable house, its entrance front,
suggestive of a Gillespie Graham asymmetrical
castle, came at a time when stylistic
experiment was rife, and is among the first and
best essays in a literate revival of 17th-century
Scots Renaissance forms.

Top *Kirkland.* Middle *Parish
Church.* Above *Hans
Hamilton's Tomb*

Dunlop House

Aiket Castle

Below *Hurlford*. Middle *Hurlford Parish Church.* Bottom *Shawhill*

Aiket Castle, 1976, Robert Clow
The restoration of Aiket, from a burnt-out unstable shell, is the most significant in post-war Ayrshire. Attention to detail throughout is first-class, and the view of Aiket, floodlit, by night, from the Lochlibo Road is dramatic.

IRVINE VALLEY

The road from Kilmarnock to Edinburgh runs up the Irvine Valley sheltered between rough, largely afforested, moorland to the north and prominent hills – **Blackside**, **Distinkhorn** – to the south. Along the Irvine lie **Hurlford**, **Galston**, **Newmilns** and **Darvel**. To the hurrying motorist, Hurlford is a crossroads, Galston all right angles, Newmilns all sinuosity, Darvel long and straight. The differences betray the origins of the towns: Galston and Newmilns long-established parish centres, Darvel a late 18th-century planned village and Hurlford a 19th-century mining and engineering village.

Hurlford

An inchoate mass radiating from the crossroads where the former roads to Edinburgh and Dumfries diverge. A propeller blade stands as mute witness to the specific skills of the long-closed Blair Iron Works. 1970s shopping facilities mark the village centre. In **Riccarton Road** is the **Co-operative**, 1904, behind it the **Primary School**, 1905, a free Renaissance essay by Andrew & Newlands. Also from the office of Gabriel Andrew is the gaunt Gothic former **UP Church**, 1898, in Mauchline Road.

Crookedholm

The transpontine continuation of Hurlford; it grew after the establishment of a woollen mill in 1817, though a dissenting chapel had existed in the 1780s. A mill of *c*.1868 survives as an *ad hoc* industrial estate. The two chief churches of the paired villages are here: **Reid Memorial Church**, 1857, and the more dramatic 14th-century-style **Hurlford Parish Church**, 1875, J & R S Ingram, boasting a Sadie McLellan stained-glass window, 1981.

Shawhill, 1820

Very neat five-bay house, the dominant feature being the large Doric porch; an older structure of cream-washed stonework is incorporated to the rear. There is also a broad-eaved square Gothick **summerhouse** of the same period.

Templetonburn, 1901, James K Hunter,
burnt-out, is a notable example of his work. An
essentially manorial house of long, low profile
moderately Scottified with crowsteps and
Georgian sashes, with essentially English
vernacular details such as red roof tiles.

Loudoun Kirk

Loudoun parish covers the north side of the
upper valley, though in medieval times the
parish centre moved upstream to Newmilns.
The remains of the choir were fitted out as a
burial vault for the Campbells of Loudoun in
1622, a plain version of the Skelmorlie Aisle at
Largs. Restoration, for the untiring 3rd
Marquess of Bute: *refecit Ioannes Marchio
Bothv Tertius*, 1898, by Robert Weir Schultz.
Bute's grandmother had been Countess of
Loudoun in her own right.

Loudoun Kirk

Loudoun Castle, 1804-11, Archibald Elliot
Elliot's first solo commission in the castellated
style, built around an existing 17th-century
core, itself enclosing a tower of *c.*1600. Work at
Loudoun ceased in 1811, owing to Lord
Hastings' dire financial problems. From the
hand of a Scottish architect it falls inevitably
within the Adam tradition by resembling
Mellerstain, though the break with classical
horizontal lines and the machicolation show an
awareness of Atkinson's Scone Palace, while it
also lacks the sense of movement that Paterson
was able to introduce at Eglinton, due to Elliot's
choice of square towers at each advance and
turn of the façade. Consequently, Loudoun has
something of a cardboard castle look, the more
so today as it stands an empty shell without
internal solidity. But whatever the repeated

Francis, **Lord Hastings**, the
client for Loudoun, was
ambitious: at their marriage in
1804 the bride, Bute's
grandmother, was given away
by the Prince of Wales. The
same year, work began on
converting Loudoun into one of
the most palatial residences in
Britain, a home befitting
Hastings' perceptions of himself
and his role in British society.
He had previously
commissioned William Wilkins
to create the splendid Gothic
Donington Hall, Leicestershire.

Loudoun Castle

Moscow, despite the Volga Burn, has no connection with the Russia. The name, accented locally on the second syllable, *Ms-cow*, is generally accepted to derive from the Old Scots *Moss haw*. The Volga Burn is a facetious nomenclature coined to strengthen the putative link.

verticals lack in subtlety is made up for in magnificence of scale and extent. For the front elevation, impressive though it may be, is as nothing compared with the long sweep of the side elevation overlooking the superb park, laid out to designs of Alexander Nasmyth. Viewed from the park, the massing of the towers of the entrance front, the long sweep of the enormous front facing the park and the asymmetrical dominance of the taller rear tower enhance its claim to the title of the Windsor of the North.

The house has been ruinous since it was consumed by fire in 1941, while doing war service as accommodation for Belgian troops. There survives in the grounds a Gothic arched **bridge**, across a dramatic gorge, presumably also to designs of Elliot. At the foot of the drive stands **Loudoun Academy**, 1969-70, Ayr County Council – a rather timid venture clad with red-facing brick.

MOSCOW
Oddly named village and telephone exchange beside the **Volga Burn**, for the motorist on the main road no more than two unnecessarily large signs drawing attention to the name, and a sprawling untidy garage. Its main charm is **Hemphill**, an attractive row of weavers' cottages of *c.*1800 which nestle close to the laneside; single-storeyed and harled, the little row is well endowed with climbing plants.

Below *Hemphill*. Bottom *Waterside School, commemorative plaque*

Waterside Mill, 1784
Built as a carding mill and now in mixed use. Opposite, the attractive little **school**, now community centre, was *Erected by subscription under favour of George 4th Earl of Glasgow AD 1823*, and is a gentle essay in provincial classicism. **28-30 Main Street**, 1943, Sam Brunton, are fowl of a different feather; a striking modern pair of flat-roofed bungalows constructed originally of Gyproc. Brunton was a pioneer in prefabricated building techniques, and experiments such as these led to the emergency housing programme after the war. **Hareshawmuir** is a much extended shooting lodge in the hills, its present asymmetrical Edwardian character obscuring earlier origins.

GALSTON
The many twists and turns of the road pattern in Galston, still a busy junction, give a new vista at every step. Although it has long been an important local centre, the town lacks any

real architectural cohesion, with the major monuments well scattered, and not strikingly obvious from near or far. The dominant images are of red stone tenements and swathes of local authority housing. The four maisonette blocks erected by the town council in *c*.1970 give the burgh, seen from afar, something of the look of an Italian hill town. Their presence cannot be justified otherwise. Coal was always important economically in this part of the valley, though weaving, especially of blankets, was prominent, while an earlier trade had been in shoes, even if by 1799, the weaving of lawns and gauze occupied the greatest number of hands.

Barr Castle, Barr Street, 15th century
A tall, solid tower, standing on a rock outcrop and slightly above road level, built for the Lockharts of Barr. Despite alterations, such as a porch and unsightly hipped roof of *c*.1899, its stern character is not enhanced by its current use as a masonic hall. Excellent, slightly sinister, house adjacent: timbered gables, Glasgow Style glass, faintly Arts & Crafts. The polychrome Romanesque **Church**, 1859, is by J Dick Peddie. Nepus gables – a regular feature of Galston's 19th-century architecture – in **Sorn Road**: 1860 and 1865. **Wallace Street**, generally unassuming 19th-century houses, has this soothing regularity jarred by the badly knocked-about former cinema, and **5-7**, the red stone Renaissance **Co-operative**, 1889.

Barr Castle! Tenantless and wild!
Dome of Delight! Dear Haunt of mine!
The shock of ages thou has foiled,
Since fell the last of Lockhart's line;
Thou, left a hermit, to grow grey
O'er swallow, crane and bird of prey.
John Wright, quoted in Paterson, *History of County of Ayr*

Left *Barr Castle*. Below *Galston Parish Church*

Galston Parish Church, 1808, John Brash
Redeemed from austerity by its pilastered doorway and simple steeple, it displays a continuation of elegant late 18th-century character. A slightly jocular attitude is struck by the ornamentation at the corners of the east tower from which the spire rises: they can only be likened to Indian clubs. A correspondent of

Kyle and Carrick Libraries

Close

St Sophia's RC Church

the *Air Advertiser* in 1809 said: *I was lately passing the village of Galston, and had the curiosity (while the horses were feeding) to visit the Parish Church lately built there: I must indeed confess that I was fully gratified on seeing one of the national churches erected agreeable to a most simple, convenient and elegant plan, which may serve as a correct model to other parishes for generations to come. The mason and wright work appear to be well executed. A Traveller.*

St Sophia, 1885-6, Robert Rowand Anderson
What would A Traveller have made of this? Freely based on Hagia Sophia in Istanbul, Anderson, with Lord Bute, and possibly Weir Schultz, brings to suburban Galston this dark red brick echo of the Byzantine Empire. The use of brick, and changes in the plan to incorporate more sittings, diminish the truly exotic feel. Bute had tried to gift a Byzantine church on the Catholics of Troon: they were having none of it. Less affluent Catholics in Galston were not in a position to turn away marquesal munificence. In **Bentinck Street**, good local authority infill at the corner of **Blair Street**, and pleasant mid-19th-century cottages facing grander late 19th-century villas such as **2**, with circular bay, hood-moulds and heavy eaves, and **8-10**, a reduced version with similar well-drawn details.

Below *Chapel Lane*. Bottom
Town House

Chapel Lane, *c*.1968,
Hay Steel MacFarlane & Partners
Local authority housing on a large site between **Brewland Street** and **Orchard Street**, with well-proportioned open spaces amid flats and terraces on the steeply sloping site. Opposite, **26-58 Brewland Street**, 1894, is an excellent, relatively unspoilt, row of Mauchline red single-storey cottages. **Orchard Street**, climbing steeply, has similar cottages: red ashlar with dormers at the top, earlier simpler and harled at the foot. **95-97** Orchard Street is faintly Gothic: a counterpoint to this fragile piece of townscape provided by a fin-windowed 1950s **community centre**. In **Gauchalland**, an excellent **Co-operative**, 1939, Cornelius Armour, a bricky cinema without the shed.

Town House, 11 The Cross, 1925,
James Hay & Steel
Conscious historicism: Scots baronial, in a Lorimer manner, competently done, though Hay & Steel are not renowned practitioners in this ultimately unadventurous architecture.

The Town House (properly the Galston Sub-Office since 1975) superintends Cross Street, a patchy widening of the street, overshadowed by the **Parish Church**, the opportunity for a civic space wasted amid bus shelters and public conveniences. Good single-storey cottages in **Titchfield Street**, particularly **22-28**, dated 1799. **Church Lane** is equally patchy, **17** a minimally Glasgow Style tenement of *c*.1900.

21 Polwarth Street, *c*.1840
Grand three-bay town house, unfortunately harled, with wide pilasters at the margins, suggestive of the work of James Ingram. The street is otherwise patchy and neglected: the coarse, and coarsened, **Brown's Institute**, 1874, James Stark, and the earlier **11-15** (former **Blairs School**) **Henrietta Street** has wall-head gables dated 1823 and 1825, and little else. **Bridge Street** is the heart of the town, its bridge across the Burn Ann, its architecture battered. At the corner with Cross Street, a nepus gable of 1803 and the excellent, but neglected, **Portland Arms**, smart Georgian with large grey ashlar and lying panes.

James Hay, 1871-1929, like Andrew and Smellie, was another of the competent and original architects of early 20th-century Kilmarnock. He arrived in 1897 as an assistant to Andrew, but soon set up on his own. His designs share Andrew's bold powerful approach, but tend to be rooted deeper in an understanding of Scottish traditional forms. He may be the architect of the notable Walker Buildings, Kilmarnock. The firm still flourishes, as Hay Steel & Partners, now based in Ayr.

Above *Brown's Institute*. Left *Portland Arms*

Co-operative, 4-8 Brewlands Street, 1901, Andrew & Newlands
A hugely self-confident essay in Renaissance, not as adventurous as their Co-operative in Newmilns, but an unmistakable symbol of the power of the Co-operative Movement throughout the valley. In **Glebe Road**, the two parts of the **Primary School**, the earlier original primary school, *c*.1875, William Railton, simple Renaissance, and the 1909 former Academy, mixing Tudorbethan and Palladian features and a Doric-columned central first-floor window. Good railings, and two good villas adjacent. Note the Glasgow Style window in **10 Glebe Road** by James Hay.

Below *Town House*. Middle *Co-operative Buildings*. Bottom *Newmilns Tower*

Cessnock Castle, from 15th century

A plain rectangular keep, extended north and east into a palatial courtyard in mid and late 17th century, with a marked Renaissance feel, notably in the imposing dormer pediment, the classical form of the door pediments and the swaggering octagonal stair-tower of 1665. Unobtrusive restoration of the decayed structure from 1890 by Thomas Leadbetter.

Sornhill, 1660

Derelict L-plan laird's country house. The overwhelmingly horizontal massing of the building is most evident when seen from the back, and where the number of large windows reveals the lack of defensive intent, and its residential nature. It requires restoration and serious architectural research.

NEWMILNS

The oldest Ayrshire burgh away from the coast, it is the centre of the Campbell of Loudoun's fiefdom. Burghal status was gained in a 1490 Charter of James IV, giving *the inhabitants of Newmylls the right to hold fairs elect bailies and other officers necessary for the government of the town*. Hereditary Sheriffs of the county, the Campbells had great influence. Serpentine and hilly, its main architectural features are grouped together in the centre.

Town House, 50 Main Street, 1739

Attractively simple white crowstepped Tolbooth, approached up a double flight of steps. Restored in 1986 by Kilmarnock & Loudoun District Council it has a single-celled first-floor room over vaulted cellars.

Co-operative Buildings, 1900, Andrew & Newlands

A unique and unforgettable first impression of Newmilns. Three-storey red sandstone Glasgow Style block on a broad gushet site with wide-brimmed tower at the hinge, marking out Gabriel Andrew as a talented designer.

Loudoun Street, a curving tunnel of red stone tenements, some by John Macintosh, retains a delicious sense of enclosure. Beyond, the villas of the mill owners and the professionals. Here more than anywhere else in the valley can be seen the almost total domination which lace curtains have in the houses of the valley folk.

Gilfoot is an inter-war local authority scheme laid out on Garden City principles.

Newmilns Tower, *c.*1530
For Pont this was a *fair and veill bult duelling decored vith plesant gardens and orchardes*, though Robertson, 1819, found it *one of those dismal square towers so frequent in this part of the country*. A small square four-storey tower with two string-courses and a base course.

Loudoun Arms, Main Street, 18th century
With its towering walls, steeply pitched and crowstepped roof and skews, possibly earlier, this is one of Ayrshire's domestic gems, its character obvious even in this rather unassuming position. Has it always been an inn or does it represent a Loudoun town house, as members of the family deserted the tower for a more fashionable life? Inter-war council housing by the Town Council in **High Street** has an attractive baronial, turreted, appearance.

Loudoun Arms

Loudoun Parish Church, 1844
A rectangular preaching box of classical mien, with a fine clock tower and steeple, which replaced a church of 1738. The architect is not recorded, though James Ingram is likely. The churchyard contains the 1823 memorial to the Covenanting martyr, John Nisbet. The urban character of this part of Main Street has suffered: the church's closest neighbours undistinguished post-war housing. Opposite are the **Clydesdale Bank**, 71 Main Street, 1829, occupying an earlier, former inn – the **Black Bull**. The **Rex Cinema**, 79 Main Street, opened inauspiciously in September 1939.

Lady Flora's Institute, 129 Main Street, 1877, F T Pilkington
A low, single-storey range built as a girls'

Flora Hastings was a daughter of Loudoun Castle – one of the Lassies of Loudoun – and a lady-in-waiting at the court of Queen Victoria. Illness led to a distended stomach, leading in turn to rumours of impropriety and pregnancy. Once these reached the Queen, Flora Hastings was banished from court. Ill, impugned and shunned, she died, proving the rumours ill-founded. The affair was badly damaging to the Queen's popularity in the early days of her reign, and the return of the body to Loudoun for burial witnessed scenes unrivalled before or since in the valley. A certain amount of contrition became apposite. The Institute, originally intended for the religious instruction of young girls, was masterminded by Sophia, Marchioness of Bute, another of the Lassies of Loudoun; some of the money being raised through the sale of a collection of Flora's poetry.

Below *Lady Flora's Institute.* Left *Detail, Lady Flora's Institute*

Morton Hall

school, with money gifted by Sophia, Lady Bute, in memory of her sister, Lady Flora Hastings. It is late Pilkington to a small budget, well-composed essay in Ruskinian Romanesque and Second Empire detail.

Morton Hall, 123 Main Street, 1896
A suite of public halls by Arthur Harrison of Birmingham is the attractive flowering of the benefaction of a Birmingham shoe manufacturer. Newmilns-bred, Harrison's English Tudor details are alien to the valley yet fit well into the cosmopolitan nature of the architectural motifs in the town.

Railway Viaduct
The viaduct leaps spectacularly across Newmilns Green, creating a townscape, of arches, greenery and the gentle rustle of the river, unique in character. The backland views of the Main Street and the industrial use of some of the arches detract a little, but in **Greenside** and **Union Street** there are typical valley mills, such as that of Muir & Co in Union Street, of c.1915.

Below *Royal Bank of Scotland.*
Bottom *Lace Mill, Ladeside*

GREENHOLM
Newmilns over the water: the river marks the boundary between Loudoun, on the right bank, and Galston parishes, and the distinction is proudly maintained. **Brown Street**, the spinal cord of Greenholm, begins with the odd **Bank of Scotland**, a crisply detailed betowered and crowstepped Victorian villa, then a goodish stretch of terraces facing one another across the wide street, and finally an excellent selection of the town's Lace Mills: generally of polychrome brick, often with red sandstone dressings.

Townhead Farm, 18th century
Tucked down **Mill Road**, and now enveloped in the burgh, this is an excellent compact farmhouse, brightly harled and crowstepped. In **Darvel Road** more mill-owners' houses, and in **Alstonpapple**, around and about the neglected **Alstonpapple Farm**, dated 1793, a final flourishing of lace-based wealth: **Parkhouse**, harled and Westmorland slated in the astylar manner of c.1905; the inter-war **Lisden**, 1928, Eric Hurcomb; and **Everton**, 1935, again by Hurcomb, continuing that tradition, and, most impressively, the huge **Westlands**, also in the tradition but writ very large and with a distinct French accent.

Gowanbank Monument, detail

Gowanbank, 1881

Double villa for Alexander and Robert Morton. On the roadside is Robert Lorimer's austere **monument to Alexander Morton**, 1927; a bust of Morton is flanked by low stone walls.

Lanfine, late 18th century (see p.C5)

Large rambling T-shape mansion, at its core a small Georgian mansion house, harled with raised rusticated dressings, largely reconstructed and extended *c.*1912-20 by James K Hunter. Particularly impressive are the **doocot** and the **bridge**, 1828, on the Darvel drive of rusticated masonry which spans the **Newlands Glen**, close to the house.

DARVEL

Darvel has not the history of the other valley burghs. As is suggested by the grid-iron road pattern, it began in the late 18th century as a planned village, chiefly for weavers, feued on Brown of Lanfine lands. Development took place between *c.*1750 and 1820, and a number of single-storey cottages, with the loom-shop windows clearly visible, still survive such as **106 East Main Street**, 1797. Many feus have been built over, especially over the last decades of the 20th century. Lace-making was introduced to the valley in 1876, and lace mills sprang up in Darvel and Newmilns. The valley quickly captured a large market, and lace, muslin and madras were exported to India and elsewhere. Though the downturn had already started, it was Gandhi's *home-spun* policy of the 1920s which finally killed the bulk of that trade. Lace-making still survives in the valley, supplying tablecloths and curtains. Darvel, like Newmilns, betrays this in its windows: all, almost without exception, have lace curtains made in the valley. The wide main street of this spruce little burgh is aligned on the

Alexander Morton, 1844-1923, was among the first cloth manufacturers to take up and develop the idea of William Morris. By the 1880s and 1890s, the variety of woven textiles available in Britain had expanded greatly, and improvements in dyeing technology allowed a wider range of colours. In his native Irvine Valley, Morton found a stagnant economy based on heavy chenille curtains. He transformed it by bringing in new machinery, introducing the concept of factory labour and turning a valley of hand wabsters to power-loom operators, producing light materials, and using innovative designs. His nephew, Gavin Morton Jun, ran the design studios. Among designers who did work for Mortons were C F A Voysey and Lindsay P Butterfield, whose influence can both be seen in Gavin Morton's own designs.

Sir Alexander Fleming, 1881-1955, was born in Lochfield, the seventh of eight children. The discovery and isolation of penicillin, for which he is celebrated, tend to obscure his previous pioneering work on bacteria and antiseptics.

106 East Main Street

Main Street and Loudoun Hill

The communities of the Valley maintain a proud rivalry. In *Discovering Ayrshire*, John Strawhorn recounts a story circulating in Newmilns that turned on the alleged meanness of the Darvel folk: *A beggar from Lanarkshire going round the doors of Darvel was getting little or nothing in the way of alms. When one further housewife refused him anything, he cried out in final exasperation: 'Are there nae Christians in Derval?' She thought for a moment then replied, 'Weel, there are Mortons and Gebbies and Clelands and Boyds – but nae Christians that I've heard of!'*

valley's chief landmark, the volcanic plug known as **Loudoun Hill**: this, the generous width of the street, and the yet existing generality of single-storey cottages, gives it a conspicuous breadth, a feeling of room to stretch oneself, in contrast to the much tighter parameters which inform the development of the other valley towns.

Darvel Central Church, 1888, Robert S Ingram
Assured Early English essay, topped by very evident tower and spire. In a county of unbuilt spires, the very existence of the spire is proof of Darvel's relative prosperity. The parish church dominates the little central **Hastings Square**, which is partly of mid 19th century, and partly modern local authority infill. Opposite are the **Black Bull**, 1840, and the **Town Hall**, 1905, T H Smith, London, described as Italian Renaissance, its street façade dwarfed by the cinema-like shed behind. In close proximity, are the town's other churches: the old **Free Church**, 1885, Baldie & Tennant, very handsome Gothic, and **Evangelical Union Church**, 1889, Robert Boyd. The architect for Darvel's council housing was William Valentine, Kilmarnock. Most notable are the lengthy blocks, with good use of vernacular details, at **79-87** and **108-110 East Main Street**.

Top *Hastings Square*. Above *Town Hall*

Co-operative Buildings, 1900, George Sinclair
Competent encrusted Italian Renaissance by a little-known Glasgow architect, presently in a bad state of repair: the block at the corner, possibly by Cornelius Armour, brings a suave touch of 1930s classicism to the areas: as throughout the Irvine Valley, the Co-op has the biggest buildings. In **Ranaldcoup Road**, **Mair's Free School**, **18**, 1863, William

Railton, takes Doric educational classical and produces something wonderfully gauche, while Darvel's **Brown's Institute**, **22**, 1872, its doors offering *Conversation etc* and *Reading Room etc*, is probably by James Stark.

Darvel Primary School, *c.*1900, Henry Higgins

Higgins was a Glasgow architect who developed a successful practice supplying schools to Board of Education and School Board specifications. This specimen, a powerful exercise which dominates the north side of the town is among his best. In **East Donington Street**, **4** is the former Police Station, *c.*1910, by James A Morris. It has a twin at Patna. Darvel has less evidence of its owners and the professionals: **Kirkland** is a large if dull villa in its own substantial grounds, and in Burn Road, **The Braes** is an attractive house, Arts & Crafts, with extensive views. Its eclectic stables, matched by an industrial building at the foot of Burn Road, has been converted into a pleasant and unusual house, **Westbrae**.

Top *Brown's Institute, detail.* Above *Primary School*

Turf Hotel, *c.*1840

Excellent and relatively unspoiled bar at east end of West Main Street. The next stretch of West Main Street mixes weavers' cottages with red tenements, such as **55-57** of 1884 and **117-119**, of *c.*1900, with excellent tiling in the closes. **49-53** are good 1920s infill. The far end of West Main Street has the best villas – on the south side, **137**, and The **Grange**, both of *c.*1905, in a free harled style. Opposite, the grey Gothicism of **140** and the blocky red crowsteps of **142** establish the parameters. Braemore, of 1910, and **158** abandon exposed stonework for, respectively, white harl and tiles, and grey harl and slates.

Turf Hotel

Long Row, **Trabboch**, is described in evidence submitted to the Royal Commission on Housing of the Miners in Scotland, in 1913, as containing *40 houses, built in five blocks of eight each. The end house of each block is of three apartments, the other of two. The measurement of the two apartment house is 14 ft by 12 ft for the kitchen, and for the room 12 ft by 6 ft. The three apartment house is not much larger in floor space … There is a washing house for every four houses, and a coalhouse and a small dry-closet for every house. There is a tiny ashpit attached to every closet. There were no doors on any of the closets when we saw them (Dec. 1913), and both closets and ashpits were deplorably dirty. Some of the ashpits were half-full of foul water and rotten matter. The paths are unpaved, parts of them badly cut up, and in wet weather exceedingly dirty. With a little attention Trabboch could be much better. Pavements before the doors would be a great help both as to appearance and comfort.*

Cumnock Old Church

Close

EAST KYLE

The heart of industrial Ayrshire. Significant production of coal began in Ayrshire in the 18th century, mostly to satisfy a growing demand from Ireland. These first pits were close to the sea, as at Stevenston, Irvine and Newton on Ayr. Exploitation of the central Ayrshire coalfield began in the 19th century, and by the end of the century coal and ironstone were being won on an extensive basis throughout this area: the colliers often housed in isolated rows where domestic conditions could be unspeakably bad. The ruinous **Long Row** at **Trabboch**, *c*.1883, not one of the worst, gives some impression of the architectural quality. Coal production continued to grow until the early 1950s, when the last Ayrshire deep mine, Killoch, was sunk, and the abortive new town, based on Killoch and another proposed mine at **Bonnyton**, mooted. Drongan is the only evidence of the new town: an estate without a centre. Killoch no longer produces coal, and the last deep mine, Barony, closed in 1989.

Interlarded with this was the iron industry. Signs of its presence generally belong more in the realm of industrial archaeology, but the complex at **Dalmellington** is rewarding architecturally, and associated residential and social buildings can still be seen at **Muirkirk** and **Lugar**.

CUMNOCK

A town of some antiquity, a Burgh of Barony since 1509, always an important trading centre and nerve centre of the routes serving this rugged upland area. Industrial growth brought change, development and renewal, leaving a largely Victorian town, dour in local grey stone. The roads converge at **Gorbals**, where the **Holm Burn** is crossed, at the heart of the little town: the **Square** outside the big parish church has always been a secondary centre, but has been less affected by recent changes, and remains aloof from the traffic system which makes it the centre of a bustling roundabout.

A **Old Church**, 1867, James Maitland Wardrop Dominating the little square, even without its intended spire, Wardrop's design is a highly competent, assured handling of early Decorated motifs, given added quality by the apsidal north end which houses the vestry. The mason work, in snecked rubble, has been finely wrought. The

Mercat Cross, a square shaft on a five-stage base, completed by a sundial and ball finial, dated 1703, repaired 1770. In the Square, **3-11** are an especially complete range of 18th-century houses, probably the finest surviving group in Ayrshire, and also boasting, at **7**, among the less distinguished modern shopfronts, a fine timbered façade of *c*.1860. The **Sun Inn** is also 18th century, with widely spaced little windows and architraves, while both the **Snug Bar**, which looks *c*.1800 but is probably older, and the **Mercat Hotel**, have 18th-century cores. The rest of the group is 19th century, including one former bank with distinctive scalloped first-floor windows, or which was refaced during that century, though the **Clydesdale Bank**, 1882-4, John Murdoch, is a fine Mauchline stone pile, the style of architecture that of the Queen Anne period. Towards Gorbals, the **Craighead Inn** and its neighbours are freestanding plain 18th-century houses, nudging up to one another, the inn remodelled in the 19th century. The disturbing aspect of the Square becomes apparent especially at the south-west corner: peer out and you discover that almost everything behind has gone, leaving the little enclosed space on its hill Italian in concept, Hollywood in execution.

Mercat Cross

Lugar Street

Lugar Street has one or two houses of *c*.1790, most obviously **16**, with its bell-cast roof, and **Riverside**, a free-standing house with widely spaced windows and an artisan doorpiece. Busier, and crouching in its restricted site, is the **Baird Institute**, 1891, Robert S Ingram, a good, substantial and elegant building in

Alexander Peden, 1626-86, covenanting minister, field-preacher and prophet, born in Auchincloich, was ejected from the Episcopalian church in 1663 for refusing to take the Oath of Allegiance. Peden rapidly became one of the leaders of the Covenanters in Ayrshire, where preaching brought thousands to remote sites – the county is replete with field names such as Preaching Brae, Peden's Pulpit and Peden's Table – and led to five years' incarceration on the Bass Rock. He died in hiding but of natural causes at the height of the Killing Times and was buried in Auchinleck. His body was resurrected by Government troops and reburied at the foot of the Gallows in Cumnock. Robert Ingram's monument marks the spot, while thenceforth Cumnock people resolved to use the gallows ground as a cemetery.

Baird Institute

Top *Lochnorris*. Middle *Bank Viaduct*. Above *Richmond Terrace*

Keir Hardie, 1856-1915, Independent Labour MP for West Ham, 1892-5, and for Merthyr Tydfil, 1900-15, became organising secretary of the Ayrshire Miners Association in 1879, and, in 1882, a journalist on the liberal *Cumnock News*. A devoted Christian, his concern for the well-being of his fellow man lead him back into full-time union work and the political arena. He tried to convert the Liberal Party from within and, failing that, established the Scottish Labour Party in 1888, and the Independent Labour Party in 1893.

Scottish baronial style. The **Lugar Bridge** is early 19th century, and the **Congregational Church**, 1883, is a compact little Gothic structure in Ballochmyle stone. **Holmside House**, *c*.1885, is a red astylar villa: **8-14 Holmside** repeat the pattern, as grey semi-villas. They sit amid some attractive new houses, including **2 Auchinleck Road**, the warm brick **4 Holmside**, and the chunky **Homestead**. In Auchinleck Road, **Lochnorris** is the large, excessive plain house built for Keir Hardie, dated 1891, with, opposite, further good 20th-century houses at **40** and **42 Auchinleck Road**. Further out, **Broomfield** has something of the simple charm of Riverside, but carries a much plainer doorpiece.

Bank Viaduct, 1848-50, John Miller
Deep in Woodroad Park, itself enlivened by the **Swimming Pool**, 1937, Robert Forbes, the viaduct crosses the Lugar on nine arches between giant panelled pilasters, a match for Miller's masterwork at Ballochmyle. **Barrhill Road** climbs past the huge bulk, its dull white harl barely enlivened by the Mauchline stone dressings of **Cumnock Academy**. Robert Ingram was responsible for the Gothic **obelisk**, 1891, commemorating Prophet Peden in the graveyard. **Richmond Terrace**, 1966, Robert Matthew Johnson-Marshall & Partners, are stylish but dated flats.

Glaisnock Street
Glaisnock Street climbs steeply southward, crossing **Gorbals Bridge**, and avoiding the Brutal **Shopping Centre**. Opposite that, **12-24** are a good run of prosperous Victorian commercial properties, while the junction with Ayr Road is marked by a Scots baronial former Bank of Scotland of 1870, turning the corner beautifully. Opposite, another notable group, a Burn-inspired block, with an outrageously heavy, and decaying doorpiece, book-ended by two baronial monsters: one the **Royal Bank of Scotland**, 1866, the other a risky but effective mix of turrets between crowstepped gables, all oversailing wide central first-floor windows. The **Dumfries Arms** looks rather naked under its small pedimented half-dormers, the rubbly stone having been scrubbed clean, while **Cumnock Picture House** injects some colour (mostly shades of green) into the ensemble. The **Town Hall**, 1885, Robert S Ingram, is a well-handled Free Renaissance effort, broadly

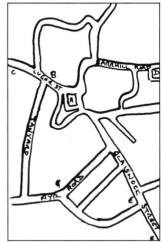

classical but going French at the edges: in front is Benno Schotz' fine bust of **Keir Hardie**, 1939, ill served by the thoughtlessly positioned

F bus shelter! **St John's Church**, 1882, is a rare Scottish example of the work of William Burges, the distinctly roguish architect who found in the 3rd Marquess of Bute a client equally remote from mainstream taste. The church does not, could not, match the results of their collaboration at Cardiff Castle, but within the dignified early Decorated apsed church, a reduced-cost version of his 1872-3 church at Murston, Kent, Burges' work, coupled with an altarpiece by J F Bentley and N J Westlake, provides a lush feast of painted surfaces, rich furniture and glorious stained glass.

Below *St John's RC Church.* Bottom *38-42 Ayr Road*

G **Crichton Church**, 1899, David Menzies Powerful, slightly sinister, dull red church pushing up a tall spire: this is exceedingly graceful, and gives an air of distinction to the little town. **38-42 Ayr Road** are a very dignified run of single-storey shop units, with delightful, if rather heavy, cast-iron Gothic arches to the shopfronts; they also may be the work of Menzies. Also in Ayr Road, **Fads** inhabits a cheery free Renaissance building, while the other side of the road is given over to a run of good small villas and bungalows in generous grounds raised above the road, while **Roseburn** is an oddly eclectic house based about a multi-sided porte-cochère-like porch. The former United Associate Church, 1831, in **Tanyard**, is the regulation rectangle, given an unusual, west façade mixing classical and Tudorbethan with devil-may-care ease. **Bankend Farm**, 1855, is a very proper Dumfries Estate farm.

Barshare, 1957-61, Robert H Matthew
A new £1m housing scheme, aimed at keeping houses away from the main roads, has been started in Cumnock. The scheme, designed by Professor Robert Matthew, is new in the architectural field in Scotland in its layout and varying designs. The majority of the 530 houses planned to be constructed in the next seven years are to be built at almost right angles to roads. A series of wide paths will run from the road to areas for pedestrians only. Different types of houses will be built next to each other to give variation in appearance. In the first development, started in October 1959, there are 84 houses of seven different types. The houses are between 3 and 5 apartments. One type of house will have timber walls and a doubly insulated aluminium roof. There will also be flat roofed houses. The intention of the scheme is to relieve the monotony of conventional layouts: we want to make the scheme 'live' by providing colour and variation and to make it easier to live in by its layout.

Dumfries House, 1754-9,
John & Robert Adam
The house built for the 4th Earl of Dumfries is a particularly fine, largely unspoilt and strangely private Adam mansion, nominally the co-operative work of the brothers Adam, but displaying a sober and correct Palladianism very much to the taste of John Adam. It is a simple house distinctively proportioned, an unoriginal Palladian layout in good taste. There is the traditional three-storey central block and two side pavilions connected by lower ranges to the centre. The 3rd Marquess of Bute thought it the homeliest of his houses, but nonetheless engaged a favourite architect of his, Robert

Barshare

Dumfries House

Weir Schultz, to enlarge the pavilions unobtrusively between 1895 and 1899. Internally, the house has been little altered, and to step into these rooms is like entering a past age, so little has anything been changed. The prevailing feel is properly Palladian, its gravitas slightly affronted by a hefty dash of rococo. In the grounds, the superb **Avenue Bridge**, contemporary with the house, boasts obelisks and a chunky central balustrade: here is gravitas indeed. There is also a **doocot** of 1671 and, towards Cumnock, the fragmentary ruins of **Terringzean Castle**, said to date to *c.*1400. **West Gates** are a delightful pair of white-harled lodges, with windows in recessed super-arches: the ruinous **Temple**, spookily exotic in its decay, may be connected with the lodge for Dumfries House exhibited by J P Gandy in 1827. **Garrallan**, old and picturesque, decays quietly, while **Glaisnock**, *c.*1835, whose style is Tudor Manorial which, whatever it may lack in prettiness is made up for by sheer size, survives as an outdoor educational centre.

Left *Avenue Bridge.* Below *Temple, Dumfries House policies*

Top *Arthur Memorial Church.*
Above *Afton Court*

90 Main Street, Ochiltree

Both in appearance and
*position the house was a worthy
counterpart of its owner. It was
a substantial two-storey
dwelling, planted firm and
gawcey on a little natural
terrace that projected a
considerable distance into the
square. At the foot of the steep
little bank shelving to the
terrace ran a stone wall, of no
great height, and the iron
railings it uplifted were no
higher than the sward within.
Thus the whole house was bare
to the view from the ground up,
nothing in front to screen its
admirable properties.*
George Douglas Brown, *The
House with Green Shutters,*
1901

NEW CUMNOCK

Straggling village at the confluence of the Nith
and sweet Afton, south of the low watershed
which separates the Ayr/Lugar system from
the Nith; thus it has more in common with the
Upper Nithsdale towns, Sanquhar and
Kirkconnel, than with the rest of Ayrshire. The
parish was erected in 1657 to better serve this
corner of the large Cumnock parish. Glen Afton
is beautiful and, as yet, relatively undiscovered
by either tourist or forester.

The Gothic Survival ruins of the 1657
Church survive, their feel not dissimilar to the
county's other Commonwealth church, Ayr,
adjacent to the disused **Arthur Memorial
Church**, 1912, prominent, oddly alien in its
robust free-style detailing: the architect was
Cardiff's W Beddoes Rees. All this happens on
Castlehill, but of Black Bog Castle not a trace
can be found. On the main road, called Castle,
are the **Martyrs Parish Church**, 1833, the
earliest documented work of James Ingram,
though the tower bears more than a passing
resemblance to that at Mauchline, finished in
1829; the **Town Hall**, 1888, Allan Stevenson,
baronial with a distinct Low Country feel; the
stylish 1930s extension to Trotter's shop and
the compact **Bank of Scotland**. **Afton Court**,
1981-2, Roy Maitland (of Cumnock & Doon
Valley District Council), is an excellent, blocky
sheltered housing complex which reinvents
vernacular details in blood-orange brick.

OCHILTREE

Douglas Brown's Barbie, a dour but likeable
village plunging down its brae to cross the
Lugar, scattering single-storey cottages and
later, improved, houses in an *ad hoc* manner.
Tacks are recorded for various late 18th-
century dates, such as 1785, 1796 and 1799.
The village has a harmonious cohesion,
enhanced by the broad street and the view.

Individual cottages are best seen as part of
this unified picture: the standard is a central
doorway, often with projecting steps, as at
64-66 Main Street, with single windows to
either side, and a slated roof over a lime or
colour wash with contrasted stone dressings.
69-89 is a fine example of the type, climbing
the slope with aplomb, while opposite **78-98** is
an equally fine group, also stepped, and
including **90**, the birthplace of George Douglas
Brown: the event recorded by a Robert Bryden
plaque and green shutters. The template for

Gourlay's house, the House with Green Shutters, is said to be **74** a free-standing two-storey house of thinly-jointed, large whin blocks. The **Church**, 1789, is an undistinguished, retiring, grey-harled block with deep rusticated round-headed windows. The old **School**, 1909, A C Thomson, is free treatment of Scots baronial, simply designed; a conventional planned Board School with typically quirky Thomson details, as on door lintels, repeated at Sinclairston, also for Ochiltree School Board, and at Whitletts.

1-5 Burnock Street

Chunky two-storey houses, bowed to suit the road pattern: **5** is decorated with the Glencain arms in a panel. The **Head Inn** is similar but affected by changing tastes, while **3-13 Mill Street** is a vernacular range of houses of character. **Burnock Holm** (see p.C7) is a little gem: single-storeyed from the front with an artisan scroll-bracketed doorpiece, from behind a three-storey vernacular house, clearly of some importance, with a wagon entrance on the lower floor. **Burnock Bridge**, 1838, has rusticated masonry and a low parapet; the bypassed **Lugar Bridge**, c.1830, is more sophisticated. **Ochiltree Mill**, 1859, is tall, and of much charm and integrity.

STAIR

Almost idyllic cluster of buildings tucked in at a bend on the Ayr. **Stair House**, 17th century, is one of the loveliest houses in Scotland, its whole fabric grouping picturesquely and displaying many vernacular Scottish traits. It is seen to advantage from near **Stair Bridge**, 1745, narrow and dignified, and the **Water of Ayr and Tam o' Shanter Hone Stone Works**, a complex of mainly 19th-century origin, with a dainty, almost invisible, **suspension footbridge** of c.1900. **Stair Kirk**, 1864, William Alexander, plain Gothic rescued from banality by its setting, and the **Stair Inn**, c.1820, its picture-

*Still **Ochiltree** sits yonder*
High on her rocky seat
And still the bonny Lugar
Keeps rippling at her feet.

Left *Stair Bridge.* Below *Burnock Holm.* Middle *Stair Inn.* Bottom *Stair House drawn by James Clark*

postcard qualities compromised by crude extension, complete the happy set.

Trabboch Mains is a stolid 18th-century improvement farm, with the scant remains of **Trabboch Castle** as neighbour. At the roofless former **Schaw Kirk**, 1843, plainness is assuaged by a delightful timbered porch. **Drongan House** (*top*), *c*.1775, is a plentifully pedimented laird's house, self-confident in its setting, and incorporating an older crowstepped house to the rear.

TARBOLTON
Battered, gap-toothed village, presided over by its impressive church, and straggling south-ward from the motte, on which a wooden castle is said to have stood, protected to the north by the now largely reclaimed **Tarbolton Loch**.

Parish Church, 1821, Robert Johnston (*middle*) The church sits on a natural knoll. The pattern is familiar: a broadly square plan, with deep clear glass windows, and, above a central projecting pedimental feature, the spire, which marks the village from afar. The minor theme is the use of thin corner pilasters to give some interest to what would else be excessively plain. The adjacent **Manse**, which must be *c*.1800, combines stout vernacular forms with a veneer of artisan classical details: a slight pediment, some urns, the odd round-headed doorway. In Croft Street there is an excellent **cottage**, perhaps *c*.1820, with elaborate carving.

The Bachelors' Club was a debating society formed by Burns, his brother Gilbert, and others in 1780: *Every man proper for a member of this Society must have a frank, open heart; above anything dirty or mean; and must be a professed lover of one or more of the female sex. No haughty, self-conceited person who looks upon himself as superior to the rest of the Club, and especially no mean-spirited worldly mortal, whose only will is to heap money, shall upon any pretence be admitted. In short, the proper person for this Society is a cheerful, honest-hearted lad; who, if he has a friend that is true and a mistress that is kind, and as much wealth as genteely make both ends meet – is just as happy as this world can make him.*

Bachelors' Club, Sandgate (*bottom*) The only survival of pre-18th-century Tarbolton, couthy: thatch over limewashed harl, with a rear external stair, acquired and restored by the National Trust for Scotland in 1938. Sentiment for Burns has triumphed over Ayrshire's innate pragmatism. The Cross epitomises Tarbolton's problem: unstopped gap sites and, where the gaps have been filled, injudicious architecture. The **Town House**, 1832, in **Burns Street**, is an unimposing relic of the burgh of barony created by Charles II: little more than an ordinary-two storey house. **Cunningham Street** merges seamlessly into **Montgomery Street**: the patchy nature of the village continues throughout. *Bachelors' Club open to the public; booklet available*

Lorimer Library, 1879, Gabriel Andrew
Chunky, red stone edifice which glares at the
street in a defrocked neo-Norman and carries
Tarbolton's architectural palm. The **Black
Bull**, *c.*1822, echoes the urn-capped pediment
of the Manse. **Daisybank**, an interesting villa
of *c.*1800, mirrors closely in its details those of
Montgomerie House.

Montgomerie House, 1804, John Paterson
(demolished)
The most grievous loss to Ayrshire
architecture. Paterson's elegant modern
mansion in the Grecian style dominated by its
full-height domed semicircular Ionic colonnade
reappears in miniature as the former Leith
Bank in Bernard Street, Leith (see *Edinburgh*
in this series). Paterson had been Robert
Adam's chief assistant.

Top *Lorimer's Library.* Above
Daisybank. Left *Montgomerie
House*

Barskimming, 1883, Wardrop & Reid
Plain neo-Georgian mansion, on older site with
a portico in a David Hamilton manner. Four-
square and exposed, it is dour and slightly
depressing. Life across the river is jollier: the
river is crossed by the dramatic **bridge** of
1788, flanked by obelisks and in its easy
elegance an apt foil for the gorge below. The
stables, *c.*1820, is a gay Gothick confection,
while the soft red rock of the gorge has been
cut and carved, tunnelled and excavated, to
create a series of paths, rooms, viewpoints and
stores: this work must be contemporary with
the house of 1771: ogival-headed openings are a
recurring feature, while crenellations appear
on one bluff near the bridge.

Barskimming stables

Mauchline Castle was the factor's house on this part of the Earl of Loudoun's estate. Here Burns came to pay rent, and the then factor, Gavin Hamilton, 1751-1805, quickly became one of his truest and closest friends: his was the encouragement that led to the publication of the Kilmarnock Edition, of which he is the dedicatee. Mary Campbell – Highland Mary – was a nursemaid in Hamilton's household.

Auchenfail is an elegant Georgian mansion built for William Cooper, a successful Glasgow merchant who bought the land in 1786. A wide, spreading house, topped by a pediment finished with armorial bearings, finding a middle ground between Auchinleck and Drongan. South of **Failford**, with its little cluster of traditional cottages, pragmatically treated, and **monument**, 1920, James Hay, obtusely plain – near this spot Robert Burns and Highland Mary took their last farewell 14 May 1786 – the soft red stone has again been cut, to form steps. **Skeoch Farm**, a worthy example of a harled Ayrshire courtyard farm boasts an Ionic porch which, despite the modern infill, is typical of good Scottish Georgian design, but which is said to have been brought from Hamilton Palace in 1925.

MAUCHLINE
Intricate settlement of some antiquity, first of importance as the administrative centre for the Ayrshire estates of Melrose Abbey, developed at the junction of the route southwards into Dumfriesshire and the east/west route along the valley of the Ayr. The winding streets which mark this can still be traced, but at some stage, perhaps c.1820, new direct roads were driven through, superimposed on the existing pattern. Mauchline stone, exploited in the Ballochmyle and Boswell Quarries of Marcus Bain, found a ready acceptance throughout the west of Scotland and Northern Ireland in the late Victorian period and beyond.

Below & bottom Mauchline Castle, 1797 & 1992

Mauchline Castle, *c.*1450
Known colloquially as **Abbot Hunter's Tower**, this was a civil residence for ecclesiastics engaged in managing Melrose

Abbey's large Ayrshire estates. It is a striking rectangular tower of two vaulted floors, the bayed vault on the first floor having an ecclesiastical feel, reinforced by the ornate window openings, and the statue niche on the outer wall. An L-shaped wing has been added piecemeal, presumably replacing the original granaries and barns necessary for the proper management of the estate. The crowstepped block, perhaps from as early as c.1690, though with a ground-floor vault which must be earlier, is linked to the tower by a pended block of c.1800. The other block is of c.1760, heightened in c.1820, when much of the current internal work was done. The adjacent **Parish Church** (*right*), 1829, is thinly Gothic, its bulk much relieved by the accomplished tower: a substantial edifice, which gives a presence to the village and forms a notable feature in the surrounding landscape. The architect appears to have been a local amateur, William Alexander of Southbar, and the construction superintended by James Dempster.

During Burns's tenancy of Mossgiel, he often crossed swords with the Church in Mauchline. Constantly rebuked by William *Daddy* Auld for his liaisons with Jean Armour, his revenge is found in *The Holy Fair*, set in the Mauchline churchyard, and *Holy Willie's Prayer* debunking the cant and hypocrisy he perceived in the attitudes of Church elders.

Castle Street

Castle Street and the **Knowe** wind deliciously, recapturing much of the character of the Mauchline that Burns must have known. **2-4** are a pair of simple stone houses, with plain openings: known as **Jean Armour's House**, they were gifted to the Burns Federation in 1915 and 1924, and restored by a noted Burnsian-architect Ninian Macwhannell. **Nanse Tinnock's** is similarly plain, with contrasted dressings. In **New Road**, some competent 1960s infill, notably the **Fire Station**, 1963, Ian McGill, blocky, uncompromising, and the **Veterinarian Surgery** of similar date, which finds greater use for contemporary detailing, equally uncompromising, yet perhaps for that reason, more respectful to their neighbours. Those neighbours include a good run of late 18th-century houses, Netherplace's simple little **lodge**, and the **Burns Memorial Tower**, 1897, William Fraser, a horribly fascinating baronial confection, a competition-winning design. The adjoining **Cottage Homes**, by contrast, have a likeable severity.

Below *Nanse Tinnock's*. Bottom *Burns Memorial Tower*

High Street

High Street mixes competent proud houses of the 18th century, such as **3**, its restoration spoilt by its fenestration, with decent single-

Top *Earl Grey Street*. Middle
15 Cumnock Road. Above
Poosie Nansie's

*Mauchline Creamery, as
envisaged in 1938*

storey cottages such as **10-12**, **The Loan**, with
its huge, steeply pitched slate roof, but clearly
originally thatched. The **post office**, 1966, is
best ignored: as an example of insensitivity to
the needs of the site, it takes some beating.

Black Bull Hotel, Earl Grey Street, 1776
The *good inn* of the village, its unfussy details
and coach-house pend picked out in black-
margined white harl. It forms the centre of
Earl Grey Street (a name which adds its own
gloss to the date at which the new roads were
run through), with more demure two-storey
houses, including **11-13** Earl Grey Street, with
four-centred coach arch below a nepus gable,
its Georgian symmetry lopsided by partial
painting of the red ashlar and the heavy
anthemioned doorway added to the right-half
hand. **Cumnock Road** has the best of the
village's villas: **15**, dominated by a squat round
tower and **19-21**, a huge double villa with odd
wings with attenuated pavilion roofs: both
needless to say, of red stone. **23** Cumnock Road
is Viewfield, a farmhouse of c.1800 engrossed
into the village and given, c.1880, cast-iron
acanthus balconies. The imposing **War
Memorial**, 1927, A C Thomson, uses the local
stone to great effect. **Loudoun Street** begins
with an attractive range of c.1800, **1-17**, more
architectonic than the work of the previous
years, which reappears in the black and white,
simply pilastered **Poosie Nansie's**. The
Haugh is an unspoiled rural backwater,
simple cottages at one with their surroundings:
the former **Creamery**, c.1900, is delightfully
flighty, the Swiss cottage style presumably
designed to imply cleanliness: similar
considerations must have been behind the crisp
lines of Alex Mair's **Creamery** of 1938, now
badly compromised by additional buildings and
the loss of its canopy.

Ballochmyle, *c.*1760, John Adam
A chaste Palladian house, which can still be
discerned in the rear elevation of the huge
extensions added 1886-90 by Hew
Montgomerie Wardrop: through the use of an
eclectic and brooding style which mixed
dominant roofs and bay windows with
Georgian and Jacobean details Wardrop was
able to pull the whole into a remarkably
convincing synthesis. The house is currently in
a deplorable condition. **Ballochmyle Viaduct**,
1848, is an object of rare splendour, leaping the
Ayr in seven arches, the central one of
breathtaking dimensions, while both the old
road bridge, **Howford Bridge**, of pleasing
rural charm, on which James Armour is said to
have worked, and the new, **Ballochmyle
Bridge**, 1962, F A MacDonald & Partners, a
sharply designed concrete single span, have
considerable merit. **Kingencleugh**, *c.*1765, is
an unusual and very pleasing specimen of an
old-world country house, given a new lease of
life, and an elephant-finialed porch, by Mervyn
Noad, *c.*1957. The adjacent L-plan
Kingencleugh Castle, *c.*1600, survives in a
fragmentary state.

Above *Ballochmyle.* Top
Ballochmyle Viaduct

Kingencleugh

Catrine drawn by J Black, 1814

The extensive cotton works at Catrine were begun *c*.1787 by the laird, Claud Alexander of Ballochmyle, in association with David Dale. Dale controlled the financial aspects of the mill, leaving day-to-day management to Alexander and the mill manager. Respectable housing was provided – but not the other Owenite facilities provided at New Lanark.

Below *Catrine Parish Church.* Bottom *Nether Catrine House*

CATRINE

There was nothing here at all, beyond the odd smiddy or cothouse, until 1787, when Claud Alexander of Ballochmyle, the landowner, in collaboration with David Dale, founded his cotton spinning works, complete with philanthropically conceived village to house the employees. The **Mill**, one of the best industrial buildings in Scotland, Venetian windowed in the manner of Mill No 1 at New Lanark, was tragically destroyed by fire in 1963. The village suffers visually as a result, and the demolition in 1987 of the bulk of the mill extensions of the 1940s and 1950s has further damaged the tight-knit feel of the little mill town lying in its perennially smoky hollow.

Catrine Parish Church, 1792

This is the major monument: it overlooks and dominates the town. Large pediment to the south elevation, and classical details of quality. **Mill Street**, **Mill Square** and **St Germain Street** comprise the core of the original village. The houses were firmly in the Ayrshire tradition: there is nothing flash or showy and certainly nothing to match the drama of New Lanark. **Brown's Institute**, 1898, Robert Ingram, has a noticeable Scots baronial clock tower. **Nether Catrine House**, a late 18th-century house of rural charm, presently in need of attention, is a Palladian villa with central pediments and urns. **Daldorch**, 1801, was the Sorn dower house: the simple contemporary three-bayed two-storeyed pile, with sash windows and central porch: the Victorian wing created a T-shape, and gave the house its present semi-Italianate feel.

SORN

Known as Dalgain until the 17th century, Sorn is one of Ayrshire's show villages, always in pristine, flowery condition. Its charm is closely linked to its major monuments, the church, the bridge, the views of the Castle. The village itself is pleasant enough, but the width of the main street and policies – sight-lines, building lines – which have pushed the opposite sides even further apart limit opportunities for the village's essence to be expressed.

Sorn Church, 1658

Rather splendid edifice, quietly assured, which sits amid the stones of its kirkyard. A Commonwealth kirk, and it has much in common with the near contemporary Ayr Auld Kirk, a plain shed with Gothic survival windows, though most details date from a Georgian-Gothic restoration of 1826, and improvements made by H E Clifford *c.*1910. The lofts are reached by three external stairs of vigorous quality. The churchyard has, seemingly like all in the county, a plaintive rustic Covenanter's monument. **Sorn Bridge**, *c.*1710, is a straight steeply hump-backed two-arched bridge spanning the Ayr at a most picturesque bend. **Dalgain Mill** is possibly of 18th-century date; **Ladeside Cottage**, with its rustic porch, flanks the bridge approach.

Sorn Castle, 14th century onwards

An ancient fabric to which a modern mansion has been added, finely situated on the crest of the precipitous bank of the River Ayr. The older part may be of late 14th century date, with additions, most obviously the corbelled parapet, *c.*1490. Additions were made *c.*1793, but the major additions were by David Bryce, *c.*1864, in a restrained baronial manner, and by

Top *Sorn Church.* Above *Sorn Bridge*

St Cuthbert Street, Catrine, borders the Catrine Voes, an attractive and unexpected series of embanked ponds in which water from the Ayr was dammed and from which it was released to provide motive power for the Catrine Big Wheels. Beginning in 1992, the Voes are being released from slow strangulation by silt and reedmace.

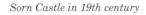
Sorn Castle in 19th century

Covenanters, such as the sixteen-year-old George Wood commemorated on the rear wall of Sorn Kirk, fought and died for their belief in Presbyterianism, as particularised in the Solemn Covenant signed at Greyfriars in Edinburgh in 1638. The Restoration of the monarchy in 1660 re-established Episcopalianism. Non-conforming Ministers, harking back to the theocracy of 1649, were ejected from their livings and banned from preaching. It was the implicit republicanism rather than religion that brought the State's wrath upon them. They took to remote hillside locations with their followers gaining greatest support in Ayrshire and the south-west, inspired by preachers such as Alexander Peden. Skirmishing between congregations and Government troops increased to the Killing Times, 1684-8, during the reign of the Catholic James VII. Wood died only a few months before the Glorious Revolution, which confirmed Protestantism as the established church in Scotland.

Harry E Clifford, 1908-10, in a grandiose voluptuous Edwardian manner at odds with Bryce's work. The **stables**, of about 1835, are particularly impressive, the standard courtyard pattern given a classical coat of pedimented arch, pilasters, wings and pavilions, while the main **Lodge** was remodelled by Clifford in a similar idiom to his additions to the house. **Cleugh Cottage** is a half-hearted evocation of a little Scottish tower house, too soft despite the large amount of rough dressed masonry employed on it: **Burnside Cottage**, known colloquially as the **Roon' Hoose**, was built *c.*1820; this chunky cottage was simply two D-shaped rooms set back-to-back: restoration in 1960 added a further wing and salvage, such as the gatepiers, from Catrine Mill.

Gilmilnscroft, *c.*1682

A stylish house of much interest, well restored in 1968 by David Somervell, pulling down most of the 19th-century accretions to the basic T-plan house of the 17th century. This had been extended, on an L-plan, *c.*1708. **Glenlogan** is an attentively restored courtyard farm, with an aedicular porch, all finished in the traditional and attractive combination of lime wash and black paint. **Dalgain** has much of the same character: the earthy unshowy nature of much of Ayrshire's vernacular building.

AUCHINLECK

A town of some antiquity, and still of some size, though the population is mostly concentrated in the housing schemes north and east of the old core. Auchinleck's **Main Street**, with its derelict castellated **Barony Church Hall**, and former Co-op with art deco arch, has seen better days. The **Barony Parish Church**, 1838, James Ingram, Catrine, is uneventful, with a tower and chancel, haughty Gothic, added in 1897, Robert Ingram. In the churchyard is the **Boswell Aisle**, a 1754 reworking of part of the 1683 church, and now fulfilling a further function as a small **museum** in memory of James Boswell.

Auchinleck House, *c.*1760

In its time, Auchinleck has been attributed to most members of the Adam clan: the evidence being that they were working at nearby Dumfries House. Possibly the work of a local mason builder, it displays an intriguing and fascinating admixture of the naïve provincial

Barony Parish Church and Boswell Aisle

Auchinleck House

and the sophisticated cosmopolitan, which well suits the home of James Boswell, the Biographer, and his irascible father-judge Lord Auchinleck. Simple five-bay structure, the central three pedimented and brought forward. The richly decorated pediment is supported on Ionic pilasters. It is not a large house: whether or not flanking pavilions and screen walls were intended is not clear: certainly within a few years taste compelled their appearance: the four pavilions, of obviously different stone, have peculiar ornamental towers, not unlike freestanding strapwork. A paradigm of restoration began in 1987: the architects are Simpson & Brown, the client the Scottish Historic Buildings Trust. Adjacent are the **stables**, a U-shaped classical range, of perhaps 1800, dour and honest, and an odd red brick **doocot** of indeterminate age. The very ruinous ivy-girt **Place of Auchinleck**, 17th century, lies much nearer the river, where there are further examples of summer-houses cut in to soft red rock, as at Barskimming and Failford.

LUGAR

A village which grew up around the iron works of the Eglinton Iron Company, founded here in the 1840s and moved in the 1860s from the low ground to the high ground currently occupied by British Coal and the District Council. Although the works have gone, a number of buildings directly linked to it survive. The **Church**, 1867, is plain and rectangular, large and commodious, and paid for by the Company, and appears to have as its core the original furnace house. The **Lugar Institute**, 1892, Robert Ingram, is an attractive, well-massed

James Boswell, 1740-95, stands as Ayrshire's second great literary genius. His father, Lord Auchinleck, a solemn, stern, unsmiling law lord, was the builder of the present house. It was not to everyone's taste, the Duchess of Northumberland confiding to her diary: *The pediments terrible loaded with ornaments of trumpets and maces and the deuce knows what; it is but a middling house but justly it is a romantic spot.* It was perhaps the result of a strict upbringing that Boswell took so winningly to wining and wenching. Boswell brought Dr Johnson to Auchinleck as they returned from their tour of the Highlands in 1773. Johnson and Lord Auchinleck failed to find any point of contact.

Hugh Logan, 1739-1802, Laird of Logan (now demolished), was so celebrated a wit that a popular book of witticisms was published called *The Laird of Logan*. The youngest of three sons, he told his father he would *follow nae trade but your ain.* His brothers died early, and he succeeded to the estate in 1759. His ready wit made him a popular guest throughout Ayrshire: *Logan's continued flow of ideas, no matter what, entertained me all the way* said Boswell of a shared journey home from Edinburgh.

L

153

Top *Lugar Institute.* Above *Craigston Square*

Bellow Mill was the birthplace of William Murdoch, 1754-1839, credited with the invention of coal-gas lighting. Murdoch also experimented with steam power, firstly in a cave below the mill house, then at Redruth in Cornwall in the tin industry, and finally in Birmingham with James Watt and Matthew Boulton, where he was the first to construct and use a steam road vehicle.

Glenbuck is the most easterly settlement in Ayrshire. Glenbuck Loch was created to provide water to the mills at Catrine; but Glenbuck's chief fame is its football team, the now disbanded Glenbuck Cherrypickers. They were amongst the top Junior teams in Scotland between the wars, their best-known player the former Liverpool Manager, Bill Shankly.

Muirkirk Parish Church

group, originally boasting skittle alley, swimming pool, library and billiard room. It too was provided by the company. The attractive, if conventional, **Craigston House**, *c.*1820, became the manager's house: **Craigston Square** is foremen's housing. **Kyle Castle**, hidden deep in the valley of the Glenmuir Water, is but a fragment: *a remnant ... with no tale to tell.*

MUIRKIRK

Isolated industrial community. The original *muir kirk* had been a chapel of ease for the extensive parish of Mauchline. The winning of coal, often through bell-pits, had been practised in these inhospitable heights since medieval times. The 18th century brought, with only a modicum of success, John Macadam's **Tar Works** and the **Muirkirk Iron Works**; the tar works failed quickly and left little trace: the iron works staggered on into the 20th century but eventually succumbed also, leaving a few ancillary buildings at Kames. Ironworks came also to hillier, harsher, Glenbuck about 1795. They too have long vanished, and this once-proud community has all but vanished, with nature, aided by the open-cast mining of coal, reclaiming it for itself.

Muirkirk Parish Church, 1812, William Stark

Worth a detour. Slightly aloof from the core of the town, Stark's battleship-grey battlemented church maintains a stern watch on goings on. Hay, perceptively, speaks of its *crouching fortified appearance, fitly symbolic of the church militant.* When he saw it it was derelict and roofless after a fire in 1949, but has been subsequently well restored, without any loss of its wonderful quality.

ALLOWAY

A small roadside huddle of cottages, the morbid heart of a suppressed parish, into which Scotland's greatest poet was born in 1759. This event has ensured the survival of one of those cottages: the others went during the late 19th century, when Alloway began to grow again, and to transform itself into a suburb of Ayr, into which it was incorporated in 1935. Growth since then has been steady with occasional spectacular bursts, while the green wedge of Belleisle and Rozelle enforces the myth that this isn't really Ayr.

The fame of Robert Burns, 1759-96, towers above that of all other Ayrshiremen. The *Ploughman Poet*, folk-song collector, satirist, farmer and Customs man, was diverted from emigration to Jamaica by the publication of his first book of poems in 1786 (The Kilmarnock Edition). A small industry recycles, records and analyses every aspect of his life. *Burns is more than a literary figure – a popular hero, whose birthday is celebrated by Scots all over the world. He sprang from the country people and their traditions and his undoubted genius owed nothing to fortune ... His birthplace has always been venerated, but it became an alehouse before 1800, and remained so still 1880 when it was acquired and restored by the Burns Monument Trustees ... Burns's character was not a complicated one: but it has been variously distorted by both admirers and detractors.* (Pamphlet sold at Burns Cottage)

Burns' Cottage, 1730
Burns' father's low sparse thatched home has great presence and obvious and proper disdain for new Alloway: the adjoining **Museum**, 1900, Allan Stevenson, is in a wholly inappropriate timbered bungalow manner. **Alloway Public Hall**, opposite, is the plain 1848 school of Clarke & Bell, substantially renewed to busier faintly baronial by Lorimer & Matthew in 1929, with lively internal plasterwork panels, *The Deil's awa wi' the Exciseman* and *The Jolly Beggars*, by Pilkington Jackson. James A Morris's 1920 exterior **War Memorial** completes the ensemble. The adjacent **Belleisle Cottages (21-31 Alloway)**, 1903, James K Hunter, with their porches and red tiles, lend an English suburban touch to the group. **1** and **2 Wellpark** and **6-16 Burness Avenue**, 1957-60, Frank Dunbar, are highly individualistic: Burness Avenue especially is a chunky terrace of rustic brick. In **Doonholm Road**, **2** is a substantial house of *c.*1800 with an exquisitely detailed Doric doorpiece, while **1** is the Jacobethan schoolmaster's house of 1849, presumably by Clarke & Bell. Doonholm itself is *c.*1898. *Burns cottage and museum open to the public; guidebook available*

Left *Burns' Cottage drawn by James Clark.* Below *Alloway Public Hall, doorway.* Bottom *Burness Avenue*

James Carrick, 1880-1940, was an architect of rare ability, who trained with James Miller and J K Hunter, developing and expanding Hunter's ease with domestic commissions, melding his English silhouettes into crafts-based best represented by the villas in Greenfield Avenue with their use of small rustic brickwork. His son James A Carrick, the best draughtsman of his generation, joined the partnership in 1936, bringing a highly tuned interest in the Modern Movement which resulted in the Mendelsohn-influenced Rothesay Pavilion, Cragburn Pavilion in Gourock and the original Ayr Ice Rink.

Below Greenfield Avenue. Middle *Mount Charles.* Bottom *Alloway Church*

Alloway's auld haunted kirk Where ghaists and houlets nightly cry (right)

Greenfield Avenue
Greenfield Avenue has a dramatic run of 1930s houses by James Carrick: these are large villas in rustic brick and roof tiles, in an English manner that seeks to recreate a past that never existed: they are **1-15** and **21-23** – whatever one may think of the philosophy behind them, highly accomplished and imaginative work. **17** is congruent design by the accomplished Alex Mair: **20** is uncompromisingly new, all glazing and flat roofs by Rowell & Anderson, 1959. **Mount Charles** is a typical boxy villa of after 1754, given an up-to-date new front in 1829 and flatted, with minimal damage, by Frank Dunbar in the late 1940s. The **Coachhouse** has also been well adapted to residential use, though it sits oddly in these groves of suburbs.

Alloway Church, 1857-8, Campbell Douglas Typical Douglas: accomplished, idiosyncratic, and enjoyable, summed up by the huge seven-light window which dominates the road front. The collection of stained glass, from Stephen Adam and J & J Kier of the 1870s, through Christopher Whall's 1922 Mitchell window, to the dainty trefoil lights by Gordon Webster, is a delight. Francis Watt in 1890 found it a *commonplace ugly structure vulgarly bedizened with cheap glass.* Behind are the **Church Hall**, 1964, William Cowie & Torry, which takes no prisoners with its direct, accessible, octagon, and the **Land o' Burns Centre**, 1975, Frank Perry, more respectful but thoroughly modern. The roofless ruin of **Alloway Old Kirk**, 1516, is frequented more for the souls in the churchyard than for its own sake.

Burns Monument, 1820-3, Thomas Hamilton The winning in 1818 of the competition for the Burns Monument was an important success

which did much to establish Hamilton's reputation as an architect. A free interpretation of the Choragic monument of Lysicrates, it is an elegant and effective essay in Grecian design by an architect whose only knowledge of ancient Greek architecture was derived from books. The nine-columned monument is raised on a rusticated triangular substructure, the monument being so placed that each side is respectively opposite one of the three great divisions of Ayrshire. At its foot is the contemporary hexagonal **Grotto** which holds sculptures by the Ayrshire primitive James Thom. The **Burns Monument Hotel** has been a plain house of c.1830, which has grown rather messily. The **Brig o' Doon**, which may be of 15th-century origin, was repaired in 1832. It is a highly photogenic, steeply climbing, yet exceedingly narrow, single arch.
Burns Monument open to the public

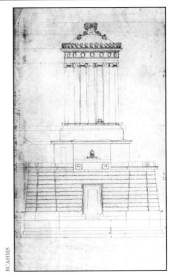

Top *Burns Monument: earlier Ionic scheme by Thomas Hamilton.* Above *Brig o'Doon*

Newark Castle, 16th century onwards
Newark's origins lie in the tall, nearly square 16th-century tower house firmly founded on a rocky outcrop. This was later extended, probably around 1687, by doubling the length, matching the old work in height. In 1848-9, the castle was again extended, this time by David Cousin with a rumbustious and vigorous Scottish baronial mansion which embraced the existing house without overwhelming it. A further addition, much tamer by comparison, was added in 1907-8 by James Miller: a restrained, accommodating addition which groups well with the existing building. **Balgarth** is a typically stylish Mauchline stone house by James A Morris; **High Greenan**, 1910, by Morris's erstwhile

Hamilton Paul's *Petition of the Auld Brig o' Doon* begins:
Must I like modern fabrics of a day
Decline, unwept, the victim of decay?
Shall my bold arch which proudly stretched o'er
Doon's classic stream from Kyle to Carrick shore
Be suffered in oblivion's gulf to fall
And hurl to wreck my venerable wall?

Newark Castle

Shooting party at Greenan Castle

Cassillis is linked with the ballad of the Galloway gypsy Johnnie Faa, with whom an unspecified Countess of Cassillis eloped, preferring his style to the fine feather beds of Cassillis:

There were seven gipsies in a gang,
They were both brisk and bonny O,
They rode till they came to the Earl of Castle's house,
And there they sang so sweetly O.

The Earl of Castle's lady came down,
With her waiting maid beside her O;
As soon as her handsome face they saw,
They cast the glamour o'er her O.

Below *Cassillis drawn by James Clark.* Right *Monkwood*

partner James K Hunter, is demonstrably in the same idiom, its uncompromising grey harl bringing out the full effect of Hunter's Arts & Crafts inspired details.

Cassillis House, 14th century onwards
The original tower was remodelled in the 17th century when a new stair tower was added to give an L-plan arrangement,while the **wall-walk** was enclosed at the same time, additions simply being added to the existing corbel table. In 1673 and 1674 Sir William Bruce advised the Earl of Cassillis on work to be done under John Hamilton, and it is tempting to link the alterations to this advice. An elegant Gothic addition of *c.*1830 is an early example of the Scottish baronial revival: it has a distinct family relationship with Belleisle and, in its curious turrets, more than a passing nod in the direction of Burn. **Monkwood**, which seems to be of *c.*1720, is a happily proportioned little mansion of much charm: its small windows faintly echoing the Italian exemplars of its Palladian roots. **Nether Auchendrane** was built piecemeal during the 19th century in a crowstepping revivalist harled manner about an existing 17th-century core.

DALRYMPLE

Rather spreading village whose character is restricted to two short streets, one the Girvan/Edinburgh road running northward from the **bridge** of 1849 built at a cost of £456 3s 2d which spans the Doon, the other Dalrymple's road to Ayr. The first is **Main Street**, where **5-19** face **2-16** and **18-24**; all are attractive single-storey cream-washed cottages, often with splayed dormers, and the ensemble is the match of any in the county. **2-28 Garden Street** repeats the format. Leases from 1799 are recorded. The Church is an undemanding Gothic box of 1849, the architect David Cousin of Edinburgh. The **War Memorial** in **Barbieston Road**, 1922, is an elegant octagonal cross designed by James Miller and executed by William Vickers.

Above *Nether Auchendrane drawn by James Clark.* Left *Skeldon House.* Below *Dalrymple Village*

Skeldon House *c.*1780

Typically elegant house of its period with advanced and pedimented centre bays to both front and rear, with fine neo-Georgian additions of 1908 by James Miller. The setting is magnificent, in a well-wooded park dropping down to the Doon. **Castle Cottage**, which incorporates the remains of Skeldon Castle, may also be by Miller. **Hollybush**, originally Over Skeldon, is a rather gawky Elizabethan house of 1853, by Robert Paton, while **Balgreen** is a fine example of a model farm, a square red stone steading by Robert Ingram.

PATNA

Patna fails to live up to its exotic name: a few houses with an 1839 **Parish Church** and hall, 1901 **United Free Church** by J B Wilson straggling up the hill, gap-toothed and

Robert Lindsay was County Architect of Ayrshire from 1940 to 1963. During the Second World War, in co-operation with W A Fairhurst, he developed a rapid-build housing system based on a reinforced concrete frame. The first experimental houses were built in Dalrymple in early 1945, and over 700 built throughout Ayrshire by 1954. From the Lindsay House was developed the Whitson Fairhurst house which was used throughout Scotland, over 3000 remaining in use from Inverness to Wigtown.

Waterside Ironworks: Above *chimneys and brick kiln.* Right *Engine House*

swamped by Ayr County Council, 1950s and 1960s houses to accommodate entire mining communities from isolated hillside spots such as Lethamhill and Benquhat.

Waterside

Fascinating industrial community, for more archaeological and socio-historical than architectural interest. An ironworks was established here in 1847, and grew rapidly, employing over 2000 men at its height before peaking and declining in the early 20th century, when the site turned with equal success to brick manufacture, as the surviving brick-built rows bear testimony. **Ardoon**, *c.*1850, is the manager's house, buried amid rhododendrons, and with a view across the valley. Works buildings are generally functional, the two chimneys are a potent landmark for the valley, and the heavily-quoined, Italianate, **Engine House** (see p.C3), 1847, extended 1865, has real quality.

The Waterside ironworks was one of the biggest in Ayrshire, founded in 1847, extended in 1866 and subsequently modernised. Coal and iron were plentiful in the hills of the Doon Valley, and an extensive system of rail lines developed to bring the raw materials to the ironworks. The lines can still be traced high in the hills, as can remains of the unsanitary isolated villages which sprang up along the lines – their sole communication with the outside world. With the decline in the coal and iron mines of the valley, the owners, Bairds & Dalmellington Ltd, successors to the Dalmellington Iron Company, switched to brick production, building two new kilns for the purpose. Brick manufacture was phased out by the National Coal Board, and the works finished their active life as a storage and sorting depot for open-cast coal. Now the Dalmellington & District Conservation Trust is developing it as an interpretative centre for the industrial heritage of Ayrshire.

DALMELLINGTON

Lord Cockburn visited Dalmellington in 1844: *When the time shall come (as come it will) when English cottages or English neatness shall be introduced into Scotland, what a village Dalmellington may be. A few old trees, irregular ground, tumbling burns, a spire, and a mill – what more is wanted?* Three years later, Cockburn grieved for progress: *It has the appearance, and the reputation of being a singularly virtuous and happy village; and I am told is perhaps the last place in Ayrshire where, with a good deal of old primitive manufacture, rural simplicity and contentment still linger. But it is now to taste of manufactures in an improved state. The devil has disclosed his iron, and speculation has begun to work it. There seemed to be about a dozen of pits sinking within half a mile of the village, and before another year is out those now solitary and peaceful hills will be blazing with furnaces, and blighted by the presence and the vices of a new population of black scoundrels. They were already lying snoring and, I presume, drunk, on many indignant knolls.* Ironworks and coal mines have come and gone. The little town remains depressed and neglected, and the peaceful and solitary hills are being carted away in the search for open-cast coal.

Kirk of the Covenant, 1846, Patrick Wilson Handsome neo-Norman church with a lofty tower, standing in a raised situation above the village. The harled **Church Hall** is the 1766 old church built by James Armour, with a little gableted porch. The old **Cross Keys Inn**, **15 High Street**, is a neglected block with a projecting gabled forewing, possibly of 17th-century origin. **30-32** is an attractive cherry-cocked pair in Straiton granite. **St Barbara's RC Church**, 1959-61, impressively massed concrete shell octagon copper-roofed and sitting under the medieval motte. The **Library**, 1982, Roy Maitland of Cumnock & Doon Valley District Council, is competent vernacular. Pleasant cottages in **Cathcartston**: **8**, with a date stone of 1744, has been converted into an **Interpretation Centre** by Cumnock & Doon Valley District Council.
Cathcartston open to public

Hollybank House, 32 Main Street, *c.*1860 Dalmellington's surgery, and its grandest house, standing slightly back from the narrow and congested street behind gates and railings. It has rusticated raised quoins, grey margins against the white painted stone, and a handsome, if over-large, porch supported on two pairs of square columns. Opposite is the much-abused **Lamloch Church**, 1851, David Millar, supported to left and right by its manse, given distinction by raised window mouldings and Peddie & Kinnear's classically plain **Royal Bank of Scotland**, 27 Main Street.
Dalmellington Cross has a rugged character; the best buildings, all more-or-less altered, are the fore-gabled **Dalmellington Inn**, 6 High Street, and the sturdy **7-9** Main Street, with its block cornice and residual wallhead chimney.

New Street, which winds between Cathcartston and High Street, is known locally, for mist-shrouded reasons, as the Crystal Palace. In High Street, one house, built in 1861, is known as Dr Jamieson's House, his bust acting as a roof finial. When fou, Jamieson was often to be found in the graveyard behind talking to long-buried parents.

Below *Kirk of the Covenant.* Middle *Library.* Bottom *Cathcartston*

Robert Hettrick, 1769-1849, the blacksmith poet, is recalled by a plaque in High Main Street:
The lovely Doon may cease to roll;
The northern blast may skreigh and howl:
But I'll ne'er cease, good honest soul,
To think on thee.

At the former Minnivey Colliery, the Ayrshire Railway Preservation Trust have been developing what is now known as the Scottish Industrial Railway Centre, an atmospheric and sooty reminder of past times in the valley. The flat-roofed brick 1950s pit-head baths and canteen are used for employment training purposes.

Craigengillan

Craigengillan, *c*.1780
John McAdam of Craigengillan, who had made a fortune as a drover, enlarged or built the house in an unadventurous Georgian manner. About 1820 a manorial entrance front was run across the house, with tall chimneys and an equally tall square tower, all minimally Scotticised, with the occasional crowstep, and, on the garden front, an odd thin round tower. The house is almost subservient to the impressive Georgian stables, with a huge domed tower above the entrance arch. At the Dalmellington end of the long drive is a Gothick **lodge** of *c*.1820.

The threat to Loch Doon Castle from a hydro-electric scheme of 1900, propounded by the Marquess of Ailsa, moved the Carsphairn poet Arthur Clark Kennedy to pen his verses, Loch Doon Castle:

> *Thy ruined wa's, thy roofless*
> *ha's*
> *Still rise above the ride,*
> *Thy shadow still ridge-mirrored*
> *fa's*
> *Upon its bosom as it cra's*
> *Lip-lapping at thy side.*

Loch Doon Castle, 13th century
Splendid, eleven-sided curtain-walled castle designed to enfold its original island site. The stonework is lavish – beautiful large blocks of well-cut ashlar attesting to the quality of the place. Note also entrance gateway with portcullis chase. Rebuilt on its current site to let the level of Loch Doon rise for hydro-electricity generation.

Loch Doon Castle drawn by James Clark

During the First World War, Dalmellington and Loch Doon were the centre of a School of Aerial Gunnery. Scant remnants of this ultimately expensive and abortive scheme can still be found.

MAYBOLE
Historic capital of Carrick, and a Burgh of Barony since 1516. Maybole Castle is the sole obvious survivor of a town whose pre-19th-century character was formed by the town houses of the landed families of the province. The little town is well situated to act as a focus for the impenetrable hills, and grew as a market centre on the main road skirting Carrick.

Close

Improving 19th-century communications allowed the Carrick lairds to exchange their old-fashioned Maybole houses for spacious fashionable residences in the Wellington Square neighbourhood of Ayr where they could rub shoulders with the rest of the Ayrshire gentry. At the same time, Maybole began to develop an industrial face based on the improvements in agriculture. Boots and shoes used a by-product of the dairy trade, while Alexander Jack established a nationally important manufactory of agricultural machinery. The town today is increasingly dependent on Ayr for employment and services: its own infrastructure has declined, while the long-awaited by-pass will remove the traffic which currently cleaves the little town. The Cassillis Street/High Street/Whitehall axis is the ancient core of the town. The pattern of feus and back lanes has been obscured by subsequent development, though something of the pattern can be seen behind 38-50 High Street. Although the town is dominated by a handsome tower house of national importance, it is predominantly 19th century, though older houses lie unsuspected behind Victorian and late Georgian refacings.

Maybole Castle, *c.*1620 onwards
Built, probably for John Kennedy 6th Earl, as the town house of the Earls of Cassillis, hereditary bailiffs of Carrick. Soaring four-storey L-plan tower, with the stair in the southern wing. Partly a pleasing light grey harl, melding well with the ashlar dressings and the rubbly crowstepped extensions added in the early 19th century to make it suitable for

Maybole

Shoe manufacture on an industrial scale began in Maybole in 1838, and grew substantially in the later 19th century taking up labour left idle by the decline in home weaving. By 1890, there were ten factories employing 1500 hands and producing 1m pairs of boots annually; but recession set in. One proprietor, Thomas Gray of the Lorne factory, threw himself from a train into the Clyde. John Lees & Co weathered the storm, diversified and traded until 1962 when a fire destroyed their premises. The last tannery supplying shoe uppers to manufacturers elsewhere closed in 1969.

John Keats paused at Maybole in July 1818, on his journey to Burns' Cottage. He was inspired by the Carrick countryside: *I'll not run over the ground we have passed; that would be nearly as bad as telling a dream – unless, perhaps, I do it in the manner of the Laputan printing press: that is, I put down mountains, rivers, lakes, dells, glens, rocks, with beautiful, enchanting, fine, delightful, enchanting, grand, sublime – a few blisters, &c – and now you have our journey thus far.*

In 1913, the young architect **Thomas Jack** emigrated to Canada. Member of the agricultural implement family, Jack had the previous year designed the McCandlish Hall in Straiton – an unexpectedly successful amalgam of vernacular and elements reminiscent of Mackintosh. It, and he, deserve to be better known.

Top & below *Maybole Castle.* Bottom *Post Office*

A **plaque** in John Knox Street records the three-day debate in 1562 between John Knox and the Abbot of Crossraguel on the doctrine of the Mass.

a factor's house and office for the Marquess of Ailsa's estate: a role it still fulfils. A veritable pattern-book of ornament, with angle turrets, dormers with semicircular pediments flanking the wallhead stack to the north-east, and similarly detailed dormers on the south-west. The southern stair wing has a corbelled top storey with a unique and attractive oriel illuminating what appears to have been designed as a prospect room. The Maybole oriel was captured by R W Billings in his *Baronial and Ecclesiastical Architecture of Scotland* and became one of the most frequently repeated motifs in the mid 19th century baronial spasm. Alongside, the Common Services Agency have built a new **Health Centre**, 1990, in a respectful, if rather twee, neo-vernacular.

High Street
High Street runs south-west from the Castle. The **Library**, 1906, by J K Hunter in Scottish Renaissance, harmonises with the castle, and the 1912 **post office** also genuflects in that direction. **82** is a simple house of *c*.1800, its gable to the street; **88-90**, *c*.1820, with thin pilasters. The **Bank of Scotland**, *c*.1810, was altered for bank use in 1875, and infill at **64** is by Kyle and Carrick District Council, with a brick-pilastered tall ground floor. The adjoining housing at **56-62**, also Kyle and Carrick District Council, is more conventional neo-vernacular.

Town Hall, 1887, Robert S Ingram
Ingram's hard-edged red stone Scots baronial Town Hall incorporates the 17th-century rectangular house, with a three-stage tower, that had been the town house of the lairds of Blairquhan. There are some lovely details to the original work. Ingram's work, with its heavy

consoled balcony, is harder, bookish. **Whitehall** is one of Maybole's best surviving groups of 19th-century buildings: **1-9**, harled with rusticated quoins and some good fanlights, facing **4-8**, more formal, ashlar, stepping down the hill, these all of *c*.1820-40, and contrasted with the generously eavesed palazzo **Royal Bank of Scotland**, 1857, by Peddie & Kinnear. The former **Police Station**, 1868, John Murdoch, is plain with an odd dab of public authority classical: the adjoining **14-16**, 1882, are improved tenements for workmen erected by the Marchioness of Ailsa, while **31** is a comfortable, unassuming 18th-century house. **4-6 Kirkoswald Road** is a pair of faintly Gothic villas, one with a grotesque finial, and **Carrick Academy**, 1925-7, J St Clair Williamson, inter-war classical.

West Parish Church, 1836-40, George Meikle Kemp
5-9 Coral Glen, a picturesque row of dormered cottages, heavily bookended, lead to the West Church. The standard T-plan preaching box, decorated by Kemp in his intense revival manner: a birdcage bellcote is corbelled out from one gable. The contemporary **Manse** alongside is probably also by Kemp. Deeper down the Coral Glen is spindly Gothic St Cuthbert's, 1876-79, redeemed by a soaring octagonal tower and spire: church, school and presbytery, with trefoil-headed windows, forming a ghetto clearly outside the town when it was built. **96 Ladywell Road**, is crisply harled, while the pink-harled **Gluepot Inn**, **Welltrees Street** is a sturdy house of *c*.1800. The **Kildoon Monument**, 1853 is an obelisk to Sir Charles Fergusson of Kilkerran, more notable as landmark than as architecture.

Top *Town Hall.* Above *Royal Bank of Scotland.* Below *Collegiate Church doorway*

Collegiate Church, 1371
Rectangular, three-bay ruin of coursed rubble with splendid ashlar dressings and details. The south door has dog-tooth, a hood-mould and the Kennedy crest above. The old Churchyard, on the site of St Cuthbert's Church, has some interesting stones. Worthy cottages at **4-10 Kirkland Street**. These monuments are mixed with decaying shoe factories and pre-war housing schemes, often cheerily detailed with residual hood-moulds and throughout the tiniest whiff of baronial, and with J K Hunter's **Cairn School**, *c*.1898, his Cotswold-domestic style applied to a broadly symmetrical plan, and executed in the local purple stone.

*Kilhenzie Castle drawn by
James Clark*

Kilhenzie Castle, a simple 16th-century
house was restored about 1850-5 with
sympathetic baronial additions for a tenant
farmer on the Kilkerran estate.

Cassillis Road
The Ayr road runs northwards from the Castle,
containing the best of the Victorian housing,
especially **23-27**, of *c.*1840, and **14-48**, of *c.*1825,
all in a warm pink stone. Regency **16-18** has a
Venetian window and attractive cast-iron
balconies and fanlights. **26** has a pillared
doorway and **44-48**, *c.*1900, is attractive in grey
stone. The **Parish Church**, 1808, by Robert
MacLachlan, has a square plan with a central
south tower of many odd little stages and an
obelisk spire, ever so slightly Aztec in feel. The
body of the church has tall lancets and
plentiful false gun loops. International Cases
occupy the faintly ecclesiastical works of
Alexander Jack: designed by Jack himself in
1852. **St John's Cottage**, *c.*1810, is a
picturesque cottage symmetrically planned
about its garden front. Delicate cast-iron
balusters and plasterwork within.

Castle Street
Castle Street has a number of worthy houses of
the 19th century and a nicely chamfered corner
at **17**: at its farther end **33** is noticeably earlier,
its steeply pitching roof suggesting that it was
once thatched. Greenside repeats the pattern:
unremarkable houses of *c.*1835, supporting one
another in an excellent group around the Town
Green: **10** has been well restored, while the

Parish Church

Greenside Inn, *c.*1900, is minimally half-timbered in the cheerful Arts & Crafts style often associated with improved public houses. The **Green** itself was relaid by Morris & Hunter in 1894. The former **Poorhouse**, 1863, John Bowman, in **Ladyland Road** is a substantial and competent building in the local pink stone. **Barns House**, **16 Barns Terrace**, is a fine villa, built in 1839, in coursed tooled rubble, with little scrolly skewputs.

Maybole Station, 1880
The railway arrived in 1859: the plain red rubble **Station** buildings date from 1880. A late Victorian development of elegant villas in spacious grounds grew up beyond the railway. Suburbia has driven out arcadia, but **Ashgrove**, 1888, Robert A Bryden, conveys something of the character: an asymmetrical two-storey house in a rather messy over-busy sub-Jacobean style. **Fairknowe**, **3 Cargill Road**, 1890, is similar but less ornate, while **Kincraig**, *c.*1875, is baronial with its little conical tower.

Fisherton
A scattered community lying above the **Heads of Ayr**. The **Church**, 1838, was substantially reconstructed by J & H V Eaglesham in 1912. It is plain and bellcoted: charming rather than especially rewarding architecturally.
Perryston, 1939, Ninian Johnston, is a successful essay in a rambling English manorial style. On the far side of **Carrick Hill** are two honest, unassuming small mansion houses: **Sauchrie**, *c.*1775, and **Otterden**, of perhaps a few years later. Both fit easily into the standard pattern of Georgian houses, and possess a distinct family likeness. The ruin of **Dunduff Castle**, a 15th-century L-plan tower, with a rectangular projection in the re-entrant, finishes abruptly just above the first floor, supporting a theory that this house, nearly finished in 1696, was abandoned before completion.

DUNURE
Small fishing village, of relatively recent date, tucked into the cliffside. Everything seems subservient to the spectacular ruins of its castle, balancing precariously on the sea's edge. The harbour was improved in 1811, its beacon tower now grotesquely weathered, and the ranges of fishermen's cottages must date from about the same period. Building leases were advertised in 1819: *as a most advantageous*

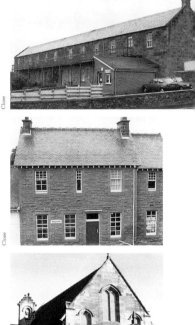

Top *Former Poorhouse.* Middle *Maybole Station.* Above *Fisherton Church*

The Electric Brae, as Croy Brae is better known, offers the optical illusion, for which countless theories have been forwarded, that the road appears to be rising, when in fact it is falling, making it seem possible that you are freewheeling uphill.

Below *Dunure Mill*. Right *Station Road*

fishing station and a place where various trades may be carried on, and a considerable intercourse by shipping may be established, it is believed to possess many recommendations. **Dunure House**, *c*.1800, is a plain bow-fronted house, sensibly dour and hunched against the prevailing winds. There are two light-hearted houses in **Station Road**: **28** and **34**: flat roofed with plentiful use of maritime references; the public rooms on the upper floor; there must be something in the air which encourages such seaside whimsy. **Dunure Mill**, *c*.1780, is striking, crisply detailed in a manner very similar to Robert Adam's Culzean Home Farm, using rubble stone rather than ashlar. If not by Adam, it must be laid at the door of someone who worked closely with him for the Culzean estate, whose lands these were. **Goatsgreen**, *c*.1963, Duncan MacFarlane for himself, is a broad U of acutely angled monopitched units nuzzling up to one another at odd angles based on a traditional cottage, *newly built* in 1876.

The roasting of the Commendator of Crossraguel Abbey, Allan Stewart, in the oven of the black vault of Dunure Castle, was part of the continuing feud between the Kennedys of Bargany and Cassillis. Bargany was a Reformer, and through his influence Stewart had obtained the Commendatorship: Cassillis was not. The latter's motive, however, was the acquisition of the Abbey and its lands rather than any deep seated objection to reform. So that *rost suld not burne, but that it might rost in soppe, they spared not flambing with oyle.* (Abercrummie) As is often the case, torture proved effective, and Stewart made over the Abbey Lands to Kennedy of Cassillis.

Dunure Castle drawn by Francis Grose

Dunure Castle

Dramatically ruined and seeming to grow from the rock itself – and equally rugged – Dunure consists of a fragment of an early tower-house, notable for its irregular plan, designed to fit its rock platform, on a tall outcrop rearing above the shore. This tower was added to, probably in the 15th century and again, further to the landward side, in the late 16th century. In

c.1610 Dunure was described as the Earl of Cassillis's residence but by 1696 was *wholly ruined*. So it is to this day, and public access to the structure is actively discouraged. There is an excellent, well-preserved circular **doocot** alongside, of perhaps early 17th century date.

Dunure Castle doocot

Culzean Castle, 1777, Robert Adam (see p.C6) A consummate example of Adam's skill at internal and external design, his ability to adapt his designs to the setting, and to subjugate settings to his designs. One of the greatest glories of Scottish architecture and, as the centrepiece of the National Trust for Scotland's showpiece country park, a honeypot for tourists.

Culzean Castle

Culzean has a truly magnificent situation, built on the edge of a bluff, overlooking the sea which washes the foot of the precipitous basalt cliffs 150 ft below. It is a thoroughly castellated design, emphasising elements such as the **drum tower**, **gun loops**, **battlements**, in a manner which is light-hearted, and not particularly Scottish in character. Essential items such as doors and windows adopt a rather more straightforwardly classical mien. On the landward side are beautiful **terraced gardens**, laid out over the old fortifications and, at the approach to the glen, Adam's **turreted forecourt** and great **gateway** entrance, a romantic design of 1790.

While the outside of the house is dramatic and a good skyline composition, the interior is a masterpiece both in its planning and disposition of rooms and levels and in its treatment and decorative handling. The various **drawing rooms**, **Dining room**, **Library** and **ante-rooms** are good-quality Adam, but, unique and of superb standard, are his **circular saloon** and

At Culzean, Adam had an opportunity to indulge his leanings towards romanticism, create architectural 'movement' and, as well, some of his most beautiful and spectacular interiors. In 1776 he was commissioned by the 10th Earl of Cassillis, who had recently succeeded to the title, to enlarge and modernise the existing castle, but one of many such houses in Scotland. Robert worked here till after 1790, gradually turning the old square castle into a fine stately home, romantic medieval outside, classical Adam within.

M

Oval staircase

The Adam castle style, comprising some of the finest buildings from the brothers, is well represented in Ayrshire – experimental Caldwell, romantic Culzean and Fullarton, to perfection of Dalquharran and the Auchincruive Tea-house. It was rooted in the romantic picturesque – no rugged landscape being complete with one, and in economy – rubble being cheaper than dressed ashlar. It is the most geometric of Adam's architecture, and according to Alistair Rowan *a highly personal idiom more exclusively the creation of the two brothers than even their refined neoclassicism had been.*

oval staircase well. The shape of the saloon was not dictated by that of the round tower. Adam himself designed and built the great drum tower in 1785 on the north, seaward, side as a classic instance of movement in architecture and then took advantage of its form to make his unusual room. It is a complete circle: its six tall windows give a breathtaking view of unlimited sea and sky with a backcloth of the Arran hills. Since the windows are placed at regular intervals in one half of the circle, the north-facing room is lit by both morning and evening sunshine. In the other semicircle are three entrance doorways, a white marble fireplace and plain niches. Both ceiling and carpet design are Robert's, not identical but a part of one theme. The ceiling is patterned in concentric circles, one of his best, and very typical, ornamented with vases, rams' heads, sphinxes, arabesques, paterae and swags. The staircase is structurally and functionally ideal, linking as it does the older house with the new. Aesthetically it is perfect; the form is oval. Three orders are used, but not in the traditional manner of selection. Here the usual Doric is on the ground floor as rectangular pilasters, but Corinthian columns surround the first-floor landing and Ionic the top. The whole scheme is in white, with restrained gildings of enrichments and pale shades for the oval lantern and delicately stuccoed walls. The whole is Italian in conception, of the later Renaissance villa theme, but the cantilevered stairs and staircase balustrade curving round the well and landings are typical Adam, with gilded metal and polished mahogany handrail.

Culzean Castle in 19th century

The other rooms are no less fine: the **Dining Room** has a fine Corinthian screen, while the **Library**, **Long Drawing Room** and **Green Room** have typically Adamesque ceilings with roundels painted by Antonio Zucchi. A huge new west wing was added, in a congruent style though of slightly ill-matched stone, by Wardrop & Reid in 1875-8. Restoration work for the National Trust for Scotland was begun by Robert Hurd in 1946, continued by Schomberg Scott in the 1950s: indenting of new stonework was carried out through the 1980s by Geoffrey Jarvis. *Culzean Castle Visitor Centre and Country Park open to the public: guidebooks available*

Culzean Visitor Centre, 1777, Robert Adam
The estate buildings are equally striking. Greatest of all is Adam's **Home Farm**, converted to the Visitor Centre in 1973 by the Boys Jarvis Partnership, four similar ranges ordered about a square, and linked by arched pends, the whole finished in crisp ashlar, and crowstepped: and the style is repeated in other buildings such as the **Powder House** and the

Much of the furniture for the saloon at Culzean was designed by Adam. An example of his attention to detail is seen in the two semicircular side tables whose inlaid satinwood tops have their straight sides subtly fitted to the curve of the wall.

Below *Culzean Visitor Centre.* Middle above *Swan Pond Cottage.* Middle below *Camellia House.* Bottom *Cat Gates*

Dolphin Cottage with its adjacent **Bath House** and **Round House. Swan Pond Cottage**, *c.*1820, Robert Lugar, is an immensely likeable churchy-Gothick cottage orné. The **gazebo**, of *c.*1790, is a battlemented look-out, on the far north point of the headland, and forms an important element in the castle group. The **Camellia House**, 1818, James Donaldson, is a delightful Gothic confection with pinnacles and crenellations. Almost lost is the 1820s **Pagoda** in the woods near the swan pond, while east of here are the **cat gates** a pair of arched and pilastered piers topped with Coade stone leopards of 1802. The Gothick **Orangery** of 1792 was restored in 1987 by Geoffrey Jarvis. **Hoolity Ha'**, of *c.*1800, develops the Gothick theme further in a crowding display of ogee-headed windows.

Thomaston Castle

Turnberry Castle is believed to have been the birthplace of Robert Bruce, in 1274. According to legend, his mother Marjorie, a widowed Countess of Carrick, kidnapped a Bruce of Annandale before marrying him in 1271. The Bruces were Normans, arriving in England with William the Conqueror. Encouraged by David I, they came north and were granted extensive lands in Annandale, before acquiring Carrick in the manner described above. Earl of Carrick is still a title of the eldest son of the monarch.

Turnberry Lighthouse

Thomaston Castle, *c*.1500
Culzean Kennels is an assured Gothick farmhouse of 1820: it has great presence. It also has in the farmyard the substantial shell of Thomaston Castle, a large L-plan castle probably dating from *c*.1500 and built for the Corry of Kelwood family. There is a square staircase tower in the inner angle of the L which rises to a corbelled-out parapet at the same height as the rest of the structure. The pend through the foot of the L suggests that entrance was first gained to an enclosed courtyard. Thomaston spreads substantially but to great artistic effect; it is simple and stunning. *It is unfortunate that such a good specimen of our domestic style of the 16th century should have been allowed to fall into the neglected and semi-ruinous state in which it now is:* many would still echo these words of MacGibbon & Ross of a century ago.

Maidens

A sprawling shapeless village of bungalows and caravans, and a sore disappointment. **Port Murray** (*below*), 1960-3, Peter Womersley, is a stunning, uncompromising, long low glass and cedarwood house, poised like a seagull on rocks.

TURNBERRY

Turnberry also has something of the same sprawling nature that afflicts Maidens, but the sprawl is broader, the houses bigger, and the architecture, usually, slightly better. There has been settlement here for many centuries, though little of any architectural meaning remains of Turnberry Castle. The adjacent **Lighthouse** was built in 1873, the **Royal Flying Corps Memorial** of 1923 is an impressive and moving design by Hugh Wallace. **Turnberry Lodge** is a neat and unusual house in a Victorian Gothic style, of *c*.1840, clearly and consciously based on the Georgian Gothic style employed widely for estate buildings at Culzean such as Hoolity Ha'. This though is all but hors-d'oeuvre for the main course: James Miller's huge **Turnberry**

Hotel complex, begun in 1904 for the Glasgow
& South-Western Railway. The style is a
combination of long neo-Georgian symmetrical
façades and plush sub-Queen Anne details.
Nothing here to frighten the horses or the
customers. The style is continued through the
numberless service buildings which spread out
northwards from the hotel: Miller was involved
in an ongoing process of additions and
alterations until the mid-1920s. De-nationalised
in 1983, the new owners have employed
Cunningham Glass Partnership to adapt it to
the higher expectations of the modern hotel-
visitor. The effect has been minimal externally.

Turnberry Hotel

KIRKOSWALD
Compact roadside village, which still retains a
few traditional cottages, though it suffers from
the A77 which hammers through, and
effectively divorces one side from the other. At
the north end, and almost physically detached
from the village, is the housing scheme, begun
by Ingram & Brown in the 1920s, and
developed slowly thereafter by Ayr County
Council. The **Richmond Hall**, 1925, James
Miller, cannot be ignored: it is a powerful
image, with a faintly nautical feel, and
demonstrates masterly ability to tailor his skill
to the expectations of his clients. The client
here was J R Richmond, for whom Miller had
earlier designed **Blanefield** in 1913, a sleek
dignified English baronial house.

Below & middle *Kirkoswald
Parish Church*

Kirkoswald Parish Church, 1777,
Robert Adam
Rusticated quoins and fine Palladian details,
though the effect has been compromised by the
removal of the harling. It is contemporary with
Culzean, and its detailing is in a different
league to Ayrshire churches of the same date:
Rowan's suggestion that Adam, touring with

Souter Johnnie's Cottage

Burns spent the summer of 1775 in Kirkoswald, receiving mathematical tuition from Hugh Rodger. He lodged with his mother's brother, Samuel Brown, at Ballochneil, where the germ of *Tam o' Shanter* took root, for among his companions were Douglas Graham, 1738-1811, the tenant of Shanter, and owner of a boat *Tam o' Shanter*, allegedly used for free trade purposes, and John Davidson, 1728-1806, the village shoemaker, Souter Johnnie. In 1775 Davidson lived at Glenfoot, close to Shanter, but built this cottage in the village in 1785. It was subdivided after his death, but taken over and restored by a local committee in 1920. With its flag floor, box beds and simple cottage garden, it exudes an authentic atmosphere.

Crossraguel Abbey gate tower, drawn by James A Morris

Lord Cassillis, his client at Culzean and a major heritor here, came across the church during construction and recommended some changes, has a plausible ring to it. **Glebe House**, 1771, an adjoining studious house with a low parapet and pilastered doorway, was the manse. **Souter Johnnie's Cottage**, dated 1786, is the best known of the single-storey cottages in the village: as a Burns shrine it is sacrosanct and has kept its thatch; the adjoining and probably contemporary **East Cairnhill** has been slated.

Souter Johnnie's Cottage open to the public (National Trust for Scotland): booklet available

Crossraguel Abbey, 1244 onwards
Crossraguel Abbey was founded by Duncan, Earl of Carrick, in the 13th century. At first only an oratory was established but some time after 1244 building of the Cluniac monastery was begun. Duncan's son, Nigel, gave generously to the foundation and interest was maintained when Robert Bruce acquired the Carrick Earldom through marriage. Even greater prominence came to Crossraguel when the son of this marriage became Robert I. In 1404 Robert III signed the great Crossraguel charter which granted and confirmed to the Abbot the lands for ever in free regality with jurisdiction over crimes of murder, rape and robbery. The monks had their own mills, brewhouses and extensive fishing rights in the Girvan. The Abbey did not remain in isolated prosperity during the Reformation though it enjoyed the protection of the Earls of Cassillis and the monks continued to occupy the monastery until 1592, probably later than any other Scottish abbey. The Abbey buildings still comprise, besides the remains of the church and cloisters with the usual ecclesiastical buildings surrounding them, an **outer court** to the south-west with a picturesque **gatehouse**, of about 1530, **doocot** and other domestic structures. There was also an **eastern courtyard** containing the **Abbot's hall**, an adjoining **tower** and **infirmary**. The foundations of the church of 1244 which contained a north and south transept can be clearly seen in the western part: it was, however, extensively rebuilt in the 15th century with a simple **aisleless nave** and a three-sided **apse**. The **sacristy** and **chapter-house** were rebuilt at the same time, each is richly decorated and rib-vaulted. A wheel stair

Right *Crossraguel Abbey Chapter House, drawn by Billings.* Above *Crossraguel Abbey: Abbot's Tower*

led from the sacristy to the library and dormitory. On the south side of the cloister garth can be seen the **refectory**. The triangular east court was probably bounded on one side by the infirmary and on the other by the Abbot's hall of which only a range of ruined vaults remain. At the south-east angle stands the **Abbot's Tower**, which is a regulation secular tower house, with vaulted ground floor and great hall above, which appears to date from *c*.1500, though it appears to have been raised and remodelled *c*.1530. This tower, and the gatehouse, have gun loops which suggests that even ecclesiastics were not immune to the internecine strife for which Carrick was notorious. The extensive courtyard to the south-west contained domestic offices. *Crossraguel open to the public (Historic Scotland); booklet available*

Baltersan Castle is a precarious survival: the stonework of this L-plan Kennedy house of *c*.1584 being in an extremely fragile state. Still just visible is the unusual top-storey treatment, with its projecting window, which was perhaps partly inspirational for the similar but more highly developed oriel at Maybole Castle.

Baltersan Castle

175

Girvan

GIRVAN

A major commercial, fishing and tourism centre at the mouth of the Water of Girvan, and now the largest town in Carrick, having exceeded Maybole during the 19th century. A place of some antiquity, with one of the few safe harbours on this coast, development has been slow and steady rather than spectacular. Industry has been predominantly sea-based, and the town still has **Alexander Noble & Sons' Boatbuilding Yard**, established here in 1946, with some weaving and a little coal exploitation in the years on either side of 1800. Improved communications, especially the coming of the railway in 1860, allowed substantial development as a place of resort from Ayr and the industrial centres of the West, though **The Avenue** reveals an earlier growth in the same market. Remoter from Glasgow than Largs or Ayr or Rothesay, Girvan has suffered more than most from the vogue for Mediterranean holidays being too far removed to benefit more than marginally from spells of fine weather. Yet the setting, beneath **Byne Hill** and **Dow Hill**, is magnificent. The original settlement was close to the tight bend in the river, in **Old Street** and **Bridge Street**, though there is but little evidence: The Avenue, running inland, was a false start, and the bulk of the 19th-century town is a long narrow grid pattern, the convergence of the two main north/south arteries softening the rigidity of effect on the flat plain. The built result is a *melange*, chiefly of late 19th century and 1930s character, with one or two buildings of real quality.

On **Byne Hill** stands a **Monument to Archibald Crauford** of Ardmillan (died 1878), an obelisk similar to Burn's at Blairquhan.

176

Auld Stumpy, 18th century
Girvan Cross marks the junction between old and new: here stood the McMaster Hall, 1911, W J Jennings of Canterbury, which incorporated within it Auld Stumpy, the 18th-century tower with pedimented clock faces and singular, crudely carved lunette openings, moved here in 1828, and the only survivor of a fire in 1939. In **Bridge Street**, **Gilmour's**, 1911, a garlanded red stone corner block, and **17-29**, 19th century, thickly harled but with decorative cast-iron guttering, while in **Old Street** the **Old Church Yard** has a notable triumphal arch entrance by James A Morris, and the **Ailsa Craig Hotel** combines a pair of three-bay houses of c.1810. **Strathaven**, formerly the Manse, is a simple harled crowstepped house of 1818. **Vicarton Street** is an attractive unified development of c.1840, hipped and gabled dormers eyeing one another warily across the street, while the **Station** was rebuilt after 1946.

North Parish Church, Montgomerie Street, 1883, William G Rowan
A dominating and powerful 13th-century Gothic design in red stone, well detailed and with a sureness of touch. Elsewhere in **Montgomerie Street** there are a number of goodish houses. **8** and **10** are both of c.1850, **8** thinly bedded ashlar with an elaborate hood-moulded doorway, **10** simpler in brick margined cream stucco; the white-painted **Queen's Hotel** is earlier. **Church Square** has a couple of rendered houses of c.1820, **St Andrew's Church**, 1870, Clarke & Bell, its pinnacled nave and polychrome broach spire a suitable counterpoint to the North Church spire, and the **Police Station**, 1923, A C Thomson, smart in a successful if heady mix of neo-Georgian and baronial with a wavy tiled string-course to give an odd modern touch. **Hamilton Street** leads back to the Cross, its two-storey vernacular mixed with a rash of banking palazzi: the **Halifax Building Society** occupies the most dramatic: a symmetrical pink and white stone French Renaissance bank of c.1870 in the manner of David Rhind with energetic and copious detailing; the **Woolwich Building Society** has a plainer structure, of c.1860, balustraded and pedimented; while the former **Britannia Building Society** is a standard wide-eaved Italianate bank with circular-headed windows of 1856, Peddie & Kinnear.

Auld Stumpy

The Avenue

The Avenue marks the first break with the old core of Girvan. Development began about 1820. The first houses are often merely single-storey cottages, but detached or semi-detached, with plain skews and painted margins, while **15-17** is 18th century, a two-storey plain small-windowed farmhouse sitting askew to the road. Later, perceptions change, and give rise to a number of large late Georgian/early Victorian houses, of which **18**, with sky-blue margins and heavy fluted porch columns, and **26** and **28**, both plain harled with consoled doorpieces, are the best. Elsewhere there are **34**, pink with another heavily fluted porch; **30**, with its castellated bay and cramped doorway; **22**, tall, dormered, black and white, but without much presence; and **20**, in a mechanical crowstepped baronial. On the north side of the street, **33**, 1875, of good-quality red ashlar, with a two-storey corbelled bay, deep eaves and simple bargeboarding; **35**, sub-Burnian, as 30, with balustrades and Glasgow Style glass. Behind these is **Girvan Bowling Club**, 1936, changing rooms and verandah to right, lounge to left: this traditional form given élan by the flat-roofed, semicircular two-storey treatment of the lounge.

Top *18 The Avenue*. Middle *30 The Avenue*. Above *Girvan Bowling Club*

Davidson Memorial Hospital, 1921, Watson Salmond & Gray

The most notable building in the street is an excellent low hospital, in grey Auchenheath stone, successfully neo-Georgian in detail, lying symmetrically about the central entrance, its name in a broken pediment, below three half-dormers, two of an unusual inverted shield form, the other wedge shaped. A number of well-built houses went up in this part of the

Davidson Memorial Hospital

town on either side of the Second World War, often, consciously or subconsciously, English, and Garden Suburban, in style: good examples are **4 North Park Avenue**, 1925, A McKimmie Gardiner, and **48 The Avenue**, 1954-5, James T Gray, with a very pinched doorway.

Knockcushan Street

Knockcushan Street has the harbour to one side, and the trappings of a seaside resort ahead, most prominent of which is the **Baths**, 1972, Cowie Torry & Partners; **19** Knockcushan Street was built *c*.1890, a long Italianate range in red sandstone, designed with a sure touch. **Knockcushan House** is an amalgam: stern mid 19th-century house aft, a touch of Gothic behind. The **Harbour Bar**, early 19th century, has good round slate-hung dormers. The **Harbour** itself was rebuilt in 1869-70 and extended again in 1881-3. This is the northern edge of the major mid-19th-century development of the town. The most characteristic examples of the architecture can be seen in **Harbour Street**, especially **5-11**, with dormers and cast-iron gutter mounts,which introduce the main features, and in **Ailsa Place** off **Ailsa Street West**, which is slightly earlier. In Ailsa Place, **2-4** are built directly on to rock outcrops. These streets contain pleasant ranges of simple one-storey dwellings, some of them attractively painted or stuccoed, of no particular intrinsic merit, but giving considerable sea-town character to the southern half of the burgh.

Top *Harbour Bar.* Above *Harbour Street*

South Parish Church, 1842

Plain, almost to the point of indifference, preaching box, its celtic-cross topped pediment front refaced in Fyfestone. The **War Memorial**, 1922, James A Morris, beached in the middle of **Stair Park** is a plain obelisk without the sculptural quality or feeling of Morris's memorials at Prestwick and Dailly, while adjacent to the park are **153** and **124-142 Henrietta Street**, 1921, Thomas Taylor (of Hutton & Taylor), Girvan's first council houses, *in the English style of street planning.* Behind the full panoply of the sea-town, in long converging streets such as Henrietta Street and **Wilson Street**, and cross streets and courts such as **Orange Arch**. Late 19th-century development of two-storey villas in **Louisa Drive**, especially the faintly Gothic **30-34**, and faintly Grecian **35-36**.

In 1944 the Town Council appointed James Wright RSW as adviser and collaborator with the architect for their post-war **housing schemes**: in 1938 a rather prosaic result of Wright's earlier collaboration had been the shape of the boating pond.

Church of the Sacred Hearts

Sacred Heart

Complex of Catholic buildings at the junction of **Henrietta Street** and **Ailsa Street**. The church (**Sacred Hearts of Jesus & Mary**) opens on to **Harbour Lane**: a plain Gothic structure of 1865 with a huge prow-like porch added in 1959 by Stevenson & Ferguson.

St Joseph's Convent, 1890, extended in 1908, huge, unelaborated red sandstone, owes something to James A Morris, while **Sacred Heart Primary School** is the former Doune School, 1874, John Murdoch, a Board building in Gothic polychrome. **Girvan Primary School** occupies the former High School, 1912, William Cowie, red sandstone boldly decorated with Renaissance details: urns, a cartouche.

Dalrymple Street

The main thoroughfare and commercial street of the town. Its architecture is messy, patchy and, with the constant rumble of traffic in the narrow street, impossible to appreciate. The

Right *Methodist Church.* Below *McKechnie Institute*

Methodist Church, 1902, Watson & Salmond, is a boldly detailed simply designed and freshly treated Arts & Crafts church of great merit where the most is made of a gable with a tracery window, low side aisle and a porch partly of timber, the **McKechnie Institute**, 1887-8, is by James McKissack. Scottish baronial handled with great verve, mixing crowsteps with a balustraded octagonal tower and Jacobethan window heads with great success: the style is Scotch Domestic with details more or less inclining to Renaissance. The **Ailsa Street** elevation is plainer with a pair of truly evil imps. The **Royal Bank of Scotland**, 1863, David MacGibbon, is *after no particular style of architecture, being what some term a mongrel.* The **Bank of Scotland**, 1879, has an elaborate Corinthian doorway, round-headed windows, six balustraded and aproned first-floor windows, all topped by a further balustrade and a Royal Arms.

The **King's Arms** is undeniably large if
somewhat cumbrous. It has a Tuscan porch to the
left, with a pilastered bay and florid cartouche
above. Elsewhere, 1930s motifs in the **Vogue
Cinema**, Stellmacs, and the **Co-operative**,
1935, Alexander Skirving, chunky horizontal
brick and stone with a ship's prow motif, all over
the most ghastly modern shopfront, Maybole-
style cast-iron work at **45**, the red ashlar and
tiled tower of **47-53**, 1896-7, and the **Clydesdale
Bank**, **36-42**, 1910, with minimally gabled bays
and low dentilled cornice in Monkreddan stone.

St John's Episcopal Church, 1859,
Alexander G Thomson
In Piedmont Road, and built of Penkill blue
whin (Thomson worked at Penkill) with
Dalmellington freestone dressings and unusual
tracery: a trefoil over a trefoil-headed window.
This building has never been truly finished,
with the transept and spire incomplete, the
transept arches infilled in concrete. The **tower**
was added in 1911 by James Chalmers. In
Wesley Road, the former **Girvan Academy**,
1948-55, William Cowie & Torry (though
design began in 1938) is a splendid example of
a 1930s genre: monumental and flat-roofed,
long horizontal bands of glazing to left and
right of the central doorway, itself recessed
between flanking round towers, all boarded up.

WATER OF GIRVAN

The valley of the Water of Girvan, a long
sinuous trail, confined by hills near Girvan,
more open further upstream, contains some of
the best land in Carrick, and in it are clustered
most of the major estates of the province.

Trochraigue, 1803 onwards
Essentially a standard Georgian format to
which has been added a rather weird baronial
wing of 1883, and substantial additions,
including a tall tower and porte cochère, by
J J Burnet between 1910 and 1923. It sits close
to the essentially industrial **Grant's Girvan
Distillery**, 1963-73, Cowan & Linn, engineers.

Killochan, 1586 onwards
*This work was begun the 1 of Marche 1586 be
Ihone Cathcart of Carltovn and Helene Wallace
his spouse. The name of the Lord is ane strang
tovr and the rytheovs in thair trovblis rinnis
into it and findith refuge.* The motto above the
door of this spectacular white gleaming L-plan

St John's Church contains a
very beautiful pierced and
carved screen. The screen's
former home was Brougham
Castle and the 1st Lord
Brougham is said to have
annexed it from an
ecclesiastical building: it is
16th-century Italian work and
was installed here in 1934.

Below *St John's Episcopal
Church*. Middle *Former Girvan
Academy*. Bottom *Trochraigue*

Above *Killochan drawn by James Clark*. Right *Killochan*

Killochan (Killunquhane in a document of 1505) – had been in the possession of the Cathcarts of Carleton since the 14th century. In 1324, Robert I granted John de Carleton a charter confirming an earlier one from his brother Edward Bruce, King of Ireland. In the drawn-out feud between the Cassillis and Bargany Kennedys, the Cathcarts supported their neighbours of Bargany, and John Cathcart commanded the rearguard at the affray in Pennyglen at which Bargany was killed.

War Memorial

tower underlines a need to mix increased domestic comfort with sensible precautions against one's neighbours and kinsmen. The result is one of the most memorable houses in the county, rising sheer from the holm. Of five storeys, with a square tower in the re-entrant, and terminating in conically roofed turrets; a second, round, tower, oddly sited at the external angle of the L, was possibly to provide a private retreat from the **Great Hall**, and, in the west gable, a little window, splayed internally and externally. Similar to one at Castle of Park, it appears to stem from balancing domestic needs (extra light for hall) with defensive precaution. Well-mannered Georgian service wing.

DAILLY
The architectural wealth of its landward areas does not extend to the village. This part of the Girvan Valley was a centre of coal exploitation, and deep mining continued in the neighbourhood until the late 1960s. Dailly was a focus for this, through the planned village, developed from the 1760s; in plan, two main streets running approximately south-west to north-east, and linked by cross lanes, and latterly through an extensive post-war scheme of Ayr County Council housing, which swamped the old village, and allowed remote unsanitary rows such as those at **Kilgrammie** and **Wallacetown** to be decanted. The **Church**, 1766, occupies a prominent site at the north end: a mainstream T-plan preaching box, deadened by dull grey harl, enlivened by the cheery tower, provincially detailed with rusticated quoins and urn finials. The church overlooks a formal square, with the **War Memorial**, 1922, James A Morris, most notable, and the **Greenhead Hotel** heading a pleasant row giving pep to the ensemble.

BARGANY, 1681

Before 1766 church and village had been at Old
Dailly, tucked into one corner of this huge
parish. The village is all but gone, the **Church**,
of the 17th century, long, narrow, belfried at
either end, largely unroofed, continues to
function as vaults for Bargany and Killochan.
Bargany, a house of many periods, is close by: it
is a marvellous house set in parkland, with the
Duke's Bridge, 1756, a graceful single-span
bridge with balustraded and solid parapets.
A U-plan about a forward courtyard, broadly
vernacular re-using 16th-century roll-moulded
windows. In 1747 the main entrance was moved
to the outside of the U, with a complete recasting
of the five-bayed north-east garden façade in
orderly symmetrical classical fashion. All this
was obscured by Victorian additions which
returned the entrance to the south-west front,
the former clarity muddled by a picturesque
confusion of architectural agglomeration, whose
history is imperfectly understood, but which
produces a house of great presence, and which
has been given further character by Patrick
Lorimer's restoration and additions of 1988-91.

Penkill Castle, 16th century

Rusticated in a wooded glen running down to
the Penwhapple Burn, Penkill was an
unexceptional house of the 16th century,
derelict and slowly crumbling away, until it
was startlingly brought to life in 1857 by
Spencer Boyd, whose family home it was.
Alexander George Thomson was the architect
for the restoration. The national importance of
Penkill, though, lies in the unique pre-
Raphaelite decoration. From the arrows
painted in the arrow-slits to the magnificent

Top *Bargany and Duke's
Bridge.* Above *Bargany*

The two Victorian poets, **Hew
Ainslie**, 1792-1878, the estate
baker's son, and **Hamilton
Paul,** 1773-1854, the coal
grieve's son, were born in the
same cottage on the Bargany
estate. Paul became a minister:
an extract from his *Petition of
the Auld Brig o' Doon* is given
on p.157. Ainslie became a
brewer and brewery constructor
in the United States:

> *I left ye, Jeanie, blooming fair,*
> *'Mang the bourocks o' Bargany;*
> *I've found ye on the banks o'*
> *Ayr,*
> *But sair ye're altered, Jeanie.*

Boyd, and his sister Alice, were
friends of William Bell Scott,
and through Scott, knew most
of the leading figures in the
pre-Raphaelite Brotherhood.
Gabriel and Christina Rossetti
were frequent visitors, each
finding the qualities of Penkill
amenable to their artistic
temperament: giving, for
instance, a new impetus to
Gabriel's poetry.

troubadour-style mural, the **King's Quair**, which winds up the stairwell, the decoration represents the pre-Raphaelites, led here by Scott and the Boyds, at their most imaginative and inventive. Much contemporary furniture, paintings, drawings, &c., complete a most remarkable and precious ensemble.

Dalquharran Castle, 1785, Robert Adam
Built for Adam's niece, and her husband Thomas Kennedy of Dunure, Dalquharran represents, perhaps even more than Culzean, the epitome of his *castle style*. There is a round bastion tower, as at Culzean, dominating the most spectacular elevation, and seen from miles about: it held the **Drawing Room** on the piano nobile, with a **Library** above. Behind was a top-lit spiral stair, no less elegant than that at Culzean. Wings in

Above *King's Quair, Penkill Castle*. Right *Dalquharran Castle*

Archibald Geikie, the geologist, was a friend of T F Kennedy of Dunure, who lived at Dalquharran, *built in a massive but rather tasteless style*. In *Scottish Reminiscences*, Geikie notes Kennedy's penchant for roast Ailsa Craig gannet (solan goose): *They had to bury the bird for some time in the garden, and when it came to be cooked, all the windows in the house had to be kept open, to let out the ancient and fish-like smell.*

Sketch design by Robert Adam c.1782 for new Dalquharran castle rising triumphantly above the old

matching style were added *c.*1881 by Wardrop & Reid. All is now ruinous and decaying, the interior decoration all but completely lost. Dalquharran is a dramatic vision in the Girvan Valley landscape, standing rigid-shouldered on its hilltop site above **Dailly**, a constant nagging reminder of what was. **Old Dalquharran Castle** lies between the mansion and the village, extensive ruins of a 15th-century rectangular tower, with a round tower and a long wing of

*c.1679: the stately castle of Dalquharran, the
building whereof is much improven by the
additions lately made thereto, which makes it
by far the best house of all that country.*

Kilkerran, *c.*1730
Built for Sir James Fergusson, Lord Kilkerran,
possibly by James Smith. The original north-
facing main front, in the recess on an H-plan,
reproduces many of the characteristics found in
Smith's houses: a symmetrically planned ashlar
block of three storeys, a central pediment with
round attic window and urns. An earlier
remodelling may have been incorporated: the old
tower of Barclanachan certainly has been, and
distends the rear façade. About 1760 the entrance
was relocated on the west front: subsequent
growth has been, fortunately, limited: elliptically
bowed wings by Gillespie Graham, 1818, and, in
the old north forecourt, a David Bryce **billiard
room** of 1854. The resultant house, in a fairytale
setting, woods behind, park before, has great
dignity and much charm. Estate buildings include
the Italianate **stables**, 1875, by Brown &
Wardrop, and some delightful Gillespie Graham
lodges in a rustic manner. **Drumburle**, *c.*1770, is
a superb Kennedy house, relying for its effect on a
great economy of detail, the curve of the doorcase
hood and of the staircase window giving character
to both of the otherwise plain elevations.

Above *Dalquharran, stairwell.*
Left *Kilkerran*

CROSSHILL
A planted village, without a strict layout.
Feuing began *c.*1808, a boom time for the hand-
loom weaving industry. Crosshill, hitherto
merely a couple of houses, became a centre of
cotton weaving, with many feus taken up by
emigrants from Ireland. The minister of
Kirkmichael in 1845 characterised the
inhabitants as *indolent, improvident and
passionately addicted to spirits and tobacco.*
Original cottages were single-storey, harled,

with a central door, domestic accommodation to one side and the weaving shop, still recognisable by its double or treble windows, to the other. Extensions, demolitions and alterations have taken their toll of the character: the best run is **15 to 91 Dalhowan Street**. Strikingly unique **War Memorial** to designs of Colonel Hugh R Wallace of Cloncaird, and crisp modern **School**, c.1968, by Robert B Rankin & Associates. **Kirkbride** is a straightforward pointy-gabled English manorial house of 1861, while **Longhill**, c.1810, is an improved farmhouse of quality, cream-painted harling and a well-judged centre bowed projection.

Top *Crosshill.* Above *Crosshill War Memorial*

KIRKMICHAEL

An old parish centre, revived c.1790 as a centre of the hand-weaving trade. **Patna Road** has the best cottages, which echo the style of Crosshill: single-storey, centre doors, the loom shop windows often distinguishable. The **Church** is tucked away, and is approached through a lich-gate c.1700, with curving gable, rusticated pilasters and panel recess over the semicircular arch, all in a pleasing rural pastiche of urban taste. The church is of 1787: the date betrays its character, which is that of a plain T-plan preaching box, with harled walls and plain freestone dressings; good treble-lofted interior with an excellent pulpit in a stripped restrained manner by James A Morris and Hugh Wallace.

Kirkmichael drawn by James Clark

McCosh Hall, 1898, John Baxter
Delicious inept Ballochmyle stone club room with clock tower. **Kirkmichael House** combines a Jacobethan wing of c.1830, in the mode of William Burn, and a block of 1861, echoing a tower house. **Cloncaird** is better architecture: a large house of 1814, incorporating the original 16th-century structure in its unusual castellated appearance dominated by a four-storey bastion in an echo of Adam's castle style. The architect may have been Robert Wallace who exhibited plans for a lodge at Cloncaird in 1819. The County Buildings in Ayr, completed 1812, had introduced Wallace, a London-based Scot, to Ayrshire nobility.

STRAITON

The most picturesque of Ayrshire villages, with two rows of single-storey cottages facing each other across the quiet narrow main street. This narrowness aids the enclosed feel, as does the memorial and gates to the former manse at the east end. A joy to walk in, its charm dependent not on formal architecture, but on the rightness of the buildings for the setting, and vice versa. **Black Bull Inn** is dated 1766; the remaining cottages must be of similar date. **Traboyack**, the old manse, is a charming, small mansion of 1795 delightfully sited in its own grounds at one end: the formal architecture is at the other, hidden from the centre by a bend and fall in the road. The **Church**, 1758, has a plain harled T-plan auditorium, incorporating the south transept of c.1510, with its **Kennedy of Blairquhan tomb**, and a window by Sadie McLellan, 1977, brilliant in design and effect. The church was restored in 1901 by John Kinross: the sombre tower added concurrently to plans of John Murdoch. The adjacent **McCandlish Hall**, 1912, Thomas Jack, is a happy marriage of neo-colonial with influences from Glasgow and Mackintosh. **Fowlers Croft**, 1984, Robert Allan & Partners: it is an attempt to adapt the informality of Straiton's architecture to modern domestic needs and to weld acceptable new developments on to a small village; it succeeds well on both counts.

Straiton

Straiton, in 1792: *The houses are neat and uniform, being all constructed on the same plan about 30 years ago by Thomas, Earl of Cassillis. The uniformity of the houses, together with the adjacent green hills skirted with wood, the vicinity of the Girvan, and a considerable number of very old trees in the churchyard, and about the village, justify those who visit this place in pronouncing it one of the most beautiful villages they have ever seen.*
First Statistical Account

Below *McCandlish Hall.*
Bottom *Fowlers Croft*

187

Right *Blairquhan.* Above
Strapwork detail. Top *Saloon*

Blairquhan, 1820-4, William Burn
Burn's design, in the then highly fashionable
Tudor-Gothic manner, is very large and very
grand. Situated on the edge of the plateau, the
basement of the rear elevation is exposed,
giving additional height to what is already an
imposing building. The entrance front, with its
dominant porte-cochère and central lantern
tower, is designed to capture the sunlight: the
drawing room and other public rooms take in
the stunning views across the park and the
river's valley. The tower is the external
evidence of the magnificent full height saloon,
its upward thrust providing a notable *coup de
théâtre*. There is an effective hierarchic
massing, stepping the house down from the

Sir David Hunter acquired
the Blairquhan estate in 1798
from the Whitefoords, who had
been badly affected by the Air
Bank Crash. After his marriage
in 1813, he turned his attention
to replacing the courtyard
mansion, comprised chiefly on
the 14th-century McWhurter's
Tower and the 1573 palace
range (of which a few fine 16th-
century details remain built
into the kitchen range, most
notably the triple horseshoes
over several windows).

public exterior through the family quarters to the service court, though the details are not especially subtle, and a certain stiffness in the design indicates a subservience of exterior design to internal planning. In 1967 Michael Laird & Partners created with great aplomb a modern **estate office** from the service wing. *Blairquhan open to the public in the summer*

Hunter Blair Monument, 1856, William Burn

The monument on Craigengower Hill commemorates James Hunter Blair, who died at Inkerman. It is a simple granite obelisk, conspicuously visible, guarding the final southward twist in the valley of the Water of Girvan. These last couple of miles before it disappears into the hills are amongst the prettiest in Ayrshire: the gorse-covered hills contrasting with the good-quality agricultural land in the valley floor. There are a number of good 19th-century farms: the standard two-storey three-bay farm, often with embracing byres, and **Balbeg**, which began life as another *typical* farm, but has been expanded, to fulfil a new role as a shooting lodge, in 1908 and 1923. The additions are in a congruent delightfully pink-harled brick roughcast, which looks well from the far side of the valley.

Hunter Blair Monument

STINCHAR VALLEY

The Stinchar's course to the sea from the Galloway Hills is a secret, sequestered journey almost untouched by the trappings of the 20th century. Other Ayrshire valleys have developed as major transport routes, but the Stinchar Valley acts as a barrier, crossed by two important north/south routes at Pinwherry and Ballantrae. Its villages are timeless, unhurrying, popular destinations for a Sunday spin.

BALLANTRAE

Busy roadside village with two distinct parts. The focus for the farming community is the tight cluster of houses about the church, while the fishing community, echoing the sea-towns of the north-east coast, lived equally compactly at the Harbour. The distinction is lessened now: an increasing demand for retirement and holiday homes has aided that process. Ballantrae's architecture is merely pleasant, and the continuous flow of ferry-bound traffic does nothing to encourage leisurely contemplation.

Lord Cockburn, was a schoolfriend of Hunter, but had a particular distaste for Burn and his architecture. In 1844, he found the house *too ostentatious and too large for the place, and, architecturally ... nothing* but admitted that he was *glad, at this my first visit to his seat, to see him so comfortably and respectably placed*.

Foreshore

Quiet can be found at Foreshore, the row of single-storey fishers' cottages at the harbour, probably of early 19th-century origin. The **Harbour** was given its present form in 1847, Arran freestone being used to create the parapetted quay with its noticeable batter. The roadside village is grouped about the **Church** (*top*), 1819, workaday stuccoed Gothic with an unmatched, rather odd, clocktower of 1891. There is a particularly fine pulpit (*middle*) contemporary with the church and a bronze mural memorial of David MacGibbon, of that great Victorian double act MacGibbon & Ross. The neighbouring kirkyard has the **Kennedy Aisle** (*bottom*), a remnant of the previous church containing the **Kennedy Monument**, *c.* 1601, a powerful tomb, if clumsily provincial in execution, similar to the more urbane **Glencairn Monument** at Kilmaurs. Built for Hugh Kennedy of Bargany, *c.*1450, **Ardstinchar Castle** survives as little more than a relatively intact ruin, dramatically situated high on a rocky bluff commanding the river mouth. At its foot is the **bridge** of 1770, twin-arched ashlar, with much dignity, that dignity rather affronted by the 1964 **bridge**. North of the village is clearly visible the stump of a **windmill**, built in 1696.

Glenapp, 1870, David Bryce

A huge High Victorian Scottish baronial mansion, whose entrance elevation, in its original form, is a good example of his control of massing, the whole composition dominated by an enormous rampant tower climaxing in a high, ogee-capped turret. The tower rises high over the surrounding lands, more Bryce-

Below *Glenapp*

baronial than genuinely Scottish in its antecedents, but its power, and originality, cannot be denied. The garden front, and the lodges, are plainer, straightforward, work, suggesting that the client, James Hunter, was not working with a bottomless purse. The house was increased in size in 1922-4 for Lord Inchcape, with consequent compromise to Bryce's tightly packed massing: the grandeur and similarities to Newark Castle suggest that James Miller may have been the architect. At **Smyrton**, Inchcape put up six picturesque cottages in 1919: a further cottage of 1959, by J H Reid of Ian Lindsay & Partners, represents a *first-class example of the use of the authentic materials of the countryside to make what is essentially a modern design.*

Glenapp Church (Butter's Chapel), 1850
Tucked into the well-wooded **Glen App** as it stretches Ayrshire down to the edge of **Loch Ryan**, a chapel of ease for the farflung Ballantrae Parish, a simple structure given character by the tasteful restoration by MacGregor Chalmers in 1910 and the stained glass by Douglas Strachan and Kelley & Co. In the little kirkyard is the **monument to Lord Inchcape**, a vast marble monolith guarded by eagles and lions, reminiscent of the colonial work of Sir Herbert Baker.

Auchenflower, *c*.1860
Well-composed group of the fine and commodious mansion house built for James McIlwraith, with its grey whin steadings, and additions of *c*.1900, in a gleaming white-harled crowstepped Old Scots idiom by James Miller. The additions were for the Hughes-Onslows, who also commissioned Miller for **Balkissock**, 1933, vaguely manorial though the time-worn charm of an ancient manor-house has been sacrificed in favour of a modern treatment: modernism restrained, with a tall slate roof and tall chimneys. Between times, client and architect had worked together at **Laggan House**, where Miller's 1913 wing, again Old Scots in a sub-Lorimer style, stands beside the gutted billiard room of the original house. From 1845 until 1902 this was the estate of Charles MacGibbon and his son David: whether either designed Laggan House is not known. **Craigneil Castle**, 14th or 15th century, sits precariously on a rocky height opposite Colmonell, its dramatic situation

Glenapp Churchyard: Top *Lion guard.* Above *Monument to Lord Inchcape*

Ballantrae was a centre for 18th-century smuggling of contraband goods from France via Ireland and the Isle of Man. They included salt: Salt Tax in the 18th century being so punitive that vast quantities entered Scotland usually from Ireland. *Large vessels, then called Buckers, lugger-rigged, carrying twenty and some thirty guns, were in the habit of landing their cargoes in the Bay of Ballantrae; while a hundred Lintowers, some of them armed with compass and pistol, might have been seen waiting with their horses to receive them, to convey the goods by unfrequented paths through the country.*

Twixt Wigtowne and the towne
of Aire
And laigh down be the Cruves
of Cree
You shall not gett a lodging
there
Except ye court a Kennedy

Gillescop MacKenedi was
Steward of Carrick in 1243, and
the Kennedy family rose to the
height of its power in the 15th
and 16th centuries, when large
parts of Carrick and Galloway
were run virtually as an
independent kingdom. Most
Kennedy families trace their
origins from Sir Gilbert
Kennedy, 1340-*c*.1408.
Somewhere along the line they
inherited a fondness for feud
and internecine strife, most
notably in the long running
disputes between the Kennedys
of Bargany and the Kennedys of
Cassillis.

heightened by quarrying operations beneath,
and indeed the north-west corner fell into the
quarry in 1886. It is rectangular in plan,
unusually without a vaulted basement, the
only vault being to the second-floor great hall.

Knockdolian House, 1842, David Rhind
An exercise in crisp neo-Tudorbethan, large,
romantically and magnificently sited above the
Stinchar. Close at hand are the ruins of
Knockdolian Castle, a rectangular planned
structure with two vaulted cellars. The
building history is inadequately explained,
though the majority of what ones sees is of
c.1650, when much rebuilding took place on, it
is believed, the foundations of a much more
ancient structure of the knightly family of the
Grahams. In 1696 the policies showed *what art*
and industry can doe to render a place to which
nature hath not been favourable very pleasant
by planting of gardens, orchards, walks and
rows of trees that surprise the beholder with
things so far beyond expectation in a country so
wild and mountainous.

COLMONELL
Roadside village of some character, most
especially in the little area around the parish
church. At the other end of the village, by the
garage-brutalised former **Free Church**, 1898,
Alexander Petrie, traditional cottages and local
authority housing eye one another warily
across the street. The council housing, pre-war
by Ingram & Brown, post-war by Ayr County
Council, is acceptable, but brings with it rule-
books on scale and space, parameters for cars
and people, which run counter to the visual
needs of the village. The contrast between the
two ends of the village is an instructive one.

Kirkhill Old Castle

Beyond the rows of cottages in **Rowantree Street** and **Main Street**, are the delights of **Kirkhill**, a neat symmetrical Elizabethan mansion of *c*.1843-5, possibly by David Rhind, in a quieter but similar manner to Knockdolian. As at Knockdolian, its ruinous castle predecessor stands close by; a handsome L-plan house with bartizan turrets, ornamental skews and, internally, a scale-and-platt stair.

Bardrochat, a house of 1893 by George M Watson, which Robert Lorimer extended in 1906-8, producing a mannered rambling Scots house with phallic bell-capped round towers and a sinuously curved Dutch gable, was the home of Robert McEwen, a notable philanthropist. McEwen threw himself vigorously into the artistic life of the village: the **Church**, which had been substantially rebuilt in 1772 and recast in 1849, was gone over, by Lorimer, in 1899. The external stair and the pulpit are his, while glass by Louis Davis was introduced. In 1922 Lorimer again designed the **War Memorial**, a particularly attractive composition in Donnington stone and whin rubble, alongside the flat-arched **bridge**, 1867, Hugh McCall, while in 1919, he had designed the **Snell Monument** at **Almont**, the lamp of learning on a granite pedestal.

Colmonell War Memorial

LENDALFOOT

A typical Ayrshire village squeezed on to the narrow strip of land between the raised beach and the sea. It is overlooked by **Carleton Castle**, 15th century, of the usual quadrilangular pattern, with vaults to the basement and great hall, each fitted with a loft or entresol, which sits on a narrowing tongue of land between two burns. **Carleton Mains** was extended in 1872 to plans of MacGibbon & Ross. The village itself has a number of pleasant limewashed single-storey cottages, of which **Carleton Fishery**, dated 1832, and **Straid Cottages**, are the most pleasing. **Carleton Terrace** includes holiday huts on feus which the Hamilton Estates began to make available from about 1933, and quickly taken up by the middle classes of north Ayrshire, Lanarkshire and Glasgow. Although consolidation and improvements have taken place, the area still exudes much of the character of that time, the opportunity to escape which increased leisure time and the motor car gave.

John Snell, born at Almont, rose to become a leading lawyer, and ultimately Seal Bearer to Charles II. In his will, he founded the Snell Exhibition Bursary, by which the ablest graduate of the University of Glasgow is awarded a place at Balliol; the Bursary is still awarded annually.

Carleton Terrace

Sawney Bean's Cave lies below Bennane Head. This large well-lit cave was home to the semi-legendary Bean family of cannibals who, it is gleefully told, waylaid and ate travellers on the road above. The cave is compartmentalised by two stone walls, the inner pierced by a doorway, the outer with a doorway, a blocked window and a fireplace. The cannibal myth is rollickingly put in Crockett's *The Grey Man*, but a more tragic perspective is conveyed by the award-winning *Ballad of Sawney Bain*.

PINWHERRY

Scattered settlement of some former importance as a route junction, with the main road into Wigtownshire crossing the minor road following the Stinchar, and the station, now closed. The only building of substantial merit is **Pinwherry Castle**, *c*.1596 and abandoned before 1800, an L-plan structure with a wide spiral stair and a corbelled-out square turret in the re-entrant, as at Baltersan. The ruin is engulfed in ivy, and it is not easy to say whether this is prising it apart or holding it together. **Daljarrock**, *c*.1750, probably incorporates an earlier structure within its Georgian skin: the house has been much tampered with, demolition after a fire in 1987 finally accounting for much of the 19th- and 20th-century accretions. Pinmore Castle, rebuilt in 1876 by Allan Stevenson, has gone: the minuscule **Chapel**, 1878, also Stevenson, survives, rather clumsily detailed. **Minuntion** is a rather fine upright little farmhouse of 1857, extended in the 1980s with great flair by Patrick Lorimer of Anthony Richardson & Partners, with a long low white wing, its neo-Victorian details and repeated bay windows catching the spirit of post-Modern design.

BARRHILL

Another centre of communication and trade, with its well-cared-for **station** on the Ayr/Stranraer line and thriving local market. The little village, tight and compact on either side of the 1811 bridge over the **Cross Water**, has some charm. There is nothing of great architectural pretension, but the congruent character of the crisply detailed, often granite, cottages, makes a virtue out of their plain-spoken honesty. The church, **Arnsheen Church**, 1887, Robert Ingram, is Scottish baronial, simple in detail, carefully proportioned and picturesque in outline. At the south-east corner rises a tower 55 ft high. The building is neat, chaste and complete in every detail and fits well within Ingram's canon of work, even if its situation is rather isolated and exposed. The **Memorial Hall**, 1924, James Miller, intended as a war memorial, is built in a simple gabled pavilion style, without the financial freedom and panache of the Richmond Hall, Kirkoswald. The **Martyrs' Tomb**, a pedimented monument with a ball finial was rebuilt in 1825 incorporating earlier fragments.

Barrhill

Kildonan, 1914-1923, James Miller

Kildonan was built on a scale that is altogether too big: too big for its setting, too big for its economic base, too big for its time and, as it transpired, too big for its owner.

Euan Wallace MP inherited the estate on condition that he made it his home. He employed Miller to design this enormous house in the English Manorial Revival style, complete with theatre and indoor tennis courts. Clive Aslet has called it *the last great country house in the Gothic Revival tradition*, and it is indeed a superb example of both Miller and the chosen style at their most sophisticated, with its long sweeping roofs punctuated by tall chimneys, its picturesque series of dormers and gablets with swept eaves, its careful harmony and balance, which sometimes suggests symmetry while narrowly avoiding it, and its subtle and considered use of fenestration, whether it be the full height bursts of glass in the great hall, or the short Tudor fashion mullioned horizontal bursts.

Kildonan was ready for occupation in 1923, the world it was designed for had all but vanished, and the interiors were never fully completed. Miller was also responsible for the **stables**, in a modern idiom more representative of Miller's canon, with its arched entrance straddled by a squat and buttressed clock tower.

Top *Miller's west elevation of Kildonan.* Above *Kildonan*

Drumlamford, 1830, W Frazer

Italian palazzo in style, Galloway granite in stone, Drumlamford, built for Rigby Wason, is a strikingly sited house whose Italian feel has been attenuated by the addition of a new attic storey. In 1838 Wason built himself another house, only some three miles away, **Corwar**, in the same style and of the same unyielding Creetown stone: presumably having outgrown Drumlamford, but finding its style congenial, he just built a new house as a greatly enlarged version of the first, creating a lochan to

Drumlamford

Black Clauchrie

Kyle and Carrick Libraries

produce the obligatory vista across water.
Corwar was extended, in a matching style, in
the 1890s, and it is this extension which stands
alone now, the original house having been
demolished in 1974. Very different, but very
much at home in this hard landscape, is **Black
Clauchrie**, a shooting lodge, 1898, by James K
Hunter; the front is predominantly Scottish,
with red sandstone, crowsteps, and
uncompromising grey harl: the garden front
has an English flavour. Dug into a sloping site,
with a huge conservatory, this house is an
attractive example of Arts & Crafts taste.

BARR

A small cottage in the village
is known as the Jam Factory.
This commemorates a post-
Great War job creation scheme
of the Revd John Barr,
involving the local housewives
in making jam to make money.

One of Ayrshire's show villages, hidden in a
particularly inaccessible part of the Stinchar
Valley, and approached from Girvan over bleak
moorlands which then suddenly open out to
reveal verdant fields and lush growth. It is the
setting rather than the architecture which
makes Barr a haunt of trippers and sketchers.
It has its vernacular cottages, and two-storey
houses, and, as at Colmonell, they eye the local
authority houses across the road. But here
there is also a burn, the **Water of Gregg**, and
trees to screen one from the other. The best
cottages are the row which includes the **King's
Arms Hotel**, of *c*.1800. The **Stinchar Bridge**,
1787, is a rusticated segmental-arched
humpback. The **Church**, 1878, Allan
Stevenson, is rather lumpen, while Alexander
Petrie's **Free Church**, now a house, 1892, is
similar to his church at Colmonell, and is no
less duller than the established church. Much
jollier is the **Village Institute**, 1913, John
Arthur, a totally alien thing of red tiles, harling
and timber gables. **Alton Albany**, *c*.1830, is a

The jam factory

Close

conventional late Georgian house, enlarged for the Hughes-Onslows in 1860 by John Murdoch, with porte-cochère, bays, wings and Tudor-style lodge in his vigorous muscular manner.

The stretch of the Stinchar eastwards from Barr is particularly delightful, the valley, wide-bottomed here, surrounded on all sides by the moorland hills, the mountains of Galloway in the distance. The architecture is a match for the surroundings, four-square harled farmhouses and steadings, the least altered still with small windows and slated roofs. At **Balloch** road and river separate, the road southwards through the **Nick of the Balloch**, an awesome pass leading to the remotest corners of the far-flung parish, the river into the plantations which cover these western slopes of the Galloway hills. Deep in the woods, reached by a track from Kirriereoch, **Cross Burn Bothy**, 1980. A competition to design a bothy was organised by Edinburgh University and the Forestry Commission in 1978 and won by the wigwam shape designed by Nichola Foot. Detailed plans were drawn up by Mike Jardine prior to construction by Youth Opportunity Programme trainees. It is designed to be prefabricated and bolted together on site. The whole building sits on three raised concrete blocks and therefore has no dampness problems: a wood-burning stove helps keep weary walkers comfortable.

Barr

AILSA CRAIG

A cliff-girt island rising dramatically to over 1100ft, the Craig, known also as Paddy's Milestone or as Brian's Stone, seems, seen from the mainland, gaunt and inaccessible. Approaching it, the traveller discovers a wide triangular apron of land, on which stands the lighthouse and its ancillary works, including the remains of a gas works and a small light railway, which was used in a connection with the curling stone quarries on the north-east side of the island. A possession of Crossraguel Abbey since 1404, the Craig passed to the Kennedys of Culzean and Cassillis in the 16th century, and ultimately gave to that family their marquessal title.

Ailsa Craig has inspired many a poet, and Wordsworth witnessed a solar eclipse of July 1833 from a steamship close to the rock:

Since risen from ocean, ocean to defy
Appeared the Craig of Ailsa, ne'er did morn
With gleaming lights more gracefully adorn
His sides, or wreath with mist his forehead high:
Now, faintly darkening with the sun's eclipse,
Still is he seen, in lone sublimity
Towering above the sea and little ships

Ailsa Craig Castle, 16th century
Of similar pattern to Kildonan Castle on Arran, a straightforward square tower, with a vaulted basement, made possible by the slope of the ground, a vaulted ground floor, a first-

Ailsa Craig Castle

Ailsa Craig is a haven for birds – most notably the dazzling white solan geese or gannets – and has Britain's fourth-largest gannetry, with over 20,000 occupied nest sites. In 1894 it was reported that *a favourite custom in excursion steamers is to fire a gun and alarm the birds which inhabit the cliffs. The scene which follows is wondrously sublime.*

Curling stones have been produced on Ailsa Craig since the 1880s when the quarries were leased by Andrew Girvan from Lord Ailsa, and continued to produce stones until 1952. Production finally ceased in 1971. The very hard fine grained microgranite, of three varieties, the Common Ailsa, Blue Hone and Red Hone, produced curling stones – polished and finished in Mauchline – of excellent quality. The best stones were said to come from the Blue Hone.

Ailsa Craig Lighthouse

Arran was granted by Robert Bruce to the Stewarts of Menteith in 1314. The male line failed in 1387, and the lands of Knapdale and Arran passed to Robert, the High Steward, husband of Marjory Bruce. The lands passed through his daughter, Margaret, to her husband, John of Islay, Lord of the Isles.

floor room with full-width fireplace and aumbry, and the scant remains of a further floor. Ground floor and first floor are connected by a straight stone stair: access thereafter was by a wheel stair. There are, as MacGibbon & Ross noted, few features by which the structure can be dated: by comparing the thin walls and internal arrangements they detected a stylistic similarity with 16th-century Border keeps. Persistent local legend gives it a Spanish flavour: either as a centre to deter Spanish smugglers or as built by the direction of Phillip II of Spain about the time when he had hopes to add the British Isles to the dominions of Spain. The **lighthouse**, 1883-6, is a thoroughly competent work by D & T Stevenson, the regular engineers for the Northern Lighthouse Board. Undeniably dramatic are the **North** and **South Fog Signals**, 1886-8, containing machinery designed by Charles Ingrey.

ARRAN

Arran attracts much praise, all of it richly deserved. This Scotland in miniature – if not quite that, then certainly a microcosm, a synthesis of Highland life and tradition – is in direct contrast to Ayrshire. For many Lowlanders, Arran becomes an unbreakable habit. There is much to see, and much to do: splendid hill walking, dramatic mountain scenery, plentiful wildlife, some fascinating archaeology. For the architectural explorer, too, there is much to see.

The great bulk of the island belonged to the Hamiltons for many years: their base on the island was **Brodick Castle**. Increasing pressure from those in search of the picturesque, both for a vacation and as somewhere to dwell permanently, was resisted until very late in the 19th century, when some development was allowed. Except in the three main villages on the east coast – **Brodick**, **Lamlash** and **Whiting Bay**, which are fairly typical small coastal resorts with a suburban character of comparatively recent development – the landscape is of a pattern established after the Clearances of the early 19th century. The development of the resorts can be readily linked to two deaths, that of Paterson, the factor, in 1881, and of the 12th Duke of Hamilton in 1895. These two had combined to ensure that few feus were made available: there was a slight relaxation after Paterson's death, but it was only after the accession of the 13th Duke that development on any scale was allowed.

BRODICK

Old Brodick is below the castle: new Brodick developed during the 19th century as increasing tonnages meant new facilities would be needed to cope with the new steamers in the Clyde.

The modern traveller meets firstly the **Tourist Information Centre**, c.1981, Baxter Clark & Paul, a jolly, effective, glass and slate oast-house, alongside a suburban **Shopping Centre** of c.1986. Tucked away is the **Harbour Office**, 1899, a simple harled box.

Douglas Hotel, c.1856
Huge, imposing hotel, with front bay and lush Elizabethan portal, marks the start of the seafront hotels. The Island Hotel is a quietly assured classical 1930s model; **Ennismor** and **Craiglea Court**, the latter now subdivided, are

Arran is well known to geologists as the ground over which the battle between Wernerian and Plutonian geologists was fought and finally settled in the late 18th century. Wernerians such as Jameson and Headrick, believed that all geological structures were created by water action, while Plutonists, of whom James Hutton was the first, asserted that some were of subterranean origin. Hutton had evolved his theories through study of the granitic rocks of Arran, and here, despite the sarcasm of the Wernerians, his arguments were to prevail. Hutton's work on Arran also led him to develop the concept of non-conformity, i.e. that many millions of years may have passed between the deposition of two adjacent strata. His theories were based on study of the sandstone and schist at North Newton.

Douglas Hotel

also from this period, but plainer, subdued. Urban character is evinced further west: red sandstone shops, with one good shopfront, and the **post office**, 1946, flat roofed and blocky, facing the **pharmacy**, 1886, station-like in its clock-adorned and wide-bargeboarded gabled baronial, and the **village hall** (*left*), 1894, an astonishing Arts & Crafts composition, large, with bursts of small-paned windows.

Ormidale was built by the 11th Duke for the German landscape painter Hering, and his adopted daughter, Jeanie. Jeanie was generally believed to be the result of a liaison between the Duke and Elizabeth Hamilton, a local girl known as the Belle of Brodick.

Below *Ormidale Hotel*. Bottom *Kilmichael House Hotel*

Alma Terrace, *c*.1856 (*above*)
In the 1850s the Hamiltons rehoused the inhabitants of the existing village at Cladach, at a greater distance from the castle. Two developments were built: **Douglas Place**, 1856, plainer, and **Alma Terrace**, slightly Jacobethan with prominent chimney stacks, overlooking the harbour. Built as cottages, it resembles many contemporary poorhouses. Douglas Place has, as neighbours **Montrose House**, 1974, flat roofed bricky sheltered local authority housing with protruding windows, and a **sheltered housing** development, 1989, Borthwick & Watson, for Kirk Care, harl-and-tile planners' vernacular.

Ormidale Hotel, *c*.1855
Famed for bar lunches and cask-conditioned beer, a dullish red sandstone villa. Opposite is **Brodick Parish Church**, *c*.1910, gable ended, squat tower and tin church hall. **Kilmichael House**, now a hotel, is an attractive late 18th-century laird's house, plain but satisfying. At **Brodick Primary School**, 1854, there is the **monument** to the Duke of Hamilton, died 1863, the kilted, rather disdainful Duke standing in front of the pretty little school, with its odd bargeboards. **Rosaburn Lodge** is a Victorian crowstepped villa, while the **Arran Heritage Museum** makes attractive use of the smithy and cottages of Rosaburn.

Arran Heritage Museum

Brodick Castle, 1844, J Gillespie Graham
This magnificent house, the base for the
Hamilton operations in Arran, sits on a hill
above Brodick Bay with wide views across the
firth. There is 13th-century masonry, but what
the visitor most readily appreciates today is
the 16th-century tower to which Gillespie
Graham added on south-west and north-west.
The tower, a Z-plan structure, was built for the
deposed regent, Lord Arran, in 1558: he
returned, remodelled and enlarged the castle in
a fashion proper to his status and the hazards
of the time. A century later, Brodick was
commandeered as a Commonwealth barracks,
and extended in a manner congruent with the
16th-century work. This ensemble, with
minimal decoration – no string-courses, for
instance, just a corbelled parapet – has a quiet
dignity. Gillespie Graham's addition takes up
this theme, set back a trifle and with large
segmental-headed windows on the piano
nobile, before breaking into the crowstepped,

Lord Cockburn, visiting
Arran in 1842, thought Brodick,
*A strong thing, with antiquity,
site and trees, sufficient to have
enabled its noble owner, if he
had chosen to spend a little of
the gilding he had wasted on
the weavers of Hamilton, to
have easily made it a fine place.*

Above & left *Brodick Castle*

The most memorable furnishings at **Brodick** are those, especially the silverware, from the collection of the arch-Goth, William Beckford who was author of the Gothic novel *Vathek*, and builder of Fonthill Abbey in Wiltshire, a bizarre Gothic monster which collapsed. Beckford's daughter married the 10th Duke of Hamilton. Although Beckford was forced by financial circumstances to sell part of his collection in 1822, a substantial amount came to his daughter, the Duchess of Hamilton. The collection was reduced further at a sale at Hamilton Palace in 1862, but what survives at Brodick is the greatest single portion of Beckford's collection to remain in single ownership.

Pirn mills manufactured wooden bobbins or *pirns*, from local trees. The one on Arran, an adjunct to the thread mills of J & P Clark in Paisley, was built *c.*1780 and functioned until about 1840: *When all the trees had been cut down, the mill ceased to function.*

and turreted western tower that encompasses the modern entrance hall, and is echoed by the smaller tower at the opposite end of the ensemble: typical unarchaeological Gillespie Graham, most reminiscent of his work at Ayton Castle, Berwickshire. Internally, the castle was remodelled as part of Gillespie Graham's remit: the style is Jacobethan: lofty elegant rooms with geometric plaster ceilings. Panelling in the dining room is English, from Letheringham Abbey in Suffolk. Splendid new timber Visitor Centre, 1992, by Page & Park.
Open to the public (National Trust for Scotland): guidebook available

Bavarian Summerhouse (*left*)
The highlight of the small, but agreeable plantsman's garden: a jolly rustic folly of mid-Victorian vintage. Outside the grounds, **Cladach**, an austere 18th-century former inn, with raised margins to its pink harl, and **Duchess's Courtyard**, the old home farm (Strabane) converted, 1989, into shops, blandly, too much of the outbuildings sacrificed to parking and landscaping.

CORRIE

Corrie is delightfully sited, huddled beneath the raised beaches on which stands **High Corrie**, the island's best example of a highland clachan: five or six cottages, harl and slate, hugger-mugger among the remnants of the runrig system: all is now holiday home and weekend retreat, but the atmosphere lingers on. The village itself, long and sinuous, relies largely on the traditional cottages of the 19th century for its character, with the occasional highlight: most notably **Cromla**, a large rambling villa, and **Corrie Parish Church**, 1886, J J Burnet, one of his two churches on the island, an

High Corrie

excellent red stone structure, burrowing into the hillside, the seaward gable buttressed in a suitably appropriate barn-like manner.

LOCHRANZA

The chief settlement of the north end of the island, lying alongside its eponymous loch, making the most of one of the few sheltered lies on the rugged coast. Pre-eminent of its buildings is **Lochranza Castle**, the 16th-century stronghold of the Montgomeries, *ane uther auld house* in 1549. An oddity is its low position, on a peninsula jutting out into the loch. This L-plan castle, roughly a double cube with a square wing in the south-west corner, has a relatively plain exterior: a few well scattered window openings, some rudimentary corbelling to corner turrets, parapets and watch rooms. Conventional internal layout: vaulted basement below hall and kitchen on first floor, private apartments above, wheel stair in the west wall.

The village has a number of substantial villas from the years on either side of 1900: the best is the **Youth Hostel**, displaying shades of Leiper, the Gothick **Kincardine Lodge**, and **Benvaren**, harled with a big central chimney rising above a first-floor balcony and Glasgow Style glass. **St Bride's Church** 18th century, is a low, harled structure with odd gabled windows, a Gothic wooden lich-gate of *c.*1930, and a nautically numinous wood-panelled interior.

Top *Corrie Parish Church.*
Above *Lochranza Castle*

West Side

Setting is everything along the west side: the hills press down less dramatically, allowing greater expansion, the view across to Kintyre and beyond breathtaking. The villages are pretty (**Pirnmill**) or commercialised (**Blackwaterfoot**). **Catacol**, a splendid row of sturdy gabled cottages, *c.*1850, designed by the Hamiltons for crofters displaced by sheep and game, enclosed within equally strong stone

The cottages of Catacol are known as the **Twelve Apostles**. The inhabitants of the clachan at the head of the Abhainn Bheag, who were being displaced to make way for deer, refused to live in them; and the row, the *hungry row*, remained empty for at least two years until tenants began to appear.

Twelve Apostles

Top *Dougarie Boat-house.*
Above *St Molio's, Shiskine*

The west coast, especially
around **Machrie Bay**, has a
fine, dramatic, collection of
stone circles. Although Historic
Scotland's guide book to Arran
offers an excellent introduction
to their archaeological and
social import, it fails to tell you
that the 15 stone circle at
Auchnagallon supported
Fingal's cooking pot.

Kildonan Castle

walls. **Dougarie Lodge** is a splendid example
of a mid-19th-century genre: turrets and
crowsteps crowding in one upon the other in a
composition of calculated abandon. Behind are
some aesthetically calculated ruins designed to
inculcate an impression of age, for this was a
Hamilton shooting lodge, not the reworking of
some timeless castle. Dougarie's **boat-house**,
J J Burnet, is a supremely competent exercise
in minimal Arts & Crafts applied to a basically
simple workaday structure. Burnet's work on
the island demonstrates a lightness of touch
that his mainland work, for all its many other
qualities, does not always achieve.

St Molio's, Shiskine, 1889, J J Burnet
Burnet's first work on the island: a precursor of
his chain of little churches that led through
Corrie, Gardner Memorial, Brechin and
Broomhill Congregational, Glasgow. Common
features which first appear here are the square,
squat tower and pyramidal roof, the admixture
of sparingly-used Gothic and Romanesque
details, and the long low cloister-like hall.

Kildonan Castle
*A ruinous ancient keep erected on a rocky
plateau on the sea-coast, at the south end of the
island of Arran. It is protected by a precipitous
cliff on the east or seaward side, and by a
ravine on the north.* Nothing much has changed
since MacGibbon & Ross so described
Kildonan, though the few features of this
rectangular structure, such as the barrel-
vaulted hall over a vaulted ground floor, that
can be identified have become more ruinous,
and more overgrown. **Drimla Lodge**, 1896, is
a peculiar brick-built house of corner towers
and balconies, best categorised as colonial.
Lagg Hotel is a pleasantly rustic hotel, with
bargeboarded dormers, and a polite extension,
in a dramatic setting, while **Kilmory Church**,
1785, is accompanied by its contemporary
white-harled manse in a remote inland site of
much charm. The church is a straightforward
chunky ashlar composition, its major surprise,
a gable window of six circular openings.
Pladda Lighthouse, 1790, Thomas Smith,
has two towers; the lower, *c.*1795, redundant at
an early age when the older tower was given a
new lantern, avoided reconstruction for a
heavier load, and consequently retains its
beautifully made cast-iron lantern floor,
murette and decorated blind panels.

WHITING BAY

The major settlement of the south end of the island, developed slowly during the 19th and 20th centuries as a place of retreat and vacation: a sheltered spot hugging the gentle curve of the bay. The original settlement was higher up, on the raised beach: **Kiscadale**, where the crowstepped mid-century **Kiscadale Inn** still stands. The modern village is little more than a string of biggish villas, the necessary adjuncts to civilised life inserted at irregular intervals. Villas include the tall Swiss **Largymhor House**, the Burnian **Eden Lodge**, the faintly Gothic **Corriedoon**, which has a good free-style addition of *c*.1900, the subdued baronial of the **Youth Hostel** and of **Grange House**, and the Arts & Crafts jollity of **Invermay**, 1905.

Stewart Memorial Church, 1910

Built for the United Free Church congregation, a plain gable-ended church with porch, Tudor windows and powerful angle-buttressed tower, faintly reminiscent of the Glasgow Style work of W D McLennan with few openings bar those, wide and flat arched, that allow the ringing tones of the bells to escape. Inside a consciously humble hall-church with a pretty open wooden roof. The old **Parish Church**, 1873, now disused, plain and lanceted sits on the main road alongside **Whiting Bay School**, *c*.1973, unabashedly modern, a grandly drafted scheme of diamonds and triangles picked out in white harl and black *margins*, complemented by a monopitched hall block and more conventional offices.

Robert Bruce sailed from Kings Cross, to the north of Whiting Bay, to Ayrshire in 1307, as the first stage in the long arduous journey that led to the crown of Scotland in 1314, to Bannockburn. The King's Cave at Drumadoon Point is one contender for the setting of the legend of Bruce and the spider.

Below *Stewart Memorial Church*. Bottom *Whiting Bay School*

Holy Isle looms over Lamlash, and the anchorage that was a natural rendezvous for Viking and the British fleet prior to 1914. Its holiness derives from St Molios, Irish missionary, disciple of Columba, and Abbot of Leinster, who died in 639. On the west side of the island is the Cave of St Molios and, towards the summit, his health-giving Well. The Gaelic name for the island, Eilean Molaise, had been corrupted by the early 19th century to Lamlash, which name was transferred about 1830 to the village developing on the shore opposite. This account of ferry passengers marooned for a fortnight in Lamlash, written in 1822, appeared in the *Kilmarnock Standard* in 1888: *For the first two or three days, we consoled ourselves for our disappointment by a variety of amusements, but they soon began to pall on the sense of their sameness; and those who are in the least acquainted with Lamlash, during the winter season, must know that (considering the passengers thus detained amounted of upwards of 60) we were soon short of every kind of comfortable food, and had now no resources but to sit moping around the fire, or betake ourselves to the mountain dew, of which we had always plenty.*

Hamilton Terrace

LAMLASH

The true capital of the island, the seat of higher education and local government, the only place on Arran – except for, briefly, at Brodick – where one can catch a true urban feel. The centre is much more compact than either Whiting Bay or Brodick, and only the obvious lack of any built hinterland (the wooded hills press down no less here) prevents that sense of an urban settlement. The harbour, in the lee of the dramatic **Holy Isle**, had long been the chief port of entry to the island: the wants of the castle, and the slightly shorter crossing to Brodick, allowed its eclipse during the 19th century.

Hamilton Terrace, 1895

The centre of the village: a long row of single storey cottages with pretty catslide dormers, and given additional emphasis by a timbered gable at either end of the row. Another attempt, as at Brodick and Catacol, by the Hamiltons, in this case the 12th Duke, to bring the crofters of the island together in cohesive and comfortable communities: this terrace replaced a row of insanitary croft-cottages. The **Parish Church**, 1886, by H & D Barclay in chunky red ashlar, has the usual lanceted gable to the road and sea, with porch, to left, and tower, to right, both set unusually far back. Some odd details, such as the quirky bell openings, but one regrets that F T Pilkington's plans of 1871 were not carried out. The congregation, one might suppose, does not share those regrets. **White House**, another Hamilton residence, has gone, leaving only a

pleasing little Arts & Crafts **lodge. Arran High School**, finished in 1941, but not opened until 1946, has the long plain horizontality of that period, mixed in with lingering classicism in the central doorpiece, and an excellent crisp 1980s extension in brick and glass.

Marine House Hotel, 19th century
An elegant classy Victorian villa, its regulation two storeys and three bays smartly harled with painted margins. The extension is less successful. A former **Church** has greater pretension than the other island churches: a tall tower and spire with spindly openings, and a nave and aisles plan picked out by the gables. The former Bay Hotel is a well-sequestered bargeboarded villa, the **Bank of Scotland** is a Dutch-gabled villa intrusively adapted to its present use, while the seafront proper boasts the elegant little **Harbour Office**.

CUMBRAE
The smallest of the triumvirate of islands that made up the ancient county of Bute. The island is shaped like an inverted heart, its only settlement, **Millport**, lying at the south end, spreading narrowly around the curve of the heart's indent. Unlike Arran, Cumbrae's physical characteristics are those of the neighbouring mainland, and the single low hill, the Glaid Stone, has affinities with north Ayrshire hills such as Law. This is good agricultural land, and the island's economy is still based largely on the production of foodstuffs from land and sea. Tourism is an important contributor: Millport ranking closely after Rothesay and Dunoon as a *doon the water* destination, though it has always been a rather more reflective, less raucous, resort. Grey of stone, the little town's considerable merit lies in an unthreatened cohesion, and not on dynamic highlights.

Cathedral of the Isles, 1849-51,
William Butterfield
Butterfield was one of the greatest and most original designers of the Gothic Revival; the greatest of his buildings are those in which his modern age Gothic is married to the ideals of the Tractarian Movement in the Church of England: Keble College, Oxford: All Saints, Margaret Street, in London. Remoteness from the opinion-formers of London has ensured

Arran High School

Arran High School is built on the potato fields of Donald McKelvie, who lived in **New Lanark** in Lamlash. In these fields, he developed and bred the potato varieties which were to take the name of the island around the world: Arran Banner, Arran Pilot, and many others still in cultivation. There is a portrait of McKelvie by Maurice Greiffenhagen at Oswald Hall (Auchincruive House).

Cathedral of the Isles

Cathedral of the Isles: Top *Cloister.* Above *Interior*

The Garrison

that his island masterpiece is relatively little known. Cumbrae's link with the Tractarians was its owner, George Boyle, later 6th Lord Glasgow, who, at Oxford in the 1840s, became involved with and influenced by the leaders in the Tractarian Movement, men such as Newman and Pusey. He returned home determined to rejuvenate the Episcopalian Church in Scotland, and naturally turned to Butterfield to make his ideas solid.

The complex of buildings began life as a theological college, with college buildings, cloisters and chapter house in addition to the church; the church was given Cathedral status in 1876. Boyle lost heavily in the collapse of the fraudulent City of Glasgow Bank in 1886: Cumbrae was sold to the Butes, and his Tractarian dream, if not stillborn, caught in a state of arrested adolescence.

The group, tightly composed and giving the impression of being much grander than they are, owes much to Butterfield's brilliance: angular, buttressed, grey stone buildings of hard geometrical forms, pulled together by the tall pyramidal steeple and steeply pitched slate roofs. Inside, the story is typical Butterfield, for though the decoration of the nave is relatively muted, the chancel and sanctuary are a riot of colour and detail. The framework is created by walls of rich polychrome tiles and windows of rich stained glass, while walls, floors, beams and, especially, the ceiling are profusely covered with stencil work, often taking its motif from the plentiful wild flowers of Cumbrae.

The Garrison, 1819

A low, long, battlemented mansion, built in the

late 18th century, enlarged and given its modest Gothic coat in 1819 when it became the chief island residence of the Glasgows. It is now the local council offices and island museum, and sits in a walled garden with Gothic archways. The faintly Scandinavian **Our Lady of Perpetual Succour**, 1958, Robert Rennie, emphasises the relationship by using Norwegian slates, while the former **West Church**, 1878, has a straightforward Gothic nave-and-aisles shell. Inside is a largely intact, and high-quality, example of the work of Daniel Cottier: stencilled designs to the woodwork, and leaded glass also by Cottier. The **Parish Church**, 1837, is unarchaeological Gothic with a battlemented tower, while also on the upper terraces are a number of good quality villas, homes to retired mariners: **Fairlie Bank**, **Springfield**, **Seaview**, **Strahoun**. **Millburn House**, 1805, is a large, two-storey three-bay harled house of conventional appearance.

Millport & Harbour

The Harbour, 1750 onwards
Captain Andrew Crawford directed the creation of the first harbour at Millport, though it was largely reconstructed in 1797. The original basin extended to the foot of **Cardiff Street**, but was filled in during the construction of the front. In **Quayhead**, some of the oldest, least formal, houses: **9** has moulded eaves and a circular stair tower to the rear, while **8**, recast afore, has a rolled skew dated 1751 behind. Good vernacular cottages are found in **Clyde Street**, **Cardiff Street** and **Creighton Street**, while **West Bay Road** has very proper boarding houses.

Kelburn Street
More of the very proper boarding houses, snaking around the bay, merging imperceptibly

National Water Sports Centre

The first sod of the then
Millport Marine Station was
cut by David Robertson, *The
Naturalist of Cumbrae*, 1806-91.
Self-taught, Robertson was one
of the major contributors to
scientific knowledge of marine
animals and fossil crustacae. It
was the desire to be in close
proximity to Robertson that had
led to the *Ark*, the peripatetic
research vessel of the Scottish
Marine Station at Granton,
settling at Millport and hence,
indirectly, to the establishment
of a land research base. The
building of 1896 was faithfully
copied in the 1939 extension, at
the insistence of the feu
superior, the Marquess of Bute.

Little Cumbrae old light is
one of only two coal-burning
lights to survive in Scotland,
the other being the 1635 light
on the Isle of May. The frequent
obscuration of the island top by
low cloud or mist led to its swift
replacement in 1793.

into the suburb of Kames. At **Kames** is the
Marine Biological Research Station, 1896,
the original building a gabled stone block
sparsely windowed on the upper floor, and
nearer the slip at which the rather prosaic
little car ferry maintains links with the
mainland, the **National Water Sports
Centre** (see p.C6), 1976, Frank Burnet Bell &
Partners, an excellently composed group of
timber buildings.

LITTLE CUMBRAE

Great Cumbrae's ancilla, highly visible in the
view from Millport, has three buildings of
much merit. The **Old Lighthouse**, 1757, is a
simple circular stone tower which relied on a
coal fire to produce illumination. Its successor,
the **New Lighthouse**, 1793, possibly designed
by Thomas Smith, is a most delightful and
idyllic station; the lantern mixes original
square panes and later triangular glazing.

On an islet off the east coast is **Little
Cumbrae Castle**, the much put-upon remains
of a 14th-century tower house, one of the
notably similar group which guards the upper
reaches of the firth (e.g. Fairlie, Law,
Kildonan), *much cast down* by Cromwellian
troops in 1653.

Little Cumbrae Castle

The author is particularly indebted to David Walker, Charles McKean, Duncan McAra and Helen Leng for their help, patience and encouragement, and to Joy Gladstone for her patience and many hours driving the roads of Ayrshire. Lena Smith dealt capably and cheerfully with incompatible computers and indecipherable scribblings.

Over the years he has also been grateful for advice, support and information from Sheila Allan, Ken Andrew, Sheena Andrew, Theodore Bruen, John Clare, Robert Clow, Kitty Cruft, Liz Davidson, Mike Davis, Frank Dunbar, Robert Ferguson, Pat Gracie, Barbara Graham, Michael Hitchon, John Hume, James Hunter Blair, Janet Kleboe, John Lord, Pat Lorimer, Euan McCulloch, Ian McGill, Jim Nicoll, Sheila Penny, Anne Riches, Roan Rutherford, James Simpson, David Smith, Gavin Stamp, Alan Stewart, Robin Urquhart, Sheila West, Fiona Walker, Frank Walker and officials of the four District Councils, and of Irvine Development Corporation, and for sustenance to Wendy Calder at the Marine Bar and Eddie and Evelyn Fisher at Geordie's Byre. The mistakes are his own.

A large number of books have been quarried for this volume. Of those of particular relevance to the architectural history of Ayrshire and Arran, the following proved most useful:

Aiton, **General View of the Agriculture of the County of Ayr**; Andrew, **Guide to Kyle and Carrick**; Andrew and Strawhorn, **Discovering Ayrshire**; Carragher, **Saltcoats Old and New**; Davis, **Castles and Mansions of Ayrshire**; Dunlop, **The Royal Burgh of Ayr**; Gray, **Maybole – Carrick's Capital**; Hune, **Vernacular Building in Ayrshire**; McKay, **History of Kilmarnock**; McLellan, **Arran**; Millar, **Castles and Mansions of Ayrshire**; Moore, **Among Thy Green Braes**; Moore, **Gently Flows the Doon**; Morris, **The Brig of Ayr**; Morris, **A Romance of Industrial Engineering**; Morton, **Three Generations in a Family Textile Firm**; Paterson, **History of the Counties of Ayr and Wigton**; Pont, **Cunninghame Topographized**; Robertson, **History of Ayrshire**; Strawhorn, **Ayrshire**; Strawhorn, **History of Irvine**; Strawhorn, **The History of Ayr**; Warrick, **History of Old Cumnock**; Woodburn, **A History of Darvel**.

National sources such as the Statistical Accounts, Hume on Industrial Archaeology, MacGibbon & Ross, and Groome's Ordnance Gazetteer were also invaluable. There are many books on Robert Adam: both Hussey and Savage have written on Lorimer, and Nuttgens on Fairlie. Most Ayrshire parishes have at least one published history, of variable quality, as have many churches. The publications of the Ayrshire Archaeological and Natural History Society, and of the Kilmarnock & District History Group can be recommended, as can the booklets produced on various communities in Cumnock and Doon Valley, e.g. Retter of Drongan.

INDEX

INDEX